3

Reward Governance for Senior Executives

In areas such as dispute resolution, visibility and investor interest, the relationship between a senior executive employee and his or her employer differs materially from the relationship that most employees have with their employer. Executives are tools which help create shareholder value. A company's decision to employ one executive over another should be based on the ability of the potential employees to create shareholder value for the organisation. It is therefore essential to get both the appointment and contract right.

Negotiating and agreeing the right contract requires an understanding of areas as diverse as valuation, employment law, tax and accounting. Covering the appointment of UK executives under contracts governed by UK law, this volume of essays is intended to help anyone involved in the appointment and termination process and other aspects of executive reward and its governance.

CAROL ARROWSMITH is Head of Remuneration and a Partner at Deloitte & Touche LLP.

RUPERT MCNEIL is HR Director, Global Retail and Commercial Banking, at Barclays Bank plc.

Law Practitioner Series

The *Law Practitioner Series* offers practical guidance in corporate and commercial law for the practitioner. It offers high-quality comment and analysis rather than simply restating the legislation, providing a critical framework as well as exploring the fundamental concepts which shape the law. Books in the series cover carefully chosen subjects of direct relevance and use to the practitioner.

The series will appeal to experienced specialists in each field, but is also accessible to more junior practitioners looking to develop their understanding of particular fields of practice.

The Consultant Editors and Editorial Board have outstanding expertise in the UK corporate and commercial arena, ensuring academic rigour with a practical approach.

Consultant editors
Charles Allen-Jones, retired senior partner of Linklaters
Mr Justice David Richards, Judge of the High Court of Justice, Chancery Division

Editors
Chris Ashworth – O'Melveny & Myers LLP
Professor Eilis Ferran – University of Cambridge
Nick Gibbon – Allen & Overy
Stephen Hancock – Herbert Smith
Judith Hanratty – BP Corporate Lawyer, retired
Keith Hyman – Clifford Chance
Keith Johnston – Addleshaw Goddard
Vanessa Knapp – Freshfields Bruckhaus Deringer
Charles Mayo – Simmons & Simmons
Andrew Peck – Linklaters
Richard Snowden QC – Erskine Chambers
William Underhill – Slaughter & May
Sandra Walker – Rio Tinto

Books in the series

Stamp Duty Land Tax   Michael Thomas; Consultant Editor David Goy QC
Accounting Principles for Lawyers   Peter Holgate
The European Company: Volume 1   General editors Dirk Van Gerven and Paul Storm
The European Company: Volume 2   General editors Dirk Van Gerven and Paul Storm
Capital Markets Law and Compliance: The Implications of MiFID   Paul Nelson
Reward Governance for Senior Executives   Edited by Carol Arrowsmith and Rupert McNeil

Reward Governance for Senior Executives

Edited by

CAROL ARROWSMITH

and

RUPERT MCNEIL

CAMBRIDGE
UNIVERSITY PRESS

CAMBRIDGE UNIVERSITY PRESS
Cambridge, New York, Melbourne, Madrid, Cape Town, Singapore,
São Paulo, Delhi

Cambridge University Press
The Edinburgh Building, Cambridge CB2 8RU, UK

Published in the United States of America by Cambridge University Press, New York

www.cambridge.org
Information on this title: www.cambridge.org/9780521871594

First published 2008

Printed in the United Kingdom at the University Press, Cambridge

A catalogue record for this publication is available from the British Library

ISBN 978-0-521-87159-4   hardback

Contents

Contributors

Carol Arrowsmith
Kathrin Kahrass
Angus Maitland
Angus MacGregor
Rupert McNeil
Emma Nicholson
Isobel Sharp
Alison Smith

Preface

This book addresses reward governance for senior executives and is aimed at two audiences.

Firstly it is intended to be a primer for people who want to learn the way many practitioners in the area of reward approach the construction and oversight of executive reward packages. Like most areas of professional practice, this activity involves a combination of art and science, and experience and judgment play an important part in reaching sensible decisions. This book also expresses a point of view about how this activity should be conducted. In other words, it is a normative as much as a positive guide; readers should be aware that some practitioners may approach executive reward in a different way but the editors make no apologies for suggesting that this is the way in which it *should* be approached.

Secondly, the reality of executive reward is that many of the decisions in any situation are taken by executive management and therefore this book is also intended to serve as a primer for executives required to take reward decisions, and shows how decisions can be taken that are fair to both executives and shareholders. There is of course an essential role to be played by those who oversee remuneration decisions, non-executive directors on remuneration committees in particular, or representatives of shareholders, and keeping the interests of shareholders front of mind at every stage in the decision making process is critical to effective decisions. In our view this works best in an environment where very clear authority has been granted to executive management to take decisions, with appropriate checks, and where every executive who takes a reward decision does so knowing that this authority could be withdrawn at any time.

We believe this book also fills a gap in the literature. While there are economic and legal texts that address some of the issues involved in taking effective executive reward decisions, the editors have not found a book which gives practical guidance on how effective decisions are actually taken. We hope that this book goes some way to achieving this.

We have approached this subject through the lens of the 'deal' – i.e. the process by which employer and executive strike a contract regarding what the individual will do and how the hiring company will reward them. This is because the deal represents the moment of truth in reward governance. It is the point when the forces of the market, the policies and pressures constraining the company, and the individual's wants and needs converge in their starkest form. Although we recognise that it is only one perspective, it is one that is applicable to the ongoing relationship between executive and employer, and to reward governance generally.

Introduction

Senior executives ('executives') are employed to help create shareholder value. When a company decides to employ one executive rather than another, it is taking a view on which one will better achieve that aim: i.e. which one will create greater value for the organisation. Once that decision has been made, a deal must be struck and documented. After it has been struck, the deal continues to evolve. This book is a guide for those involved in that process.

The best, most effective deals, which means those most likely to enhance shareholder value, are those which are 'fair' to both parties. These are deals where, with appropriate checks and balances, the executive's 'price' is the market price for someone with that skill set, ability and potential for creating shareholder value.

Chapter 1 sets out a framework for constructing executive rewards and how this can be used to compose a 'term sheet' for a senior hire from which a contract can be constructed

Chapter 2 discusses the practicalities of converting a term sheet into a legally enforceable agreement. It ends with a set of questions any reviewer of a service contract should ask as they review it.

Chapter 3 explores the most effective ways to reach robust and fair values for the various elements of the remuneration package.

Chapter 4 describes the various forms of executive reward commonly found in UK listed companies and discusses the process of determining the package.

This leads onto Chapter 5 which illustrates the ways the package can be optimised in different commercial contexts. This forms part of the important process of tailoring the deal to the given business situation, influencing the form of awards, as well as the nature of performance conditions.

Chapter 6 examines the wider impact of the remuneration policy and how this may appear to shareholders.

Chapter 7 reviews the development of the governance framework within which these decisions need to be made.

At this point, it may be helpful to explain why this book is focused on arrangements involving senior executives. For the purposes of this book, senior executives are individuals whose individual contributions will have a material impact on the creation or destruction of shareholder value. They tend to be more common higher up the organisational hierarchy. They also tend to be scarcer than candidates for less senior roles.

Why does the employment of executives require a different approach? A practical reason is that there is usually more scope for 'customised' deals which are less constrained by wider corporate reward policies. But the principles discussed in the following chapters should be applicable to any individual hiring decision, particularly as the customisation we refer to is better viewed as the product of rigorously enforced, but pragmatically elastic, policy, rather than individually negotiated anarchy.

Appropriate elasticity in reward policies and reward structure is important because the relationship between a senior executive employee and his or her employer is likely to be more complex than many other employment relationships, given the number of remuneration elements in the package and their potential value. The sums at stake in a dispute involving senior executives are likely to be out of the scope of tribunals and the UK's unfair dismissal regime, taking disputes into territory where high-profile litigation may become a material risk. This makes those involved tread a little more warily, even if, in principle, it is invidious to treat executives more flexibly in disputes than other employees. The executives involved are less likely to be local nationals which creates both opportunities and risks, particularly in terms of tax status and the treatment of international relocation. There are also more likely to be unique features of the executive's current package which need to be accommodated in the construction of the new deal, particularly around compensation for the forfeiture of existing awards and special covenants. Finally, individuals at this level are more visible than other employees, and contracts and their terms are more likely to be in the public domain, whether through requirements to put terms on display or to set them out in shareholder documents. A properly constructed deal should be able to withstand intense scrutiny and this is considered in Chapter 6 where the factors and issues which need to be taken into account when reporting the deal and explaining it to the outside world are discussed.

Most organisations apply a more rigorous process of governance for roles at the senior executive level. Typically, this will be through the remuneration committee on behalf of the board. But the remuneration committee is only part of the picture. It is the capstone on a process that needs to be closely integrated with the other parts of a company's control environment. Chapter 7 explores how processes can be put in place to allow executive remuneration to be governed in an effective and adaptable way.

There are a few things which we have deliberately left out of this book. We have not covered the identification of executive talent or the selection process, nor have we covered the process after the deal is signed when the successful candidate is being integrated into the organisation. Both of these parts of the hiring process deserve their own discussions elsewhere. We have also not specifically addressed the issues around executive terminations.

This is because, as far as possible, the termination of the contract should be considered as part of the construction of the deal in the first place and is therefore effectively covered in the sections on package construction. On termination, the terms of a deal should unwind in a smooth, elegant and mutually agreed fashion, but terminations are always difficult and, in Chapter 2, we discuss some of the flexibility that can exist.

Getting to the right package is an art as well as a science but there are tools that can be used to make the process easier. These tools facilitate what is ultimately a negotiation: a negotiation to acquire the services of someone who can create shareholder value. Having explained the focus on executives, why is this book structured around the issues that arise during the hiring process, the 'deal'? As stated in the Preface, striking the deal is the moment of truth in reward governance. It is the time when reward governance processes are stretched to their fullest: hiring managers want the deal done and may lose their objectivity in the heat of the deal; others, rightly, are hyper-vigilant in case policies or interests are compromised. But the hiring process uses tools which are needed whenever the contract between an individual executive and his or her employer needs to be revisited and refreshed. This is reflected in the way that the context broadens in the later chapters of this book. These cover a wider range of situations beyond the hiring process, but they all rest on the foundation laid at the outset, when the deal is first struck.

Does this mean each deal is unique? To some extent it does but, in reality, governance processes provide a wrapper around each deal and mould them into a finite set of shapes, which mean that, outside the buyout, individualising reward packages, even for executives, is hard to do. And, perhaps more importantly, we should remember that the business context should determine the extent to which diversity can be accommodated and the choices available to attract suitable talent.

1
Striking the deal

RUPERT MCNEIL

The starting point: getting to the 'number' which represents the executive remuneration package

This chapter identifies the steps that must be taken when hiring an executive. In doing this, it is helpful to look at the deal as a process which leads to a single monetary amount (the 'number').

The number is the value of the final package that employer and candidate both sign up to. It is an abstract concept. It represents what an informed and independent observer would consider the value of the package to be, taking into account what will be paid, when it will paid and the likelihood that it will be paid.

In reality, the employer and the candidate may have different numbers in mind. For example, they may have different views on how likely it is that a particular part of the remuneration package will actually be paid. In practice this means that the number will always be, for practical purposes, a range, reflecting the different values that could be assigned to the package's individual components. But for purposes of explanation, and negotiation, the idea that both candidate and employer are effectively engaged in a process of convergence on a shared idea of the value of the package is a useful tool. It is the best representation of both the value of the deal to the individual and its cost to the company and its shareholders. It is the basis of the investment decision made by both parties, and is a function of what needs to be paid to secure the individual in the given labour market, as well as representing an amount that the company believes it can afford.

The identification of the number is the first step in a four-step process:

1. First the candidate's current package is deconstructed into its component parts and its 'number' determined.
2. The company then reaches a view, based on a range of factors, on what the uplift needs to be on that number to secure the individual in their new role. That can start with a new number and then involves determining how to deliver that new number using the various reward components available: from salary and pension through to bonus opportunities and stock awards.

Figure 1.1 *Getting to the term sheet*

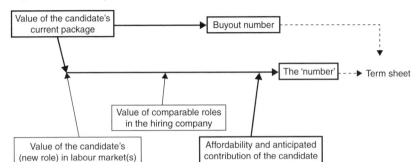

3. The third step is deciding on how those components will fit together, taking into consideration current reward policies, investor guidelines and, always, affordability.
4. Finally, the package that is comprised of those components needs to be recorded; ideally in a term sheet and then in a legally enforceable employment contract.

This process should allow the candidate and the employer to answer the following essential questions, which represent the essence of their contractual agreement:

- What are the components of the package?
- What is the maximum amount of value that the executive will receive under each component?
- What conditions need to be met for any amount to be received?
- When will each amount be received?

The final step is to document all of the details in a 'term sheet' from which the contract can be prepared, with all material issues having been dealt with in the negotiation process. The steps needed to reach the point where a term sheet can be prepared are illustrated in Figure 1.1.

Deconstructing the current package

When analysing an executive's remuneration package, the simplest starting point is to split the current package into amounts which relate to awards or payments which have been promised, but which will be lost if the individual leaves (the 'buyout'), and the 'run rate' of the package, which is what the individual will earn each year, or over some other period, if he remains with his current employer. These are two distinct categories and confusing them unnecessarily complicates the process of getting to a fair value for the package.

For example, the salary that the candidate currently receives is part of his 'run rate'. It is an amount which he expects to receive over a period of time. It will need to be replaced, in some economically equivalent form, in the new package, and on an ongoing basis, i.e. on a 'running basis'.

Alternatively, the candidate may have accumulated amounts under, say, a pension or incentive plan, which he will forfeit if he leaves his current employer. The value of this amount will need to be replaced, but only once. Replacing this amount would form part of a buyout, i.e. paid on a one-off basis.

The buyout

Buyouts can typically be of two types:

- Amounts where receipt at some future date is essentially guaranteed, i.e. there are no conditions attached to the future payment, other than the individual's continued employment. An example would be a deferred share award, where the shares will be transferred to the award holder if he is still in employment at a given date. These can be referred to as 'earned amounts'.
- Amounts where receipt remains uncertain, because a condition has not yet been tested. An example would be an award which has been made but where some period of the performance period remains before the final performance measurement takes place. These can be referred to as 'unearned amounts'.

The distinction between earned and unearned amounts can be quite subtle. For example, some bonus plans will allow awards to be retained by an award holder who leaves, provided they are not leaving to join a competitor. In other cases, an award may still technically be subject to a performance condition but will effectively have vested because the performance condition has already been substantially met and the likelihood that it will not vest is small.

In practice, buyout issues primarily arise with unearned amounts, and non-cash benefits. This is primarily because of potential disagreement over the assumptions that should be used for calculating the underlying value of the award (see Chapter 3, for a discussion of valuation techniques that can be employed and different approaches to underlying assumptions). For share awards and share option awards, a key assumption which affects the value of the buyout is the share price which should be used, i.e. the share price of the shares underlying the award. There are basically three approaches which can be used when dealing with this assumption:

- taking the spot price on a designated day (e.g. the date of the term sheet or the date the contract is signed); or
- using an average share price, e.g. over the three-, six- or twelve-month period ending on a designated day; or
- using a 'high price', e.g. the twelve-month high.

Someone negotiating a hiring package may have a mandate to use any of these three techniques. The second of these is likely to be the safest approach.

On the basis that market expectations of future dividend yields and share price movements are, in theory, taken into account in the share price at the point of measurement, no further assumptions about the underlying shares are required for awards made over whole shares.

For share options, the additional assumptions that need to be agreed are determined by the valuation method used. There are two typical approaches. The first uses the intrinsic value, or embedded gain, of the share option, by simply deducting the gain per share from a current share price calculated on one of the three bases discussed above. This is the simplest method, and, usually, represents the lowest value per share under option. Using this basis, for share options where the exercise price is higher than the current share price, no value will be recognised.

The second approach uses an option pricing model to determine the value of the option. Essentially, this involves calculating the present value of the expected future gain. For a given share price / exercise price combination, the size of that gain is assumed to increase, in most[1] cases:

- the longer the exercise period remaining (because there is a greater likelihood that the share price will rise above the exercise price);
- the higher the 'volatility' of the underlying share price (because this is assumed to indicate the possible extent to which the share price will exceed the exercise price when it rises above it);
- the higher the 'discount rate', or risk-free rate of interest, used to determine the present value of option gain that may ultimately be received, (because the higher the discount rate the lower the present value of the amount that needs to be paid to satisfy the exercise price when the time comes to exercise); and
- the lower the dividend yield, i.e. the expected level of dividend payment expressed as a percentage of the current share price (because the higher the rate of dividend payment, the more value in the share price will have 'leaked out' to shareholders ahead of option holders exercising these options).

Agreeing what figures should be associated with these assumptions has become less contentious since the introduction of option expensing into accounting standards and the more widespread use of the calculations which this requires. Figures for each of the assumptions needed to value an option over a quoted company's shares now need to be set out in the financial

---

[1] These are the author's layman's rules of thumb, applicable in most commonly encountered situations. But where these variables have either very high or very low values relative to each other, different effects can occur. Valuation experts would rightly criticise these as generalised and grossly simplified.

statements of any company reporting under either US or International accounting standards. While there may be debate on whether these are the right assumptions at the time the deal is being struck, the common starting point can now be a set of audited numbers for each assumption.[2]

Despite the use of published assumptions, the debate on assumptions used in option pricing discussions most often focuses on the remaining life, or term, of the option for valuation purposes. The published figures required for accounting purposes use the 'expected term', i.e. for the population of option holders reported, what is the expected time between grant and exercise (usually based on historic exercise patterns). Using this figure will usually produce a higher value per option than using the earliest date on which an option can become exercisable and a lower value than the latest date on which the option can be exercised, i.e. the date the option will expire (many candidates' preference).

Pragmatically, anyone negotiating a buyout of options should have a high and low figure in mind, driving the range within which they have a mandate to agree a buyout value for those options. The aim should be to go for the basis using the expected term and the other published parameters. But it is important not to underestimate the emotional dimension of holding an option, which is not wholly rational from an economic perspective. Some people may place additional personal value, for example, on the apparent status conferred by being an option holder. Others may be highly risk averse and place a correspondingly lower value on holding an option. Being flexible about the basis of valuation can recognise that emotional dimension. But whichever approach is used, it should be replicable and defensible. Any of the above approaches, in the right circumstances, can be both of these.

It is important to ensure that the awards being bought out have actually been forfeited. A term sheet and contract should require 'best efforts to exercise' what can be exercised and make payment for the buyout conditional either on evidence from the awarding company that the award concerned has been forfeited, or on receiving confirmation from the candidate's representative advisor that this is the case.

A final aspect of share option buyouts relates to 'earned' awards. Although these awards are not forfeited, it can be argued that there is a lost 'time value' as it is likely that they will need to be exercised within six months of cessation of employment. Using an option pricing model approach, the shorter exercise period would result in a lower value. It may be reasonable to compensate for this lost time value by calculating the value using an option pricing model and then deducting the intrinsic value from this value.

---

[2] After taking into account the impact of performance conditions, one of the variables to which option values are most sensitive is volatility. A very legitimate basis of debate in an option valuation exercise is whether historic volatility should be used as the input or either 'implied volatility' (derived from the values of traded options on the same underlying share) or volatility figures (either historic or implied) from comparable companies.

Another aspect which is common to various unearned amounts is the conditionality associated with each award. Often it is easier to assess this for share-based awards, where performance conditions tend to be more objective and the likelihood of achieving them can be more easily assessed. In some cases, the impact of the performance condition on the value of the award may already be factored into the value shown in the published financial statements (e.g. if the condition is based on 'relative total share-holder return' or some measure of share price growth). This is discussed in more detail in Chapter 3.

The position is harder to assess for more discretionary awards such as annual bonus opportunities. For annual bonuses, the hiring company is far more dependent on extrapolation than for share awards. A much greater proportion of the information required is not in the public domain. This is an area where it will be necessary to apply judgments, based on a sensible assessment of the candidate's performance and that of their employing company (e.g. assume a lower range of potential bonus payment for a non-critical executive in a company that is not hitting its targets and is regarded unfavourably by market analysts). It can also be informed by the historic pattern of bonus payouts received by the candidate (for which it is also reasonable to ask for evidence, or to retain the right to do so). This is discussed in more detail below.

There are also areas where some elements of a candidate's 'run rate' package are best wrapped up in the buyout, taking them off the table for discussion about what the hiring company will offer as ongoing arrangements. These may include the value of defined benefit pension entitlements (where the hiring company offers a less generous pension arrangement) and 'expatriate type benefits' not offered in the hiring company. Both of these categories are discussed below.

The final decision on structuring a buyout relates to the form in which the buyout will be made. A commercial approach, and one candidates will typically consider to be 'fair', is to try to match the forms of award as closely as possible, so that share awards are matched with share awards in the hiring company and cash is matched with cash, and that, while the only conditionality is likely to be continued service with the hiring company, the dates of receipt match the vesting dates of the substituted awards, as far as possible.

Expatriate benefits

Expatriate benefits are, as described above, a form of award that it may be convenient to deal with as part of a buyout, in preference to including them on a continuing basis. In dealing with a candidate, expatriate benefits offered by their current employer can be a significant incentive for the individual to remain in their existing organisation. Predominantly, these benefits cover housing (with employees receiving either a subsidy towards housing or provision of accommodation leased on their behalf by their employer), and education for school-age children. 'Home leave' ('furlough' in the USA) flights are also common, as well as the benefit of services such as home search and educational support, and support with preparation of tax returns in the host and home country. There are important psychological aspects to expatriate-type benefits. In particular, their true cost to the employer is often not fully transparent to the individual receiving them, even when they are received in cash form (because they are communicated as a net (i.e. after tax) rather than gross (i.e. before tax) amount). However, the astute candidate will be acutely aware of this fact and they will want to ensure that, in terms of their cash in hand, and their standard of living, they are not worse off in any way if they lose these benefits.

The best way to cross the 'expatriate benefit chasm' is to make a very clear distinction in the company policy between 'true expatriates' and those who are simply being compensated for the disruption and expense of relocating. True expatriate benefits are best limited to the genuinely internationally mobile, and for a cadre of people who accept that part of their employment deal is that they can be moved, often at short notice, and certainly on a frequency of no less than once every two to three years. These people need the help that an expatriate programme of benefits can provide. Crucially, their peers and co-workers should understand why their packages are different and that the difference is justifiable. For example, most expatriate programmes operate some form of 'tax and cost of living equalisation', which attempts to put the employee in the same cash position as they would have been, in spending power terms, if they had remained in the home country. This has two benefits: it is essentially fair (these are home-based employees temporarily assigned to the host location) and it goes some way to cushion the shock of the return to home base with minimum 'withdrawal symptoms' from loss of disposable income.

This leaves a wide category of people who will need to relocate to join a new organisation, and for whom the process will be very disruptive. For these people, there are several approaches which can be adopted. The first is to pay them a relocation allowance, either in cash or through services provided in kind. This can be a one-off, and as such is probably most effectively treated as a one-off buyout cost, paid together with share awards. The second is to provide a period of adjustment, when the individual essentially receives expatriate-style support (housing and schooling, for example), for a limited 'localisation period', but all other aspects of the employment are structured as if the individual was a locally hired employee.

The position is more complex for individuals currently benefiting from an expatriate programme (quite common for executives hired out of large US corporations). If they can be transferred into an equivalent programme in the hiring company, the problem can be quickly and easily solved (although not necessarily in a way that is conducive to good reward practice or cost control). A better option is to take a pragmatic view of the value of the programme, on an expected value basis. To do this requires agreement that the expatriate benefits are not a perpetuity that the candidate will receive indefinitely. If that agreement cannot be reached, an unbridgeable impasse is likely, unless the new salary and benefits on offer are sufficient to bridge the gap on their own. If agreement can be reached, a pragmatic view needs to be taken on how likely it is the individual would be in a position to receive expatriate benefits from his current employer in coming years. A working assumption is that anyone being hired at this level, on the trajectory of a high-performing executive, would expect to remain on expatriate terms for a limited period, before being reassigned back to home base to a more senior role. If that is the case, the fairest approach is to calculate the expected present value of the expatriate package and discount it not just for time, but also for a factor reflecting the likelihood that the individual will be in receipt of the benefit over, say, a five-year period. This delivers a value which can then be included in either a buyout figure or an overall figure representing the total run rate (and including the impact of increased salary in the new role).

Having suggested that senior executives should not be given traditional expatriate-style benefits for an unlimited period, it is important to recognise there are some distinct 'expatriate-style' benefits that this population should receive as part of their employment terms.

The first is tax preparation assistance. This is not simply because it is a benefit that can be provided at a relatively low cost, and one which recipients value. It also provides an important risk mitigator, by ensuring that there is no embarrassment arising from differences of view over tax liabilities. In this respect, for the hiring company, it retains an important degree of reputational control.

The second is a repatriation provision. This ensures that the individual feels confident that, if anything goes wrong (and they are not the cause), there will be free transport for them, their family and their possessions back to their home base. Well-drafted clauses will provide some flexibility on when this can be drawn down (to minimise concerns about the school year, for example) and will make sure that it only applies where the individual does not have an equivalent provision provided by a new employer (i.e. it remains valid only for as long as the individual does not obtain new employment in the host location).

Pension benefits

Another set of reward elements which complicate valuation discussions are pensions and retirement benefits. New employment tax regimes in the UK and USA have simplified the pension benefit situation. Defined benefit plans linked to an individual's final salary on retirement have become less common. Increasingly, executives will participate in defined contribution type arrangements or arrangements which are closer to defined contribution than traditional defined benefit plans based on final earnings.

This means that most executives should have a good sense of what the annualised value of their existing pension entitlement is, typically expressed as a percentage of their annual salary. In this case, pension can be added into the overall run rate value. However, to do this on a like-for-like basis, the tax-protected element of most pension entitlements needs to be accounted for, given that a proportion at least of any annualised pension value is likely to be viewed as free of tax (although the tax is usually deferred as pension payments will usually form part of a pensioner's taxable income). This means that, for example, £100 paid in the form of a pension contribution is likely to be worth two thirds as much again (£165) as the same gross amount paid in the form of salary. For executives currently benefiting from a pension entitlement in the form of a final salary promise, the position is harder to determine. The value of that benefit does not lend itself as readily to annualisation, being driven by a wider range of factors including age to retirement, the features of the plan itself (including the rate of accrual for each year of service, the treatment of inflation on the benefit pre- and post-payment and the availability of a pension for dependants). To assign a value to this when calculating the value of a package is likely to require an actuarial assessment of the annualised value of their current pension entitlements, which can be done objectively and usually reasonably cheaply. The product should be a letter from the firm providing the advice.

Two further issues regarding pension benefits are worth discussing. The first is the treatment of medical benefits, life insurance and other 'welfare benefits'. For US nationals this forms a key part of the value attributable to a pension promise, in the form of post-retirement medical cover. One approach is to take the strictly local view and assume that, as the benefit is not on offer to the local executives, it should not be available to anyone else, unless they pay for it themselves. The other view is that this is such an important part of the socio-economic proposition of being an American that it should be available to all Americans. How the latter is achieved can vary, but can include using a US employing subsidiary (which provides the pension and other welfare benefits) or making some other provision into which these employees can be placed. For other benefits, it is often easier not to express these in cost or value terms but in terms of the benefit that is being delivered. Life insurance (usually expressed as a multiple of salary) is probably the most common example. The second is the impact of nationally specific differences, most commonly encountered in the form of the 401(k) plan in the USA and the generous provision available for retirees under the French social security system. In the case of the 401(k) plan, employees in US corporations are often given the opportunity to save through a programme which allows them to acquire stock in their employer on a tax-deferred basis. In some cases, the amount of saving is supplemented by an employer contribution. Despite parallels with certain share purchase programmes (e.g. UK Save As You Earn schemes), this is best regarded as part of the overall pension proposition available to the US employee and should be treated in the same way as other pension contributions when valuing the package. In the case of French employees, the issue usually emerges when the individual wishes to remain in the French social security net, which, historically and at the time of writing, has a significantly higher cost for the employer than UK or US rates. However, this represents, largely, the price of more generous earnings related state pension benefits. Given this, the social security contribution should be factored in to the value of the deal, as it represents the true cost to the employer of the package being offered to the candidate.

The run rate

Having calculated the buyout number in a fair and reasonable way, the next step is to calculate the run rate. This represents the annualised earning potential with which the hiring employer is seeking to compete. The run rate usually breaks down into five basic components:

- salary (and other forms of fixed reward, such as a special allowance that may be paid to people living or working in certain locations);
- bonus (i.e. an amount which may be paid annually depending on performance in a given year);
- long-term incentive ('LTI' – i.e. an annual award that may be earned depending on performance over a period of more than one year, either in instalments or at a single 'vesting' date);
- benefits (particularly car, expatriate, relocation and 'welfare' benefits, such as life insurance);
- pension entitlements.

It is important to take a consistent and economically realistic view of the run rate and the 'value' it represents, and which needs to be matched or exceeded by any new package.

This is best done by taking a simple view that the value of each component is a function of:

- the value that can be delivered;
- the time at which at which it will be delivered; and
- the likelihood that the maximum will be delivered (given performance or service requirements).

Essentially, this involves calculating the probability that an amount will be received and adjusting its value to reflect when it will be received. For example, if a bonus has a 75% chance of being received, and the long-term award has a 50% chance of vesting and, if it does, it will be received after three years, then annualised value of the package would be 75% plus the present value of 50% of the long-term award. The present value of the latter can be calculated by dividing 50% of the award (its expected

13

value) by the discount rate raised to the power of the number of years until it can be received (i.e. if the discount rate is 5%, dividing by 1.05^3). On this basis, if the bonus and the long-term incentive are both equal to 100% of salary, the expected value is 75% of the bonus plus 43%, i.e. 118% of salary.

That number can then be compared with the other factors that need to be considered in reaching the number that the employing company will table as part of the 'deal':

- the value of the candidate's new role in the labour market: 'the market rate'; and
- the value associated with comparable roles in the hiring company: 'the internal rate'.

The value of the role in the labour market can never be assessed with complete precision. But various sources can be used to derive the market rate, or benchmark, for equivalent roles. The first reference point should always be a reputable data source, which broadly means one which provides either data for the given role in a sample of organisations covered by an established remuneration survey, or data for the given role for named individuals disclosed in published financial statements. The latter, while arguably the best and most reliable data source, will usually only be available for individuals on the main board of a company or their most highly paid direct reports. This means that the core of any benchmarking exercise will be a remuneration survey.

The first observation to make about using a remuneration survey is that there will never be a perfect match between two jobs in two different organisations. In many cases, the best estimate of the market rate will be obtained by combining market data for several roles, possibly from several surveys. The second is that extreme care also needs to be taken to check that the sample on which the market rate (commonly referred to as the 'market benchmark') is based is large enough to be relied upon (although for senior roles, practicality may mean accepting much smaller sample sizes than would normally be considered adequate by most reward professionals for less senior roles).

It is also important to interpret the data in a rigorous way. Most survey data, for example, will show three key categories of information, and for each will show the key data points of sample median (usually the most useful figure, and representing the 50th percentile point, i.e. the point which splits the sample in two), the lower quartile or 25th percentile (i.e. the point which separates the bottom 25% of a sample from the top 75%), the upper quartile or 75th percentile (the point which separates the top 25% of a sample from the bottom 75%) and an average figure.

The three categories are:

- salary;
- total cash (being salary plus cash bonus);

- total direct compensation (being total cash plus an annualised value for long-term incentives, usually being the 'input value', i.e. the expected value of the award at the date it is made[3]).

An important point to note is that the data points for the medians, lower and upper quartiles and averages for each of these categories will not necessarily relate to the same role, i.e. the median salary may be paid to individual X in company A and the median total cash may (probably will) relate to a different individual Y in company B. The most obvious implication of this is that one cannot derive, for example, the median bonus amount by simply subtracting the median salary figure from the median total cash figure.

This means that it may be better to derive the market benchmark in terms of the total direct compensation rate for a given role. This then requires a careful assessment of what typical market practice would be for delivering that value in terms of the mix of salary, annual bonus opportunity and long-term incentive. The advantage of using this approach is that, if the assumptions are reasonable, it allows an offer package to be constructed that is essentially neutral as to structure because it incorporates the effects of timing of payment and the likelihood that payment will be made.

Understanding the market data is critical to determining the reward package. The sample underlying any statistical presentation of remuneration data is made up of data points relating to individual roles and incumbents in those roles. In some cases organisations participating in the survey may provide data for more than one incumbent for a role.

Each data point used to derive the market benchmark is a function of two variables: (a) the closeness of match to the role being benchmarked; and (b) the outcome of each negotiation between incumbent and employer.

Figure 1.2 illustrates how a data set can be visualised in this way.

Appreciating the reality of market data and how it is compiled can provide helpful perspective when you are trying to reach the number required to close the deal. In particular, this means recognising that market data represents a range of possible compensation values for any given role.

One particular feature of survey data should be highlighted. The first is that the figures shown are commonly what has actually been paid or awarded. This raises a particular issue for annual bonuses, where the amounts shown do not indicate the actual range of earning opportunity available to each individual in the sample. For example, a total cash figure of £100,000 with an associated salary of £50,000 could be associated with a maximum bonus of £50,000, or with an on-target bonus of £50,000 which could have delivered £100,000. There are two ways of dealing with this. One is to look for data on bonus opportunity (usually reported as a percentage of salary for on-target and

---

[3] For example, the expected value for an award for which there is a 50% chance that it will be received would be calculated by multiplying the maximum that would be received by 50%, as in the example above.

Figure 1.2 *Visualising market data*

extent to which role surveyed had package value set in labour
market in equilibrium and bargaining power of individuals and
employers matched

'Largest' roles: more
complex and/or requir-
ing higher or more
specialised skills than
others in the sample

*some data points will relate to
packages in this quadrant,
where package value may be
driven by ability of employer to
tap into a higher skill labour
market (e.g. for professionals
who see these roles as
entry points for other
career opportunities in
the organisation)*

**Highest value
packages are likely
to be in this
quadrant**

Roles with best
fit to job being
benchmarked
and where
labour maket is
in equilibrium

extent to
which role
surveyed is a
good match
for the role
being
benchmarked

'Smallest' roles: less
complex and/or requiring
fewer or less specialised
skills than others in the
sample

**Lowest value
packages likely to
be in this quadrant**

*Some data points will
relate to packages in
this quadrant, where package
value may be driven by factors
such as individuals' potential
for other roles in the organisation, and/or perceived risks of
being employing by hiring
company*

Hiring company had stronger
bargaining position (e.g.
because demand for roles in
this organisation and/or roles
of this type is high)

Candidate had stronger
bargaining position (e.g.
because demand for skill of
this type was high among
prospective employers)

maximum performance). This data is commonly available in larger surveys.
This range can then be applied to the salary figure, to give a range of bonus
opportunity. Another approach is to make a working assumption that the
median performer in the sample will receive the median total cash amount
and that the high performer will receive the upper quartile amount. The salary
component can be assumed to be the median salary. The same approach
(median to upper quartile) can also be used to reference the long-term incentive component of the 'market rate'.

Having established the market benchmark, the next stage is to check the
value of comparable roles within the organisation: the 'internal rate'. If the
appropriate data is not available to the individual conducting this process,
the process owner should check that the line manager and/or functional
head is happy with the relativity to other roles at the same level or within the
same team. Typically there will be differences, sometimes significant ones.
The extent to which an organisation gives greater weight to either market
data or internal comparisons is cultural. In some organisations the issue of
internal relativity is of central importance, while others place more emphasis on the market data available at the time of hiring. We would usually give
most weight to the market data, but it is important to be able to justify the
variance. For example, some functions (e.g. risk management or particular
geographic sales skills) may carry a premium at the time of hiring. There

may also be subtle differences in the skill set of the individual that may justify the difference. Identifying and documenting any variance can also be valuable to support future pay decisions.

The final stage is to look at the market data (and the internal peer comparison) and reflect on whether this represents good value, in terms of what the individual will be able to achieve. Signs to be alert for include those where the market data is significantly different from what the individual is currently receiving. If the candidate has a much lower number in their current package than the market data indicates for that role (on a total compensation basis) the decision to hire is effectively a promotion decision. It may be worth trying to mitigate the risk by increasing the performance-related proportion of the offer, so that the individual is only paid if they deliver. This can be sweetened by a first-year guarantee, without inflating salary unnecessarily. In dealing with these issues you are also mitigating the risk for the candidate. To be over-paid, particularly on fixed compensation, in a new job is often not a comfortable place to be.

At this point the information on the candidate's current package, the market data and a rigorous check on affordability and contribution should allow a final number to be offered. This is, after separately addressing any buyout, the expected present value of the package which will be offered to the candidate (with some margin built in for negotiation). The next step in the process is to decide how to deliver that number.

First the available reward components need to be reviewed. Generally there should be very limited variation in the components used across a group of executives of broadly equivalent level and role. If the hiring process involves a very senior executive, which we would generally limit to either a Chief Executive Officer ('CEO') or a major division head, then there may be some bespoke components in the reward package. But bespoke arrangements for more junior positions create a host of potential problems, from administrative difficulties to problems of precedent. This point is worth emphasising because hiring managers can find the prospect of a bespoke incentive very seductive (superficially it can look much aligned with how the role will contribute to shareholder value). But these arrangements beg many questions and need as much care in their construction and documentation as plans covering thousands of employees. Anyone at any level asked to put in place such an arrangement should ask for a copy of the rules, or at least the budget in order to get some rules drafted and approved. Without rules, which give an arrangement a sound and agreed contractual basis, acrimonious and expensive arguments of interpretation are more likely to occur, and will be harder to resolve: particularly when events occur which were unforeseen at the time the arrangement was entered into.

This does not mean that incentives cannot be individualised. This is harder to do for long-term incentives, easier for annual bonuses. But for annual bonuses, retaining some discretion is recommended as to what, if anything, is paid, unless the bonus for the first performance period has been guaranteed.

Chapter 4 discusses different ways of configuring the executive reward package in detail. But for present purposes it is simplest to assume that the main flexibility that will exist will be around the relationship between salary, bonus and LTI, with the parameters for performance conditions and time horizon of payment defined by the existing company policy. In most cases, the components available under current reward policies will be consistent with the expectations of investors. But checking to ensure that these have not changed, particularly for high-profile hires, is always recommended.[4] An issue which can cause problems in discussions with candidates is the treatment of uncertain events, contingencies, such as the treatment of a change of control and payments due on termination of employment. This is an area on which investors have increasingly strong views. Broadly, investors look for termination payments to be kept to the minimum contractually necessary, and avoid either 'paying for failure' or delivering 'wind fall gains'. This logic is impeccable. Shareholders should bear costs proportionate to the results delivered. This means that it is reasonable to restrict the bonus opportunity available to a terminated executive, and restrict what they can retain in terms of LTI awards. Unfortunately, the logic from the executive's side is also powerful. An executive wants protection against lost opportunity and against what may be a no-fault termination.

Helpfully, as explored in Chapter 2, the legal obligation to mitigate a loss under a contract and to compensate only for economic loss that cannot be so mitigated provides a clear limit on what can be paid under the contract. If this is combined with provisions which, at a maximum, link the amount of damages payable in lieu of lost earnings over the notice period to salary, benefits and an amount for bonus that is broadly at the on-target level, or based on an average of recent years' payments, or better still discretionary (and prorated for time served within the performance year), and if long-term incentives are prorated for time and vest, subject to performance conditions at the originally intended date, a fair result should be achieved for both executive and shareholder.

In some cases, a candidate may request a special protection associated with a feature of their current contract. As far as possible, resisting these requests or providing the assurance required in a more creative way is recommended. For example, questions about change of control protection can be very effectively answered by a chief executive looking the candidate

---

[4] For example guidance has been produced by the Association of British Insurers (ABI) on pension entitlements for senior executives. This guidance may well affect the decisions UK companies take on what pension arrangements to put in place for a new hire.

squarely in the eyes and reassuring him/her that he/she himself/herself does not need one and has not got one.

At this point the substantive discussions with the candidate should have been completed, although realistically further issues will arise as the contract is finalised. So what needs to be done before a term sheet can be tied off? Two sense checks are needed. They represent the acid test of the package being discussed. The first is to ask what the package would look like if it entered the public domain. In some cases that will always be the case and the package will appear in the company's statutory disclosures. That merits a full dry run and a review of a dummy disclosure to see what it will look like, in its own right and when compared with both peer roles that will be disclosed in the same document and also disclosures for equivalent roles in obviously comparable organisations.[5] Disclosure requirements are discussed in more detail in Chapter 6.

The second is to consider a number of 'what if' scenarios. In many cases this will have been done as part of the discussions with the candidate, but it is worth running through systematically again:

- What will happen if the share price moves within a range of say +/−50% of the current price? What will this do to the buyout of the existing package or share-based incentive awards?
- To what extent can the proposed package deliver amounts that vary significantly from that received by peers involved in delivering the same performance objectives?
- What happens if it goes wrong? What will be paid when?

Asking and answering these questions will provide some comfort that the various contingencies have been addressed.

To conclude, it is worth making an observation on two of the most insidious, and related, deal-breaking behaviours. The first is a phenomenon that some people have dubbed 'micro greed'. This is the tendency for candidates, and executives generally, to focus on small elements of their current package well beyond what is economically rational. This can include gilt-edged elements of relocation or international mobility packages (from gym membership to home leave flights) or non-cash benefits (like a second car).

The second is best explained by reference to the much-quoted 'parable of the boiling frog'. The 'Boiling Frog Moment' occurs in the course of a package discussion when the incremental impact of changes to each

---

[5] An interesting and encouraging trend in larger corporations is to publish full details of the package of executive officers in the hiring announcement. This is reassuringly transparent and lets the organisation set the context within which the figures will be viewed. Angus Maitland discusses media management and control of news flow in more detail in Chapter 6.

element is added up to deliver a figure far higher, in value terms, than is reasonable or intended.

The best way of dealing with micro greed is to fall back on policy and assume that one will not concede an item which is not available under current benefit policies for the category of employee that the executive will be joining. If it is in the current package, either the buyout or, better, the run rate of the new package should absorb the pain of the lost benefit (e.g., 'pay for the extra flights out of your salary'). But this needs to be carefully applied. In some cases what could seem to be an example of micro greed could be a reasonable request and one that the hiring company would be wise and magnanimous to agree to. This is more often the case with international hires. Huge goodwill and loyalty can be secured by a family-friendly and compassionate approach to relocations, for example, such as easing the move of a family pet or being flexible about housing, provided the cost is transparent.

The best way of dealing with the 'Boiling Frog Moment' is to avoid it! This is most easily achieved by ensuring that one person owns the package discussion end-to-end and that this person runs frequent and complete checks on what is currently on the table (and that what is on the table in the candidate's mind matches exactly what is on the table in the hiring company's mind). It is also important to identify areas still under negotiation and value those elements so there is a clear view of costs for the preferred choices of the candidate and the hiring company. Additionally, it may be that the 'Boiling Frog Moment' can be fixed by a frank conversation with the candidate. It is not comfortable or elegant to have such a conversation and particularly to do so in a way that does not look like a 'bait and switch' tactic on the part of the hiring company. But it can be done, albeit that it serves as a tough test of the quality of the relationship. A sensible candidate, and one still interested in the role will (a) have sensed that the offer had become too generous, and (b) understand that being overpaid for the job will not serve their longer-term interests in the organisation. They will then see that being paid significantly above either true market peers or ability to contribute is likely to damage their 'franchise', i.e. the way in which they are perceived by others in the organisation, and particularly the extent to which their presence and activity is perceived to add value for shareholders.

The final step is to summarise what has been agreed in a term sheet.

A term sheet is not necessarily a legally binding document (although an offer of employment does not require a signed contract and so without the proper caveats it could potentially be sued upon if breached). But both parties should view it as at least morally binding.

At a minimum the term sheet should set out the following:

- The job title, the reporting line and the candidate's name (or code name).

- The salary, on an annualised basis, and the anticipated start date from which entitlement to salary and other benefits will accrue (although start date may be shown as 'to be mutually agreed'[6]).
- The bonus opportunity, including:
  - when it is typically paid;
  - the target award and, if applicable, the maximum;
  - any guaranteed portion (and that, if it is not guaranteed, whether it is discretionary);
  - any part deferred into shares (including the treatment of dividends earned on the deferred shares).
- The structure of any LTI opportunity, and the size of any guaranteed award in respect of the first year.[7] There should also be some way of communicating the basic terms of the plan, including performance conditions. This can be done at high level in the term sheet or as a 'frequently asked questions' type summary or other explanatory annexe to the term sheet. Ideally, the guide provided to other participants can be used. This is particularly important because the contract will not typically contain the scheme mechanics (as awards under long-term plans are usually the subject of a separate contract and may, in the UK, be made by trustees rather than by the company itself[8]).

The term sheet should also show:

- the notice period (on both the employer's and the employee's side);
- the benefits programmes and what they offer (a summary is usually sufficient); and
- the details of any buyout of the legacy package, including timings and amounts (and any forfeiture provisions).

---

[6] The start date can take on an added significance if, as part of the buyout arrangements, there is some form of sign-on conditional on starting at a certain date. We remain pleasantly surprised at how effective these can be in getting someone at their desk on a designated day.

[7] We recommend that the award sizes that are shown, including guarantees, are genuinely representative of what the candidate could expect to receive on an ongoing basis and that expectations are properly managed. We also recommend leaving some flexibility to add a small amount onto a guarantee when bonuses are actually paid. This gesture has a good motivational effect in our experience, for example where a candidate expecting a guaranteed bonus of £10,000 is awarded an additional bonus of £5,000 at the end of the year.

[8] For candidates not yet familiar with UK practice, where the use of offshore employee benefit trusts is common as the vehicle for making share-based awards, it can be helpful to introduce in the term sheet the concept of the 'recommendation' and that the employing company will be contracting with the candidate that it will be making a recommendation that an award be made, rather than making it itself. All English employment lawyers and most experienced US employment attorneys will understand, and explain to their client, that the prospect of a trustee not granting on the basis of such a recommendation is at worst very remote.

The aim of the term sheet should be to give the drafting lawyer all they need to prepare the contract which is specific to the individual candidate.

The term sheet should also contain very clear wording regarding any outstanding matters that must be concluded before the final offer can be made, or on which any offer will remain conditional. We would expect this to include:

- the requirement for any medical or drug tests;
- the requirement for any regulatory approval (e.g. clearance from a financial regulator);
- The requirement to pass satisfactorily a credit, criminal record and reference checking process;
- any final approvals required as part of the governance process, e.g. a board or remuneration committee approval; and
- a final signed contract.

The term sheet having been agreed, the process passes over to the lawyers.

2
Documenting the deal

ANGUS MACGREGOR

The term sheet forms the starting point for documenting the deal between the candidate and the employer. But it needs to be converted into a legally enforceable contract, which ensures, as far as possible, that, whatever happens to the relationship between the candidate and their prospective employer, both sides know exactly where they stand in terms of their financial and other responsibilities.

This chapter discusses the practical and legal issues that can arise when converting a term sheet into a legally enforceable contract.

That contract document, and any associated materials, form part, but not all, of the 'matrix of facts' that underpins the contract. It is this broader matrix that will be considered by a court if a disagreement between the two parties escalates into legal action.

Additionally, any contract at main board level also needs to be prepared in the light of investors' expectations. In the UK, the two major representative bodies for the communities of institutional investors, the Association of British Insurers (ABI) and the National Association of Pension Funds (NAPF), have prepared joint guidance on what they expect to see included in, and excluded from, senior executive contracts. This chapter assumes that companies will seek to comply with what are, generally, a sensible set of principles.

Preparing the ground

Where will a draftsman start when converting agreed terms into a contract? Generally, the draftsman will seek comprehensiveness, clarity and concision, in that order.

A starting point can be the staff handbook of the employer, which should set out mutual responsibilities. By referring to this document, the draftsman is linking the executive contract to a key part of the terms and conditions of all employees. And as this document will typically be updated on a regular basis, it will be incorporating an update mechanism into the individual's specific contractual terms.

The draftsman will also be aware of the constraints imposed by the term sheet itself, and by any issues raised in the discussions to date. Usually, he will be working with a term sheet, and discussions, which have been clearly flagged as 'subject to contract', but he will be very sensitive to the fact that in employment law a verbal contract is as binding as a written agreement, albeit potentially harder to evidence.

There are likely to be other conditions which need to be satisfied before the agreement can be finalised, and the draftsman will want to ensure either that these are satisfied before the contract is signed or that the contract can be varied or terminated on short notice if, subsequent to the contract being signed, these conditions are not met. These conditions may include:

- satisfactory completion of reference taking;
- negative drug screen;
- proof of right to work in the UK;[1]
- credit checks;
- regulatory approval; and, critically,
- that there are no restrictions which would prevent the candidate working for the new employer.

In an increasingly litigious employment environment, the last of these is particularly important. The new employer will want to be assured that there are no covenants or other restrictions, usually relating to employment with the individual's current employer, which would either prevent them joining the new employer or, more likely, prevent them joining before a certain date.[2]

The inclusion of these conditions in the contract itself, or ideally also in the initial term sheet, makes sure the candidate is aware of what is expected and that they are able to give thought to whether they can meet all the conditions. Failing to run these checks can have serious consequences for both employer and candidate. In the worst case, they can leave the candidate and employer subject to fines from regulators or to actions for damages or injunction from a former employer claiming breach of the candidate's existing contractual obligations, or the inducement of a breach of those obligations by the prospective employer.[3]

The draftsman will also want to make sure that:

- in being comprehensive the contract has drawn a line under any other potentially enforceable agreements; this will usually be done by a

---

[1] As required under Section 8 of the Asylum & Immigration Act 1996.

[2] In some cases, restrictions may be set out in the previous contract which are, in legal terms, unenforceable. For example, the candidate's former employer may have set them at a length which any UK court would consider unreasonably long or a geographic reach which is too wide. The UK courts will tend to oppose these as a restraint of trade.

[3] Some candidates may seek some form of comfort letter or indemnity from a prospective employer, to protect them if their current employer pursues them for a breach of covenant. Such letters and/or indemnity provisions expose the new employer both to a potentially large financial exposure and to the risk that the former employer will use them as evidence of inducement of a breach. A better approach is to ensure that the candidate has taken legal advice on what existing obligations, if any, he is under.

generic clause that cancels any previous agreements, in whatever form; and

- in being clear, it establishes the precedence of the contract over any other documents which may form part of the contractual matrix, such as the staff handbook[4] or the generic rules of pension plans and share schemes.

A final consideration for the employer is who will 'case manage' the finalisation of the contract. Practice varies on this. In some cases the hiring manager, i.e. the candidate's prospective boss, will remain closely involved: effectively instructing the draftsman. In other cases, the hiring manager may prefer to keep the negotiations at arm's length and rely on a Human Resources ('HR') or legal colleague to oversee this stage, or act as the main intermediary. Ultimately, this may be a matter of personal taste. But it is helpful to be aware that this can be approached in different ways, and configured to accommodate the preferences and strengths of the hiring manager.

Main provisions of the contract

At a minimum, the contract will incorporate the statutory particulars of employment required under Section 1 of the Employment Rights Act 1996. But typically, for a senior executive, more onerous provisions will be included, providing additional protection for the employer.

The draftsman will be able to bear several things in mind:

- whether there are any specific provisions that need to be included, for example, because the individual is, or may be required to be, a director of the employing company or any associated companies;[5]

---

[4] This allows the employer to apply, for example, expedited disciplinary and grievance processes that may be swifter than those which would normally apply to the wider employee population. It can also ensure that, in the event of a dispute, the executive cannot connect his terms to a collective agreement with trade unions that may also apply to the wider employee population.

[5] The most critical additions for prospective directors' contracts are to capture the term of their appointment as such and any provisions for removal as a director, and, from the individual's perspective, what indemnities are provided to protect them from litigation in respect of (non-criminal and non-negligent) acts performed while a director. In most cases, the draftsman will refer to the relevant articles of association of the companies concerned, to ensure that specific requirements are captured and processes for appointment are followed. Some candidates may also seek separate insurance ('Directors' and Officers' liability insurance') alongside the indemnity. While this is an increasingly common additional protection, less common is the further protection of the extension of indemnities and/or insurance beyond termination of the employment contract. A further wrinkle for directorships is the requirement to disclose remuneration of directors, including those of subsidiary companies, in any UK report and accounts. It is important that anyone becoming a director is made aware of what aspects, if any, of their remuneration may enter the public domain in this way.

- whether any one-off payments, such as those that might be associated with the type of buyout referred to in Chapter 1, can be captured in a separate schedule: leaving the main contract terms to cover the 'run-rate' remuneration that will apply on a regular basis;
- whether there are any special flexibilities and restrictions that need to be accommodated, for example, requirements for the individual to be internationally mobile.

He will also be considering a fourth factor, alongside comprehensiveness, clarity and concision: flexibility. As far as possible, the contract should be able to accommodate the full range of commercial circumstances that may arise over the course of the executive's career with the new employer.

In general terms, the draftsman will need to make sure the contract answers the following key questions:

- When does the agreement start?
- What are the time commitments involved?
- Where will any disputes about the contract be heard?
- What potential changes in the employment relationship need to be captured?
- How will the contract be brought to an end, by either party? And if it is, what restrictions will apply?

When does the agreement start?

There are effectively two start dates. The first is the date that the agreement takes effect, i.e. the date of the contract, when it is signed. The second is the date when the individual can actually start working for the new employer. Where there is a difference, as there is in most cases, the draftsman will be sensitive to the risk that the individual may never reach the employment date, for example because either a condition of some kind (e.g. legal right to work) is not satisfied or they receive a counter offer. This will influence when any one-off payments are actually made, and also whether there is an overriding cut-off date which, if the individual is not working by that date, expressly causes the frustration of the contract.

Footnote 5 *(cont.)*

In terms of providing for removal of an employee who is also a director, generally the employer's wish to terminate the office will be connected with a termination of the employment. But they are separate. This separation can be addressed by providing for a power of attorney in the contract, usually as a schedule, which provides that, if an individual refuses to resign as a director after they have been given notice of termination as an employee, the employing company can act on their behalf for the remainder of their time on the board. If such powers of attorney are included, the contract will need to be executed as a deed for these to be effective.

What are the time commitments involved?

Under the Working Time Regulations 1988 (WTR), employers are required to take all reasonable steps to ensure that their workers do not work more than forty-eight hours a week (averaged over a seventeen-week period). However, it is normal for executives to opt out of the average maximum 48-hour week if certain conditions are met. But an even more robust approach is to deem senior executives to be among those whose working time is neither measured nor determined under the WTR and can instead be determined by the worker himself. Where this is the case, the 48-hour restriction will not apply. Nevertheless, while opt-outs of this kind remain lawful, there is significant debate at European Union level on whether this should be the case and the situation should be monitored. For this reason, some draftsmen will recommend that any opt-out is only obtained after a reasonable period has elapsed after the start of employment, to avoid the risk that undue pressure could be seen to be exerted to obtain the opt-out at the outset.

Where will any disputes about the contract be heard?

For UK-based companies, the contract will usually be drafted on the basis that it is governed by the law of England and Wales, reflected in the 'jurisdiction' clause. This enables the parties to agree at the outset of their contractual relationship which courts will have jurisdiction to hear any disputes arising from the contract.

The drafting of these clauses is usually wide, to cover all situations. Most employers go for a choice of exclusive jurisdiction, which attempts to prevent the employee from bringing proceedings against the employer in any country except England or Wales. If the employee attempted this, the employer would be entitled to apply to have the proceedings stayed. There is no certainty here, as courts are not bound by the terms of the contract.

Some forward-thinking employers also now include a clause which provides that the parties will attempt to settle any dispute, complaint or disagreement arising from the contract by mediation. This can be more efficient for both parties, but as mediation is meant to be entered into on a voluntary basis it may not be enforceable as a contractual term.

What potential changes in the employment relationship need to be captured?

The individual will usually seek comfort that they cannot be demoted once appointed to the role (and, if they are, this will be a dismissal without cause which will trigger severance payments). They may also seek reassurance that no-one can be appointed alongside them, making the role 'joint'.

The draftsman's concern here will be to ensure that the way such protections are phrased does not fetter the employer and prevent business reorganisations which may reasonably be expected to occur.

A further change that candidates may seek reassurance on is the status of the contract in the event of a change of control of the employing company. Generally, UK companies will take the position that the lengthy notice periods characteristic of UK senior contracts are more than sufficient protection if this occurs, in contrast to the abrupt way in which, say, many US contracts can be terminated. Few companies in the UK, therefore, include provisions dealing with change of control. And most companies carrying out due diligence look for such provisions with particular vigilance.

How will the contract be brought to an end, by either party? And if it is, what restrictions will apply?

The most complex part of the draftsman's task is likely to be the termination provisions. Essentially, he has to make sure there is a balance between the need to protect the earning potential of the executive and the commercial needs of the employer.

Termination provisions will, accordingly, have three dimensions:

- time – how long after either side has said they want to terminate the agreement (i.e. 'give notice of termination') will (a) the employment relationship, and (b) any other obligations, cease?
- money – what is a reasonable and clear way of calculating what amount of money, if any, should be paid by the party (in practice, typically the employer) doing the terminating to the other?
- restrictions – what will either party be able to do after termination?

The dimension of time will be expressed in terms of a notice period. Usually the employer will be required to give more notice that they wish to terminate than will the employee. At the level of the senior UK executive, this will typically be between six and twelve months. But the contract will usually specify some circumstances where no notice need be given, such as where the employee has committed an act of gross misconduct.

The notice period will determine the point at which the employment relationship ends, together with the duties that the employer owes to the executive as an employee (e.g. in terms of health and safety).

The notice period is also essentially a protective period during which the employee remains under an obligation to follow the reasonable instructions of the employer. This is a fairly simple and enforceable principle when considering a one- or three-month notice period, as it is difficult for an employee to argue that this is restrictive. But longer periods carry more risk for the employer that the employee will be able to argue that they are unduly restrictive, and are keeping them out of the market place. To be able to mitigate this risk, the employer will need to demonstrate that it requires that length of time for good commercial reasons which reflect its legitimate business interests, such as repairing client connections, rebuilding a business strategy or preventing the 'poaching' of valuable employees.

The challenge for the employer is also how to maintain this period of restriction without having the employee on the premises. It is this challenge that has produced the uniquely British invention of 'gardening leave'. Similar in some senses to 'house arrest', gardening leave means the employee is still employed but considered to be fulfilling their duties from home, or anywhere which is neither the current workplace nor any other workplace.

In many cases companies do not wish to terminate a contract by serving notice on executives, rather they wish to accelerate the point of departure. In these circumstances the company must either reach a negotiated settlement of damages for breach of contract or make provision for a PILON ('payment in lieu of notice'). This is a provision that allows the employer to accelerate the date on which the employee ceases to be an employee, by making a payment in compensation for what the employee would have received had they worked to the end of the notice period. PILONs take various forms, they may be paid in instalments or a single lump sum and may be restricted to salary or extended to include an amount in lieu of benefits in kind or, less commonly, bonus for the period of the employment forgone. PILONs have many attractions to both sides, particularly by providing certainty. They are usually only triggered at the choice of the employer. The challenge they raise is in maintaining the enforceability of restrictions, discussed below.

The dimension of time will determine the quantum of money on termination. The key legal concept which shapes the dimension of money, however, is that of 'mitigation'. Under English law, parties have an obligation to mitigate any losses they have under a broken contract and company directors have a fiduciary obligation to minimise the cost of any termination. In an employment context, that means that, if the employee obtains employment during the period, say, when they are receiving payments under a PILON, the payment can cease, because the new employment mitigates the loss for which the PILON was compensating.

Both the ABI and NAPF rightly expect companies to enforce mitigation obligations vigorously. However, notwithstanding their expectations, individual employees will often resist any attempt to make mitigation a contractual requirement. Instead, there is often a request by a candidate for the inclusion of a 'liquidated damages' clause, which provides for a fixed amount to be paid on termination without any requirement for mitigation. But even where this is the case, there may be some scope for the two parties to negotiate the period during which liquidated damages might be paid (usually part of the notice period, such as the first half of, typically, three to six months), after which any payments must be subject to mitigation.

The third dimension, of restrictions, varies somewhat, dependent on the practice of the industry concerned. In the investment banking sector the notice period, together with any express confidentiality provision and requirements relating to protection of intellectual property, are really the only common restrictions. In other sectors, additional provisions around non-solicitation of clients and employees are also common. The key question an employer needs to ask before imposing a restriction is whether a court will be able to satisfy itself that the employer needs it to protect its legitimate business interests. If not, the risk is that all the restrictions could be struck out as a restraint of the employee's trade.

The restriction that is likely to be least controversial is the restriction on the solicitation of employees by the exiting employee. But these restrictions need to be used sparingly, and limited to those realistically in a position to effect solicitation: team leaders, managers and senior executives. Broad brush application of this restriction, e.g. to all employees above a certain level, can dilute its effectiveness.

Non-solicitation of clients, and, more broadly, non-dealing with clients, flies closer to the wind of restraint of trade than non-solicitation of employees. As does non-competition, i.e. not working for a competitor or, on the employee's own account, in competition with their former employer.

It is also best for these restrictions to activate on the serving of notice, i.e. any period of restriction runs concurrently with the notice period and, typically, some months beyond.

The uncertain enforceability of these restrictions may be what prompts many employers to look at other ways of maintaining some leverage over former employees. One simple but effective way is through deferred compensation, such as deferred portions of annual bonus, which are forfeited if the holder goes to work for a competitor. These types of 'financial' restrictions, often through use of share plans, have not been tested in the courts, so should be treated with some caution.

Finally, there are restrictions which the employer can impose with impunity. These include a requirement of confidentiality and a requirement for protection of the employer's intellectual property,[6] including works created by the employee during the course of his employment.

The final check

When the draftsman returns the contract, the employer and candidate will want to do a final check:

- Does the contract as drafted reflect the spirit and letter of the term sheet?

---

[6] Intellectual property can be protected by including in the contract a provision that the employee assigns the rights of the work to the employer. If this is done, the contract needs to be executed as a deed for this assignment to be effective.

- Are there any circumstances which could arise, which we can reasonably anticipate, which would create problems under this contract?
- If it all ends tomorrow, is it clear what happens?

If the answer to any of these questions is 'no', send it back.

3

Valuing the package

EMMA NICHOLSON AND ALISON SMITH

Chapter 1 introduced the concept of the 'number' representing the value of an executive remuneration package. In determining this 'number', different valuation techniques and methodologies can be used. This chapter explores these different methods and the relative merits and shortcomings of each. In doing this it will become clear that these methods rely on various assumptions which may vary at any given time and in different situations. Whilst the 'number' is a practical and useful way of distilling all relevant information into a simple and easily understood reference point, the reality is that the best result is likely to be an acceptable range around the 'number'.

Overview

The main purpose in determining a 'number' which represents the value of the package is to allow a comparison of the value of different arrangements. This may be to determine the value of the existing arrangements of a potential recruit or to ensure that a package is competitive relative to the rest of the market. It is important to be clear on the purpose as this may influence the methodological approach to be taken. As we will see, there are many ways of valuing different elements, some of which are highly complex, but when considering how to deal with some of these things there are some basic points to keep in mind. Any methodology should be easy to understand and explain; it should be consistent and it should be possible to replicate it; most importantly, it should be defensible. Figure 3.1 provides a framework for thinking about the methodology to be adopted.

The valuation approach should take into consideration the effect of different features of the various elements of remuneration. For example, it should take into account the fact that £100,000 cash salary now has more value than a potential £100,000 cash bonus which may lapse if certain conditions are not met or £100,000 of shares that would be forfeit if employment ceased before the end of a specified period.

The process of valuing the package aims to incorporate all of these different features to allow the various elements of remuneration to be compared on a like-for-like basis.

Figure 3.1 *A valuation framework*

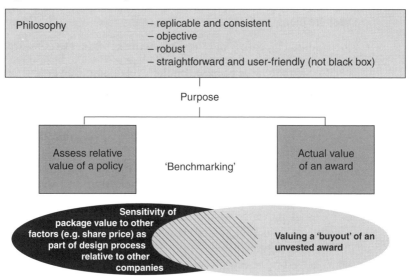

There is no perfect technique for valuing the remuneration package and the different components can be treated differently. The most difficult elements of the package to value are shares, share options and other non-cash benefits (e.g. retirement benefits). This is mainly due to the fact that these elements are often delivered at the end of a number of years (for shares and share options typically three years, for pension benefits even longer) and the value that will be delivered may depend on the future share price performance of the company. Future share price performance is of course dependent on many factors and is very difficult to predict. An additional problem associated with shares and share options is that there is often a wide variety of different design features (particularly performance measures) which make it even more difficult to compare the elements on a like-for-like basis. For example, how do you assess which is more valuable – a grant of £100,000 of share options with a total shareholder return (TSR) performance measure compared with the same-sized grant with an earnings per share (EPS) performance measure?

However, the difficulties are not limited to shares and share options. Valuing a cash annual bonus plan where the payout is subject to the achievement of performance targets requires an estimation as to whether the targets will be achieved, which will involve a degree of subjectivity. In addition, it could be argued that even the actual salary of an individual which is paid in cash and is not deferred in any way is related to the performance of the individual and therefore is not directly comparable between individuals and companies.

Potential approaches to valuing short- and long-term incentive and share plans

When valuing incentive and share plans the key issues to consider are:

- Should the value be based on the level of actual award made in a given year or the potential that might be earned? The former may be easier in that this information may be more readily available but it may be more volatile on a year-on-year basis, given that the level of award made to a given individual in a particular year may be due to factors other than performance, for example larger awards than normal might be made to reflect promotion, or a new appointment. The latter represents the company policy on incentive and share plan awards and may be more helpful in benchmarking across different companies. It indicates what level of award would normally be made, all other things being equal. However, this information may not always be as readily available.
- The vesting of any incentive or share award will normally be based on certain performance targets being met. These targets will vary from company to company, and sometimes between individuals in the same company. They may be based on internal financial or business measures, or may be based on performance relative to other companies. However the award is to be valued, it will be necessary to make some judgments about the probability of achieving the performance targets. This can be done by making an assessment for each company based on historical and/or, for example, using a stochastic technique, such as 'Monte Carlo' simulation and projected performance. When benchmarking a number of companies, this can be time-consuming and subjective and may not be consistent between companies. Another alternative is to look at performance generally across a relevant index or comparator group of companies and apply a consistent probability to all companies.
- The final value of a share award will be based on the future share price performance which is an unknown. One option is to look at the expected share price performance of each company by looking at historical share price movement and volatility. Another option is to look at general share price growth across an index or a comparator group of companies and apply the same assumptions to each company.
- The risk of forfeiture. An incentive award may be earned but deferred for a number of years. This award may be forfeit if the participant leaves the company. In other cases the award is dependent not only on still being employed at the end of the deferred period but also on whether certain performance targets have been achieved. It is important to be clear on how this impacts the value of the award.

In some cases it may be appropriate to take into account the risk of forfeiture where this is based solely on remaining in employment. For the purposes of benchmarking the packages of different companies, it is probably reasonable to assume that all participants will remain in employment and therefore it may not be necessary to build this into the valuation. However, where the award is based on the requirement to achieve specific performance targets, this can clearly have a significant impact on the valuation.

- The vesting period. Although the majority of deferred bonus plans and long-term incentive plans require a three-year vesting or performance period, this is not always the case. This will of course impact the value of the award since this will affect the present value and allows a longer period for potential share price growth. However, this is unlikely to make a significant difference to the final values and it may be simpler to assume a three-year vesting period for all awards.
- There are other design features in long-term incentive plans such as re-testing of performance conditions or further retention periods at the end of the performance periods. These can be built into the valuation methodology but will add a level of complexity which may not be worthwhile. It may be simpler to value everything on the basis of a three-year performance and vesting period.
- A payment made now is worth more than one which is deferred for a period of time and therefore it is normally appropriate to discount deferred payments by an appropriate factor to reflect the present value of the award.

These different ways of looking at the value may be equally valid in all circumstances but, in general, if the aim is to value the package of a specific individual for the purpose of recruitment or for a new appointment, then taking the individual awards and a company-specific approach to performance may be more appropriate. If the purpose is to conduct a benchmarking exercise across a number of companies in order to review the competitiveness of a company's current arrangements, then it may be more appropriate to base the value on policy and take a standardised and consistent approach to the expected performance of all companies.

The most common approaches to valuing the package are called 'expected value' and 'projected value':

- *Expected value* – An expected value for a situation with a number of mutually exclusive possible outcomes is the sum of the probability of each possible outcome multiplied by the potential value. It therefore represents the value which might be expected, on average, if the same situation was repeated many times. Note that the value generated by this approach may not be expected in the general sense; it may be unlikely or even impossible. For example, the expected value for an annual bonus which is equally likely to vest in full (i.e. 100%) or not at all (0%) is 50%, which is not one of the possible outcomes.

The expected value takes into account factors such as vesting restrictions, probability of achieving performance goals, risk of forfeitures, etc.

The expected value provides a 'number' for the package and the expected value of an opportunity is what a rational person might pay for that opportunity.

- *Projected value* – The projected value calculates what the value of the package would be in a given set of circumstances. Instead of looking at the average value of a given element, the projected value approach considers the value of the element assuming that on-target performance is achieved and that this would be accompanied by share price growth of x% or that outstanding performance was achieved and that this would be accompanied by a higher share price growth. Assumptions still need to be made about the probability of achieving performance targets but the level of vesting that would be achieved for this level of performance is usually readily available. For a given level of performance and an assumed share price growth, it is then possible to calculate the value at the end of a given period.

  This provides a reasonable range in which the value of the package may fall.

Other approaches which may be considered and may provide useful or simple ways of comparing individual elements of a package are as follows:

- *Face value* – The face value of an incentive share award is the share price at grant multiplied by the number of shares or options which are granted.

  This approach could not be used to value and compare the remuneration packages of different companies with different types of share plan in place because it is not possible to compare a performance share and a share option in this way. Market value share options with a face value of £100,000 are not equal in value to performance shares with a face value of £100,000 because the share options are worthless unless the share price increases whereas the performance shares always have value.

  However, this approach is very straightforward and transparent and can be used to compare the award levels in different plans. For example, if you have a performance share plan you can quickly compare the face value of the typical award level with other companies operating performance share plans.

- *Intrinsic value* – The intrinsic value represents the value of an incentive at a particular point in time. For example, for a share option this represents the current share price less the exercise price. It would not be appropriate to benchmark the package using the intrinsic value because this number is affected by the share price movement on a daily basis. It would also be meaningless to look at the intrinsic value of share options at grant because they would have no value. However, it can be helpful to consider the intrinsic value when determining the 'number' for buyout purposes, because it provides a snapshot of the value of the incentives at a particular point.

It is important to remember when considering the different valuation approaches, that none of them precisely value the package and will only provide an **estimate** of the value. In addition all of the approaches rely on a set of assumptions and therefore the estimated value that they produce will only be as reliable as the assumptions that are used. The old adage of 'garbage in, garbage out' applies.

Figure 3.2 provides an illustration of the different values for two share incentive awards:

- share option grant: 100% of salary (no performance conditions);
- performance share award: 100% of salary, 30% vesting for target performance and 100% vesting for upper quartile performance.

The chart illustrates the range of values that could be assigned to the different share awards and shows how the different approaches could be used together to determine an appropriate value for the package. It demonstrates that the expected value tends to sit somewhere within the range produced by the projected value. It also shows the volatility of the intrinsic value; and the weakness of the face value approach which does not differentiate between performance shares and options.

Valuing each element

We can now examine each element of the remuneration package in more detail and show how an expected value and projected value approach could be used to determine the value.

Salary

Base salaries are fixed annual payments, which are paid in cash and which are not related to company performance. The value of a salary is therefore relatively straightforward.

Salaries are usually reviewed and increased annually and companies conduct this process at different points during the year. Therefore, for benchmarking purposes, salary data will normally be aged by the prevailing rate of salary inflation, to ensure the information is up to date. It is important to use an appropriate aging factor and to ensure that this reflects to some degree both historical data and trends on salary increases and future expectations. The aging factor should be realistic but conservative to ensure that the aging process is not responsible in itself for ratcheting up salary levels.

Figure 3.2 *Expected value vs projected value*

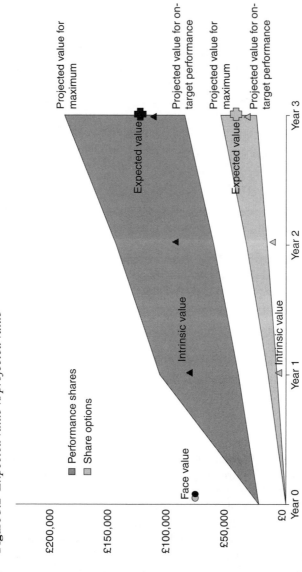

The value of the salary will be the same under both an expected and projected value approach.

Benefits in kind

The range of benefits that may be provided, as well as their relative importance as part of an overall executive's package, are considered in more detail in Chapter 4. Aside from pension arrangements (which are considered at the end of this chapter), benefits rarely make up a substantial proportion of the remuneration package of an executive director. Therefore, we have not considered in any detail how these would be valued in order to determine the 'number' for a package.

For executive directors, the simplest way of valuing the benefits is to use the value disclosed in the remuneration table in the remuneration report. However, it is important to note where additional untypical elements have been included in this disclosure, such as relocation allowances, housing and education allowances.

This ignores the debate about whether the benefit should be valued based on the cost to the company or the value to the individual, or indeed the perceived value to the individual, which may be different. These issues become more important when benchmarking all employee remuneration, but at executive level benefits are a much smaller element of the total remuneration and therefore less of an issue.

The value of the benefits, if included, will be the same under both an expected and projected value approach.

Annual incentive plans

The annual incentive or bonus is typically a cash payment paid out annually subject to the achievement of performance targets over a single financial year.

It is difficult to compare precisely the annual bonus plans between different companies on a like-for-like basis, because it is almost impossible to assess how stretching the performance targets are. For example, one company may set targets so that the maximum bonus would only be paid out if the company substantially out-performs a stretching budget, whereas another company may set the targets so that the maximum annual bonus will be paid out if the company meets an achievable budget.

Projected value

For projected value purposes, the value of the annual bonus is based on the company's annual bonus policy. For example, a company may have a maximum annual bonus of 100% of salary with 50% of salary payable for achieving on-target performance. For the projected value for on-target performance, the value would be 50% of salary. Where a company does not disclose the level of bonus paid for on-target performance it is possible to make assumptions based on typical market practice. The maximum of 100% of salary would be included in the projected value for maximum performance. This approach does not solve the problem of assessing the level of stretch in different companies' targets but compares what would be payable for on-target performance on a consistent basis.

Expected value

There are a number of approaches which may be used to determine the expected value of an annual incentive:

- Target level or 50% of the maximum. This assumes that this is the value which is most likely to be paid out (as with the projected value approach, this does not solve the problem that companies set targets with varying levels of stretch).
- The most recent actual annual bonus. This assumes the level of payout in the last financial year provides the best indication of the likely level of payout for the coming year. The disadvantage associated with this approach is that it is not possible to compare companies on a like-for-like basis. In addition it does not allow for the fact that a particular company, or individual, may have had a very good or very bad year, or the fact that the company may have set the targets on a different basis for the coming year.
- Three-year-average annual actual bonus payments. This works on a similar principle to using the most recent annual actual bonus. However, the average smooths the volatility of bonus payments. The disadvantage of this approach is that it is based on out-of-date information.

Deferred annual incentive plans

Participants may be required to defer part or all of their annual incentive for a fixed period (typically three years) into shares in the company. The final value of this award will depend on the share price at the end of the deferred period. Basing the value of the deferred bonus on what this share price might be would make the deferred portion of the bonus appear more valuable than an up-front cash award. Clearly from the perspective of the participant this would not necessarily be the case. Given that, as long as the participant remains with the company there is no further risk of forfeiture, it makes more sense to value this award in the same way as a cash bonus with the value discounted to reflect the present value of the award.

Annual incentives – matching shares on deferral

Where matching shares are awarded at the end of the deferral period, these will usually be subject to further performance conditions and, from the point of view of valuation, can be considered in the same way as an award of performance shares as described below.

Long-term incentives

Long-term incentives are the most contentious element of the package to value due to the number of assumptions that have to be made in order to derive a representative value. The reliability of this value is clearly dependent on the appropriateness and reliability of the inputs. It may often be necessary to use historical information as an indicator of future behaviour and to drive the assumptions.

Projected value

The projected value of long-term share incentives is based on a projection of the potential gains under a number of different scenarios which might, for example, include on-target (which might be thought of as median) performance and superior (which might be thought of as equivalent to upper quartile) performance. It may also be helpful to look at the value of the maximum that might be paid which may be different to superior performance. Different share price growth assumptions will accompany each of these. The difference between the value under each scenario will therefore be based on the share price growth and the proportion of the award that is expected to vest. The final value will be discounted to reflect the present value.

Share price growth assumption

The share price growth assumption is particularly important for valuing share options as they only have value if the share price increases (share awards have inherent value in the underlying share price).

The starting point for the assumption will usually be historic share price growth and this may be measured over a broad market (for example FTSE 350, AllShare), a specific industry sector, a specific type of company (for example high-growth companies) or a specific group of comparator companies. It may be appropriate to look at each company individually, although it is important to note the dangers associated with trying to compare values that have been calculated using different bases. There are situations where it may be considered appropriate, for example an executive being recruited from a low share price growth industry to a high share price growth industry, or from overseas. In this case it may be appropriate to compute the two packages using different share price growth assumptions reflecting the fact that the executive may stand to make much larger gains on shares granted with high share price growth potential than those with lower share price growth potential.

Usually where share price growth assumptions are applied over a period, a present value discount factor is also applied.

41

Figure 3.3 *Example of projected value*

$$\text{Target projected value} = \frac{(\pounds100{,}000 \times (1 + 10\%) \times (1 + 10\%) \times (1 + 10\%))}{((1 + 5\%) \times (1 + 5\%) \times (1 + 5\%))} - \pounds100{,}000 = \pounds14{,}977$$

Figure 3.3 illustrates the projected value for a share option (face value £100,000) with a three-year vesting period and with share price growth at 10% p.a. and with a discount factor of 5% p.a.

Performance conditions

Where awards have performance conditions attached, the next step is to consider the likelihood of the awards vesting under each of the scenarios.

In the UK the level of vesting will usually be determined by achievement against performance targets. This will be usually be scaled with the full award vesting for 'maximum' performance and a portion (e.g. 30%) vesting for a threshold level of performance ('on-target' performance). Usually vesting will be on a straight line between these two points.

The maximum projected value is obviously the maximum level of vesting. For the on-target projected value, one approach would be to assume that the threshold level vesting is equivalent to target performance. For superior performance, one approach would be to take the level of vesting for upper quartile performance which may be relatively straightforward for a TSR-based plan but is more difficult to assess for other performance measures. The weakness of this approach is that it assumes companies set equally stretching performance targets.

An alternative to this approach is to determine for each performance metric what level of performance would represent 'on-target' and superior performance. This would be applied to each performance schedule on a consistent basis to determine the level of vesting at this prescribed level of 'target' performance. For example, using historic EPS data it may be determined that, for a given market or industry sector, on-target, or median, performance is growth of Retail Prices Index ('RPI') + 5% p.a. Upper quartile performance might be more like RPI + 10% p.a.

For TSR measures, where performance is measured relative to positioning within a group of companies, it is much easier as most plans have a threshold level of vesting for achieving median performance and most plans specify the percentile with the market that is required for maximum vesting, making it easy to calculate the level of vesting for upper quartile performance.

Where more bespoke performance measures are used, it is much more difficult. It may not be appropriate or possible to perform historical analysis for all potential measures and in these instances it may be necessary to rely on each company's assessment of 'target' performance.

Figure 3.4 provides an example of the projected value for a performance share award (face value £100,000) with vesting dependent on TSR

Figure 3.4 *Projected value under three performance scenarios*

Face value of shares at grant	£100,000		
Target			
Share price growth	(100,000 × (1+10%) × (1+10%) × (1+10%)) / ((1+5%) × (1+5%) × (1+5%))	=	£114,977
Level of vesting	30%	=	30%
Target projected value	114,977 × 30%	=	£34,493
Superior			
Share price growth	(100,000 × (1+15%) × (1+15%) × (1+15%)) / ((1+5%) × (1+5%) × (1+5%))	=	£131,379
Level of vesting	(75% − 30%)/(90% − 30%) × (100% − 30%) + 30% =		82.5%
Superior projected value	131,379 × 82.5%	=	£108,388
Maximum			
Share price growth	(100,000 × (1+20%) × (1+20%) × (1+20%)) / ((1+5%) × (1+5%) × (1+5%))	=	£149,271
Level of vesting	100%	=	100%
Superior projected value	149,271 × 100%	=	£149,271

performance relative to the FTSE 100. Of this award, 30% vests for median TSR performance and 100% vests for upper decile performance, with straight line vesting in between.

The projected value at target, superior and maximum has been calculated based on the following assumptions:

- target share price growth – 10% p.a.;
- target TSR performance – median within comparator group;
- superior share price growth – 15% p.a.;
- superior TSR performance – upper quartile with the comparator group;
- maximum share price growth – 20% p.a.;
- discount factor – 5% p.a.

Dividends

Where awards carry entitlement to dividends that are paid during the vesting period, investor guidelines suggest that remuneration committees should take the expected value of dividends on awards into account when determining the size of long-term incentive awards.

It may be appropriate therefore to include the potential value of dividends that would be paid in the 'value' where awards carry this entitlement. This requires an assumption about likely dividend yield. This can be applied on a company-by-company basis or by applying a general assumption based on the whole market. In the absence of any other information in relation to forward-looking dividend policies, historical analysis of dividend yields may provide the best basis for any assumptions.

Expected value

Instead of looking at a projection of the potential gains under a number of different scenarios, the expected value provides a weighted average of the values for each scenario based on the probability of each potential outcome.

To value share options there are a number of option pricing tools which can be used, such as the Black-Scholes formula, binomial ('lattice') model or Monte Carlo simulation.

The Black-Scholes methodology is the simplest and probably most commonly used approach. The formula, which was originally developed for valuing traded options, takes a number of key inputs relating to the shares of the company (share price volatility and dividend yield) and calculates the value which might be expected given these inputs. The binomial model and Monte Carlo model use these inputs along with other assumptions (e.g. share price correlation and the typical behaviour of participants in terms of when they exercise the options).

Following the adoption of International Financial Reporting Standard ('IFRS') 2 and Financial Reporting Standard ('FRS') 20 which require companies to recognise the fair value of all share incentives as an expense, nearly all companies are using one or more of these methodologies to value their share incentives. Fair value is defined as the estimated price of a share-based payment in 'an arm's length transaction between knowledgeable, willing parties', which in effect is the same as the expected value.

When valuing share incentive awards, an expected value approach will typically build in a number of additional variables, including performance targets and vesting schedules, employee forfeiture rates, discount factors, etc.

The basis for the expected value of share awards is the share price, with adjustments to reflect whether there is an entitlement to dividends, performance schedules and forfeiture rates.

The extent to which the output of each option pricing model represents a reasonable 'expected value' for the share option depends entirely on the appropriateness of the inputs to the option pricing tool. Each of the commonly used inputs for determining an expected value are examined below.

Share price volatility

Share price volatility is a measure of the amount by which share price returns fluctuate in a period (this will generally take into account the value of dividends as well as share price growth). Generally the higher the volatility, the higher the value of the option.

Historical volatility may provide a good starting point to determine an assumption about future share price volatility. Depending upon the purpose of the valuation, different approaches may be applied. For example if the valuation is for buyout purposes it would be appropriate to focus on the volatility of the specific company. If the valuation is to provide a comparison against a large number of companies, it may be simpler to consider the historical share price volatility either across the whole group of companies, or on an industry basis, and apply a consistent number across all companies.

It is important to consider whether there is anything that might have affected the historical volatility which is unlikely to reoccur in the future. This is particularly important when looking at the volatility for a particular company. For example, when a company is newly listed it may have a high share price volatility for a number of years, after which it will begin to settle down. Where a company is newly listed or unlisted, it may be more appropriate to look at the volatility of other companies within the same industry sector, or a more general market, in order to get a more realistic view of future volatility.

Share price volatility is measured over a particular period. Usually it will be appropriate to consider the share price volatility over a period commensurate with the vesting period for the incentives in question (typically three years).

Dividend yield

The dividend yield represents the value that leaks away from options or shares when dividends are paid during the vesting period. Therefore an assumption about the dividend yield should only be used where awards do not carry an entitlement to dividends during the vesting period. Generally the higher the dividend yield, the lower the value of the options.

Where there is information available about a company's forward-looking dividend policy, it would be possible to base the dividend assumption on this. Alternatively, historical dividend yield information would provide a good starting point. Again it would be important to consider whether it was appropriate to make the assumption based on a specific company or to make a more generalised assumption (based on an industry sector or the whole market) that could then be applied to all of the comparator companies.

Figure 3.5 summarises the impact each of these factors has on the expected value of a share award.

It should now be clear that the expected value will vary depending upon the assumptions used. However, the following example in Figure 3.6 shows the expected value of a share option using some standard assumptions.

Performance conditions

As with the projected value approach, it is important to consider the probability of the awards vesting based on the achievement of performance targets.

45

Figure 3.5 *Impact of input factors*

Input	Impact of increasing input on expected value	Intuition
Share price	⋂⋂⋂	Increased share price while exercise price is constant, the option will be more in the money and have more value
Exercise price	⋃⋃⋃	Increased exercise price while share price is constant, the option will be more out of the money and have less value
Volatility	⋂⋂⋂	As volatility increases, there is more chance that the share price rises above the exercise price
Dividends	⋃⋃⋃	If you're not entitled to dividends, value is leaking away from your shares/options whenever dividends are paid
Time	⋂⋂⋂*	The longer the time, the more chance of the share price rising * *except with high dividends*
Interest rate	⋂⋂⋂	You need less money today to be able to have the exercise monies at the time of exercise. Therefore, the option has more value

Figure 3.6 *Expected value of a share option*

The expected value of a market value share option using a Black-Scholes model and the following inputs – volatility of 25%, dividend yield of 2.5%, interest rate of 5% and expected life of 5 years – would be *c.* **25%** of the face value of the option.

The assumptions relating to performance conditions are even more important for an expected value approach than a projected value approach. The projected value approach provides a range of potential outcomes, generally including the maximum potential, whereas the expected value provides one number which is based on the weighted average probability of vesting.

Using similar approaches to those used in the projected value approach the probability of different levels of vesting can be determined. There are then a number of ways to determine the weighted average probability of the level of vesting.

Where there are a fixed number of potential outcomes (e.g. ranked TSR), a simple approach is to assume that each outcome has an equal probability. Figure 3.7 illustrates this approach where TSR performance is measured relative to a comparator group of nine companies, with 30% vesting for median performance and full vesting for being top of the group.

Figure 3.7 *Example of simple weighted probability*

Position within group	Probability	Vesting	Weighted average probability of vesting
10	10%	0%	0%
9	10%	0%	0%
8	10%	0%	0%
7	10%	0%	0%
6	10%	30%	3%
5	10%	44%	4%
4	10%	58%	6%
3	10%	72%	7%
2	10%	86%	9%
1	10%	100%	10%
			39%

An alternative, illustrated in Figure 3.8, would be to estimate the probability of achieving different levels of performance. For example with EPS it could be assumed that it is 50% likely that EPS growth would be greater than RPI plus 5% p.a., but only 25% likely that EPS growth would be greater than 10% p.a.

The difficulty lies in determining the probability that each level of performance would be achieved. A combination of an analysis of historical data and brokers' forecasts could form the basis of these assumptions.

For less common and more bespoke measures it may be necessary to apply a more standardised approach to determining the inputs. For example, it might be assumed that there is a 75% chance of target vesting and a 50% chance that the maximum will vest.

One other factor that should be taken into account is that good performance will usually be connected to good share price performance. This is clearly the case where the performance measure is linked to share price, such as TSR. However, good performance against earnings based measures

Figure 3.8 *Estimating the probability of a level of vesting*

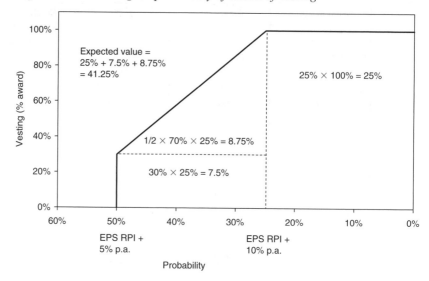

Figure 3.9 *Expected value of a performance share award*

The expected value of a performance share award (with entitlement to dividends) which vests dependent on TSR performance relative to the FTSE 100, with 30% vesting for median performance and maximum vesting for upper quartile performance, would have an expected value of *c.* **55%** of the face value (assuming share price correlation of 25%).

is also likely to be reflected in the share price. This means that where the maximum targets are achieved the value of the award is actually greater than the maximum award level because there will also be an associated increase in share price. The correlation between good performance and share price growth is usually applied to the expected value as an uplift factor. This factor may be based on analysis of the historical correlation between levels of performance and share price growth.

The Monte Carlo simulation is a more sophisticated model which can be used to generate an adjustment which can be applied to the expected value to reflect the probability that performance targets will be met. The Monte Carlo model runs very many (e.g. 10,000) simulations of 'random numbers' to generate an adjustment.

The example in Figure 3.9 shows the expected value of a performance share with a typical TSR performance measure and based on some standard assumptions.

Employee forfeiture rates

It is possible to incorporate the fact that awards are generally subject to continued employment into the expected value. It can be argued that it is inappropriate to adjust the 'value' for this fact as this is a feature which is under the employee's control. For a general benchmarking exercise, it is likely that the same discount would be applied across the board as virtually all long-term incentive plans are subject to continued employment. This discount would have little effect as it would equally decrease the value of most incentive arrangements.

Expected value vs projected value

While it has never been as common in the UK, the US market has always tended to think about remuneration packages in terms of expected value.

The great advantage of the expected value approach from a benchmarking perspective is that the output is one number per company. The ability to produce one value for comparison is particularly useful at recruitment or where new incentives are being introduced and existing arrangements are being bought out.

Under an expected value approach where company-specific factors are used to value incentives (for example, using company-specific historical share price volatility), the expected values will be as much a function of the share price characteristic as of the remuneration policy and award levels. For example, a company with high historical volatility would have a higher expected value on their options than a similar company with lower volatility, even if the award levels, the performance conditions and the vesting schedules attached to the options were identical.

Is this a problem from a benchmarking perspective? Imagine a scenario where the expected value in a company's incentives was lower than the expected value of a benchmark company. As a result, the company increases the award levels to move in line with the benchmark. But what if the high benchmark had been driven by the historical share price characteristics of the benchmark company (such as a high share price volatility), rather than higher award levels? This would mean that award levels were driven by the historical characteristics of benchmark companies rather than by the incentive opportunity that exists in those companies. In addition, benchmarks may change, sometimes quite drastically, year to year, as a result of changes in company-specific valuation inputs rather than as a result of any real change to remuneration policies within those companies.

Generally a projected value approach compares the potential value that can be received under each package for a number of different performance scenarios. In each scenario, the same level of assumed share price growth is applied to each company. This means that, for each scenario, all companies are compared on a like-for-like basis.

Under an expected value approach, all the relevant information about an incentive award is condensed, through the calculation, into just one number. This process involves a number of subjective decisions about the nature of the incentive, and in particular about the performance targets and vesting schedule. For instance, how stretching is one set of EPS targets when compared to another? Because a number of the inputs are intertwined in reaching the final value, it can be difficult for the user to 'unwind' the calculation in order to get an understanding of how the stretch of the performance targets has been interpreted.

A projected value approach suffers from similar problems to expected value when it comes to assessing performance targets. There is usually a degree of subjectivity when interpreting a company's disclosed targets and vesting schedules. However, because a number of performance scenarios are valued, there can be more transparency around how the targets and vesting schedules have been assessed.

When benchmarking executive packages using an expected value approach, it is difficult to compare the stretch in different packages. That is, it is difficult to compare the 'shape' of the package (i.e. the risk in the package, the range of potential payouts, and the extent to which it is geared to performance).

The stretch of a vesting schedule is an input into the valuation under the expected value approach. All the information about the shape of a vesting schedule is condensed, along with the other valuation factors, into just one number. This information, although having an impact on the value, is essentially lost to the user. As a result, two packages may have very different levels of stretch while having exactly the same expected value. It is therefore difficult to use expected values to make any comment on the gearing in a package.

A projected value approach would show the potential payouts under a number of performance scenarios, including different share price growths. It is therefore often easier to compare the stretch in a particular package against the stretch in comparable companies' packages.

Consider the example in Figure 3.10 (which ignores all valuation factors except the stretch of a vesting schedule).

In addition to giving information about the shape of the package, the projected value approach will also highlight the maximum potential value that may be delivered under a set of arrangements. The one big disadvantage of an expected value approach is that the maximum liability may not be clear. This is particularly a problem when comparing packages with varying levels of stretch, for example between the UK, where performance targets are common, and the USA where they are not. The expected value of UK packages will be reduced by the performance measures, whereas the US packages will not. This means to match US and UK packages on an expected value basis, the value of incentive awards for the UK must be much higher, which can cause problems if the maximum awards vest.

Figure 3.10 *Impact of the vesting schedule*

Incentive A = an award of shares with a value of 100% of salary. These shares are not performance-related and therefore always vest.

Incentive B = performance shares with a value of 200% of salary. These shares use a profit-based performance measure. The vesting schedule is such that there is a 50% chance of 0% vesting and a 50% chance of 100% vesting.[1]

The expected value of both Incentive A and Incentive B (ignoring other valuation factors) is 100% of salary.[2] Therefore, both incentives have the same expected value. But Incentive B clearly has more stretch and risk associated with it.

Using projected value, the Incentives might be compared at, say, two performance scenarios, Target and Maximum. At Target (again ignoring other valuation inputs), the value of Incentive A is 100% of salary, while Incentive B is valued at 0% of salary. At Maximum, Incentive A is again valued at 100% of salary, while Incentive B is valued this time at 200% of salary.

The projected value approach gives more information to the user about the shape of a particular incentive.

---

[1] In this example, it is assumed that there is no correlation between the probability of vesting and the value received if the award vests.

[2] It should be noted that the expected value of Incentive B is actually a value that can never occur in practice (i.e. the only possible amounts that could vest are 0% or 200%). This is often cited as a weakness of expected value methodologies in general.

It is important to remember that all of these approaches can only provide an estimate of the value of the package based on a set of assumptions and none of the values represent an amount which the executive could go out and spend.

As we have mentioned, no approach provides a perfect solution for all benchmarking scenarios. When considering the valuation approach to adopt it is important to consider which approach provides the best solution for each individual benchmarking exercise, for example:

- when trying to value an existing package in order to buyout the arrangements on recruitment, the main focus will be on obtaining a single value for the package that can be used for negotiations;
- when designing the package for a new recruit or the main board as a whole it is important to look not only at the value of the package but also at how this is structured, the extent to which it is related to performance and the potential maximum that may be paid out.

The conclusion must be that, in most situations, it is beneficial, if not essential, to consider a number of data sources using a variety of methodologies in order to arrive at the best answer.

Pensions

So far in this chapter we have focused on methodologies and valuation techniques that can be used to value the performance-related elements of a remuneration package. There is one other element of the package that is not performance-related and can have a significant value: the pension provision.

The two main types of pension arrangements in the UK are defined contribution plans ('DC') and defined benefit plans ('DB'). These are discussed in more detail in Chapter 4.

Under DC arrangements the employer contributes a fixed amount to a participant's pension scheme each year. This is usually expressed as a percentage of salary and it is therefore easy to include the value of this in the overall value of the package.

However, it is not easy to identify the value of the DB and there are many ways in which this can be done.

Many executive directors are still members of DB plans although this is becoming far less common. A DB plan is a 'promise' on behalf of the employer to pay an income in retirement usually linked to pre-retirement earnings. The most widespread DB plan is a commitment to pay a pension based on final salary (often defined as the average salary over a period prior to retirement).

Under a DB plan, the benefit delivered is based on the number of years of service and the individual's salary at the time of retirement, leaving or death. The final pension is designed to provide, say, two thirds of final salary. The accrual rate determines what the pension on retirement will be. A 1/60 accrual rate means that 1/60 of salary accrues each year and this would mean that an employee would have to work for forty years to achieve a two thirds salary pension. An executive director is more likely to be eligible for an accrual rate of 1/45 or 1/30 which is clearly a more generous provision. The pension on retirement is therefore the number of years' service multiplied by the accrual rate multiplied by the pensionable salary.

The value of the benefit therefore depends on a range of assumptions including the age of the employee, the length of service, the accrual rate, the expected rate of salary increase and the expected age of retirement.

In order to value the pension benefit accurately, it will be necessary to involve an actuary and it will require as much information as possible about the pension plan for the individual or company under consideration. This information may not be readily available, although some companies disclose sufficient information in the remuneration report to allow an accurate valuation.

As with the valuation of incentives, it is also important to be clear on the purpose of the valuation. The value of the pension for two individuals participating in identical pension arrangements will be very different due to their different ages, length of service and expected retirement date. One important decision to make therefore is whether to value the pension benefit of a specific individual, or to value the pension policy based on a 'straw man' approach.

In order to derive a value from readily available data using a simple approach there are a number of options but it is important to remember that none of these will accurately value the pension benefit for any specific individual. They may, however, provide a general market benchmark which may be sufficient.

One way of valuing the pension provision is to determine the value of one year's worth of pension accrual for each director, allowing for earnings growth up to retirement. The value derived is analogous to the charge required to operating profits under International Accounting Standards, in respect of the pension benefits earned in respect of company service over the year.

This method would take the transfer value disclosed in the remuneration report and divide this by accrued service (some companies disclose the years of pensionable service; where this is not disclosed it may be necessary to use the number of completed years of service). This is increased to allow for expected future salary growth (adjusted by forecasted RPI) over the remaining years of service to normal retirement (where the normal retirement age is not disclosed it is probably reasonable to assume a standard age of sixty). If the director is required to make a contribution this should be deducted. Where an executive is affected by the earnings cap, any contribution made during the year to additional funded arrangements, or payments made to personal pension plans or as salary supplements, should be added. Where there is an unfunded promise, this is usually taken into account in the transfer values disclosed.

Other ways of calculating the pension value include using the increase in accrued pension which is also disclosed in the remuneration report. The downside of this is that the value is based on the current year only and this may not reflect usual practice. Dividing the transfer value over the past years of service has the effect of smoothing out any large salary increases or changes in accrual rate over the period of service.

There are some disadvantages to using this method. For some individuals the derived value may be understating the real value of the pension benefit, for others it may be overstating it. However, in the absence of sufficient data for each individual director to enable an accurate actuarial valuation to be derived, this methodology may be a way of providing a consistent, simple and logical way of obtaining an indication of the value of the pension for a general market.

And a final thought

Remember that the values produced by these methods do not necessarily represent the accounting or the actual cost for the company or the perceived value for the employee. These costs should be balanced against each other.

The accounting cost of a share award is based on the grant date fair value of the awards and the application of accounting policies. The actual cost for the company will depend on the funding arrangements that are used and may represent an actual cash cost or, where newly issued shares are used, dilution suffered by the shareholders.

The perceived value for the employee may be influenced by cultural values and the personal situation of the individual. In some cases the culture of the company or the industry may assign a high value to equity incentives; in other situations an individual may place a higher value on the value of the cash benefits they receive each year. Other factors may also affect the value an individual assigns to an incentive award, for example they may assign a higher value to the portion of a bonus that is subject to personal rather than corporate targets as they perceive they have greater influence over the ultimate payout.

Ideally the company will want to maximise the perceived value, whilst minimising the associated costs. However, beware the situation where it seems that the perfect balance has been achieved. It is more likely to be that an error has been made in the calculation or a cost associated with the delivery of the benefit has not been accurately identified or assessed. For example share options satisfied using newly issued shares would appear to have no actual cash cost for the company, yet may be perceived to have a high value for the executive, allowing them to benefit from any future growth in the company. However, there is a cost for the company and the shareholders through the dilution suffered following the issue of additional shares.

4
Constructing the package

ALISON SMITH

This chapter explores the typical elements of executive remuneration, ranging from salary and pension provision to bonus and long-term incentive opportunities. It begins by examining the principles of benchmarking and data analysis and focuses on some of the pitfalls associated with using market data. This is followed by an in-depth analysis of short- and long-term incentive plan design and the tax, accounting and regulatory issues associated with such plans. One of the key aspects of any bonus or incentive plan is the choice of performance measures and the setting of targets, and the second half of this chapter explains the most common performance measures and some of the issues that can arise when using them. The chapter concludes by looking at how the different elements are balanced and how this varies by size of company and type of business.

This chapter is followed by an exploration of how these different elements come together in different commercial contexts and how the package can be constructed to support the business strategy in a variety of different phases in the life of an organisation and the principles behind good remuneration design.

Determining the policy

The first point to make is an obvious one: the remuneration policy should support the business strategy. It can be argued that the behaviour of the senior executives who are required to execute the business strategy is driven, to a greater or lesser extent, by remuneration and there are a number of well-known examples that demonstrate the truth of this argument. It is also true that senior executives are not solely and simply driven by money. But if the two elements are not aligned, this will at best deliver less than optimum results and at worst possibly destroy the business. For example, if the business strategy relies on long-term relationships with customers but the senior executives are paid bonuses which are weighted towards the number of new customers signed, there is an obvious mismatch and the business may falter or even ultimately fail because the focus will be on finding ways to get new customers to sign a contract and there will be little focus on ongoing customer service and relationship building. It is important to 'test drive' any proposed change to remuneration policy to ensure that the right behaviours are being rewarded and to forestall, where possible, any unintended consequences, and the inherent 'moral hazard' that exists when anyone – in this case ultimately shareholders – pays someone else to do something on their behalf.

Successfully aligning remuneration policy with business strategy is a dynamic activity as the policy will need to change and evolve during the life cycle of the business. The policy must also be flexible enough to deal with exceptional circumstances such as the recruitment or retention of a key executive.

Why is determining the remuneration policy difficult? Primarily because of the tensions between market pay practice and how much you need to pay in a specific situation, the linkage between remuneration and performance and the balancing of the expectations of individuals and shareholders. It is also worth bearing in mind that the culture and values of the organisation will play a part. Some companies may value internal equity above market competitiveness and so will be more willing to shape pay structure and levels firmly around an internally consistent corporate model rather than allow flexibility from role to role in line with the varying external markets; some companies may have a much stronger culture of performance-linked remuneration than others and so are happy to deliver appreciably less than 'market' when performance is disappointing but want to pay handsomely for great performance. Yet other companies may have a strong culture of fairness and transparency and so need clear and unambiguous reasons for internal differences.

There are a number of questions to be addressed when determining the remuneration policy.

- What is the appropriate market with which to compare remuneration?
- Within this market, where should we aim to position ourselves on total remuneration?
- Are the different elements of our package more or less generous than those of our comparator group and are the differences appropriate?
- What is the appropriate balance between fixed and variable reward in our business?
- Given the balance and the competitiveness of the different elements, where should we position salary and the other fixed elements, like pension benefits?
- What do we want to achieve with our incentive plans?
- What is the appropriate balance between short- and long-term reward?
- How highly geared should the incentive arrangements be?
- What performance do we want to reward and how stretching should the targets be?
- How do we determine the stretch in performance targets?
- What role should pensions play?
- How do we deal with unexpected and exceptional circumstances?

The answers to these questions will vary at different stages in the life of an organisation, although the answers will typically lead to a combination of different elements of remuneration.

The elements of pay

Fixed elements of remuneration

Basic salary

In the UK, salary is the foundation of the remuneration package and determines many other elements of the package (both incentive awards and pension provision are often expressed as a percentage of salary). It is therefore important that the salary is positioned appropriately. This does not mean that the salaries of your executive directors should necessarily be positioned at market median. And, in any case, you need to decide what constitutes 'the market'. Salary levels have become of increasing concern to shareholders. Figure 4.1 illustrates why.

The impact of these increases is clear – if the typical executive director in 2001 received ten times the salary of the average employee, in five years this multiple has increased to twelve. Given that other elements of the package are based on a multiple of salary, the gap, in absolute terms, is ever widening.

Salary benchmarking
The origin of the word 'benchmark' is a mark hewn on a wall or a 'trig point' on the summit of a mountain whose height above sea level has been carefully measured and which can therefore be used to assess the heights of

Figure 4.1 *Basic salary increases*

Year	Median salary increase for executive directors in FTSE 350 companies	Increase in seasonally adjusted average earnings index	Average increase in RPI
2001	9.8%	4.4%	1.8%
2002	9.7%	3.6%	1.6%
2003	7.5%	3.6%	2.9%
2004	7.1%	4.2%	3.0%
2005	6.5%	3.9%	2.8%
2006	6.8%	3.7%	3.2%
2007	7.0%	3.7%[1]	4.5%[1]

[1] First two quarters of 2007.

surrounding objects or buildings. In other words, a benchmark is simply a reference point against which comparisons can be made and conclusions drawn.

Salary benchmarking requires the identification of a reference point in an appropriate market, of which there may be more than one. There is no single 'right' reference point and it is important to recognise that there is therefore no such thing as 'the benchmark salary'. Because of this it is important that data are interpreted sensibly and that good judgment is applied when carrying out a benchmarking exercise.

The best an organisation should aim for is an appropriate market competitive range. This should be based on the role, not the individual. Once the range is established, it requires a judgment as to where within the range an individual should be positioned. It is not always necessary or appropriate to position salaries at the midpoint, or median, of that range even if the market data are drawn from highly relevant comparators. Many other factors should be taken into account, such as the length of tenure and performance of the individual, internal relativities, succession planning, retention risks and other more or less generous elements of the package.

For example, if the individual is new to the role and the performance is as yet unknown, then it may be reasonable for the salary to be positioned towards the lower end of the benchmark range. If the size of the organisation has increased significantly due to a takeover or merger with another company the current salary of the chief executive officer (CEO) may look low in comparison with a benchmark based on the size of the combined organisation. But it may not be appropriate to adjust the salary until the transaction has had time to bed down and a judgment can be made on whether the integration has been successful. If an executive director is appointed as the CEO elect with a planned handover period, it may be appropriate to set the salary at, or above, the upper end of the market-competitive range for the current role as an executive director, given that promotion to the CEO position will be within a twelve-month period and the individual might reasonably expect at that time to be positioned at the lower end of the market-competitive range for a chief executive.

The potential dangers of benchmarking are recognised by investors. The Association of British Insurers guidelines on executive remuneration state as a core principle that 'Executive remuneration should be set at levels that retain and motivate, based on selection and interpretation of appropriate benchmarks. Such benchmarks should be used with caution, in view of the risk of an upward ratchet of remuneration levels with no corresponding improvement in performance.' The detailed guidance on base pay and bonuses makes it clear that just adopting a policy of paying at median is not appropriate: 'Remuneration Committees should ensure their policy on base pay is fully communicated to shareholders. Where a company seeks to pay salaries at median or above, justification is required.'

Job matching

When analysing salary data to benchmark a particular position it is important to ensure that jobs are compared on a similar basis. It would not be appropriate to benchmark the CEO of a large company against a market of salaries for smaller companies any more than the opposite.

In an informed and rational pay market, typically evidenced in medium- and larger-sized organisations in a mature economy, the salary of the CEO of a company is related strongly to the size and industry of the overall organisation. Obviously there are also other, usually lesser, influences on basic salary – such as sector, geography and the performance of the incumbent. There is also a good, although not as strong, correlation between salary and company size and industry for other board positions. The size of the company could be measured by turnover, market capitalisation, number of employees and so on. While basing the analysis on just one measure of financial size may be considered too simplistic, introducing too many additional factors may add a level of complexity which is unnecessary. However, we would suggest that taking one measure of the financial size of the business ignores some very important factors. An example is the complexity of the business; all other things being equal, a pharmaceutical company is clearly more complex than a retail operation. Another example would be the degree to which the company operates internationally; again, all other things being equal, the complexity involved in managing an international business is clearly greater than operating in the UK only. A combination of relevant factors will produce a better benchmark.

Below the board, factors other than responsibility for financial and human capital dimensions start to become more important, such as the amount of specialist knowledge and experience required to do the job, the amount of thinking and creativity needed and the extent to which influencing, selling or other interpersonal skills are required. Therefore, below the board, some element of more detailed and analytical job matching will be required to ensure that jobs are being compared on a like-for-like basis. There are numerous proprietary job evaluation and job matching systems available. Some are based on comparing jobs with similar job titles, some rely on matching jobs to multi-levelled generic capsule job descriptions and some are in-depth job evaluation systems which score the jobs against a number of factors in conjunction with additional statistics about the size and complexity of the organisational environment.

Methods of analysis

There are two main methods of analysing data: regression analysis and ranking analysis. Both of these methods are valid ways of looking at the data, and in many cases it will be appropriate to look at both.

59

Regression analysis

Regression, or trend line, analysis measures possible relationships between two variables. In the case of salary benchmarking, the relationship in question will be salary and some measure of company or job 'size'. Figure 4.2 shows a trend line for the top full-time executive of a company, with the company size shown on the horizontal axis and the salary on the vertical axis. The idea of the trend line is to find a line which best describes the data available. It is a line which 'best fits' the data. Once the trend line has been calculated for a particular sample of positions, it is then possible to use it to predict the salary for a CEO of any company provided that the size of the company can be identified.

There are a number of types of regression line – linear, logarithmic, power, etc. But the regression analysis should be seen as no more than a tool to assist in best representing the data and there is always a danger of putting too much emphasis on the statistical predictive power of a particular method. It is always necessary to look at the data carefully: a statistically 'good' fit does not necessarily mean that there is a true relationship between the two variables or that the line is a good representation of the data. There are many occasions, particularly with small samples, where a trend line is not an appropriate way of analysing the data.

Having said that, the main advantage of the trend line method is that it takes into account all of the data: each data point will impact on the trend line. This can also be a disadvantage in that one significant outlier in a small

Figure 4.2 *Example of regression, or trend, line*

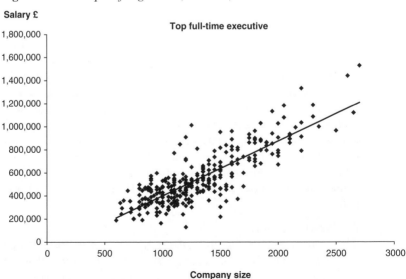

Figure 4.3 *Example of outliers*

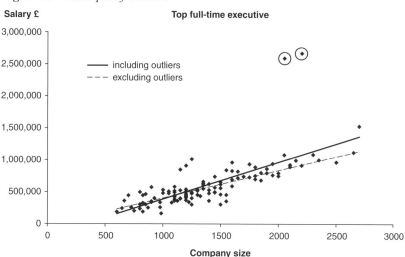

sample of positions may have a disproportionate impact and it is always worth checking any outliers to ensure that the data are correct. Figure 4.3 illustrates the impact outliers may have on the trend line. The highly paid outliers cause an upward shift in the trend line which could be considered inflationary if then used for benchmarking purposes.

A further disadvantage of the trend line approach is that, unless the sample is well spread and of sufficient size, there may be very little correlation between the variables. With small samples it is usually inappropriate to try and identify a relationship in this way. However, provided the limitations of taking a trend line approach are known and understood, a regression analysis of market salaries provides an excellent objective starting point for salary decision making.

Ranking analysis

This method of analysis relies on grouping data into bands of companies or jobs of a similar size. For each band the median, quartiles and sometimes deciles can be calculated for all of the data within that band, thereby providing a good indication of the spread of the data. The median is the middle point of the sample. The quartiles separate the top and bottom 25% and the deciles separate the top and bottom 10%. The upper quartile is often called the 'Q3', or the 75th percentile, and the upper decile is called the 'D9' or the 90th percentile – these separate the top 25% and top 10% from the bottom 75% and 90%, respectively. The lower quartile – 'Q1' or the 25th percentile – and the lower decile – 'D1' or the 10th percentile – separate the bottom 25% and 10% from the top 75% and 90%, respectively.

It will be necessary to identify appropriate bands within the data sample. This will depend on the spread and size of the data sample. Each band needs to have sufficient data points for the statistics to be valid, but if the spread of data contained in the band is too wide the statistics may be meaningless, or at least misleading for the purposes of salary benchmarking. Many published surveys use this method of analysing the data, but as different surveys contain different samples of data, the bands will typically not be the same, thereby making it difficult to compare the data in different surveys.

It is difficult to give a precise number of data points needed in each band in order to provide a reliable and representative median, quartile or decile. This will depend on how robust the sample is and the spread of the data within that sample. As a very broad rule of thumb, it would be preferable to have a minimum of five data points in order to provide a median, eleven data points to provide a quartile, and around twenty-one data points to produce a decile. However, where the spread of data is quite narrow, quartile and decile numbers may be considered reliable in smaller datasets than this. Reputable data surveys should always indicate how many data points are included in any given analysis, preferably for each band of the analysis. It is also worth noting that there are different methods of calculating quartiles and deciles, although in practice this is unlikely to affect the results to any great extent.

Remember that the median is just the middle number and, depending on the spread of the data, may or may not be representative of the sample. This is a particular problem if published data are being used, where it is not possible to see the details of the spread and size of the sample. The median tends to be more robust than the mean because of the impact of any outliers on the mean but where samples are small, or very widespread, the median may not be a helpful number. Figure 4.4 illustrates this. When using the ranked analysis, it is very important to ensure that the sample of data is appropriate. If, for example, the sample is based on a small sample of companies of very different sizes the median is likely to be unrepresentative.

Over-zealous use of the median in a comparator group can provide an unstable basis for comparison. For example in Figure 4.5, if CEO 'C', paid

Figure 4.4 *Example of small data sample*
CEO salary £ p.a.

Sample data	Ranked data
£395,000	£975,000
£250,000	£750,000
£975,000	Median – **£395,000**
£199,000	£250,000
£750,000	£199,000

Figure 4.5 *Example of impact of change in one data point in small data sample*

CEO salary £ p.a.

	Year 1		Year 2
A	£750,000	A	£750,000
B	£680,000	B	£680,000
C	£610,000	D	£600,000
D	**£600,000**	C	**£495,000**
E	£495,000	E	£495,000
F	£491,000	F	£491,000
G	£490,000	G	£490,000

£610,000, was replaced by a CEO paid at the level of 'E', the median would move from £600,000 to £495,000 in the following year.

In most samples of salary data for a particular size and type of role the data tends to cluster around the median. Above the median there is typically a wider spread of data than below. This means that the median is likely to be more robust than the upper quartile. The reason for this is that, for any given job in a group of companies of broadly similar size and complexity, there is, in practice, a minimum salary that can be paid whereas there is unlikely to be a maximum, and this causes the data to spread out above the median.

The main disadvantage of the ranking method is that the company or job size to be benchmarked is unlikely to fall neatly in the middle of the band; if the size of the company or job is towards the bottom or the top end of the band it will be necessary to make an adjustment to the benchmark to take this into account.

Where a ranking analysis is used, it is always helpful to look at the trend line analysis too, as this is a quick way of identifying any outliers in the data.

Targeting median or upper-quartile pay

Many companies will have a stated policy of paying at median, or even at upper quartile. It is quite easy to fall into the trap of assuming that if you adopt a policy of being market median on all elements of pay, this will give you an overall median package. This is even more problematic with the upper quartile which, as explained above, is likely to be more volatile than the median. Figure 4.6 demonstrates why adding together the median, or upper quartile, for each element does not equal the median or upper quartile of the total compensation.

Figure 4.6 *Example of adding together median or upper-quartile elements*

	Base salary	Ranked	Annual bonus	Ranked	Long-term Incentive Plan (LTIP)	Ranked	Total compensation	Ranked	
1	£273,584	£723,077	£113,498	£1,250,000	£528,340	£6,113,587	£915,422	£7,906,869	
2	£315,000	£708,461	£115,000	£655,116	£4,322,867	£5,933,792	£4,752,867	£7,226,605	
3	**£495,000**	£653,500	£490,000	£603,018	£778,488	£4,322,867	£1,763,488	£4,752,867	
4	£723,077	£510,000	£1,250,000	£490,000	£5,933,792	£3,173,567	£7,906,869	£3,548,567	
5	£500,000	£500,000	**£245,000**	£486,000	£2,228,990	£2,228,990	£2,973,990	£2,973,990	
6	£345,000	**£495,000**	£655,116	**£245,000**	£816,763	**£1,810,111**	£1,816,879	**£2,804,894**	
7	£510,000	£412,522	£603,018	£220,000	£6,113,587	£1,610,433	£7,226,605	£2,683,611	
8	£290,000	£345,000	£85,000	£115,000	£3,173,567	£816,763	£3,548,567	£1,816,879	
9	£708,461	£315,000	£486,000	£113,498	£1,610,433	£778,488	**£2,804,894**	£1,763,488	
10	£653,500	£290,000	£220,000	£85,000	**£1,810,111**	£528,340	£2,683,611	£938,337	
11	£412,522	£273,584	£58,500	£58,500	£467,315	£467,315	£938,337	£915,422	
M	£495,000	£495,000	£245,000	£245,000	£1,810,111	£1,810,111		£2,804,894	
Q3	£581,750	£581,750	£546,509	£546,509	£3,748,217	£3,748,217		£4,151,717	
M	£495,000 +		£245,000 +		£1,810,111 =		£2,550,111		91%
Q3	£581,750 +		£546,509 +		£3,748,217 =		£4,876,476		117%

Useful questions to ask

Some of the questions that need to be addressed when deciding whether a benchmark is appropriate include:

- What is the appropriate comparator group against which to benchmark salaries? Factors to be taken into account will be the size of the comparator companies, the complexity of the business, the industry sector, the degree of internationality, the number and type of employees, the management structure. It may include looking at companies from which you might recruit people, or to where you might lose people.
- Should you look at more than one benchmark? It may be helpful to have a benchmark for a broad, general market, a second reference for a narrower industry market and even a third reference for a specific group of comparator companies.
- Should you use the same comparator groups for all your executive director positions or should you treat them all individually? This may depend to some extent on the type and location of jobs. For example, one of the board positions may be very sector- or company-specific and not a common board position, or the job may be located in another country. It may also depend to some extent on the culture of the company: some companies are focused on the rate for the job and are comfortable with the pay differences that this approach may generate within the executive team, whereas others value team harmony to a greater extent.
- Will shareholders perceive the comparator group(s) as appropriate?

What if you use several benchmarks from various published surveys and data providers and they give different answers? This may be due to a number of factors:

- the basis of the statistics may be different;
- the effective dates of the data may be different;
- the methodology for comparing companies and positions may vary from one provider to another;
- the sample and quality of the data may vary from one data provider to another and may be weighted towards smaller/larger companies or specific industries; or
- the position may be a unique position where there is no established market.

In practice there will always be differences between the benchmark salaries derived from different survey data providers, and in some cases these differences will be significant. It is therefore important to take a view on which are the most relevant and robust data points and use judgment to derive the appropriate market competitive range.

Having determined an appropriate market range, it is then appropriate to consider the positioning for each individual role. This should be consistent with company policy but needs also to accommodate the level of skill and experience of the incumbent.

Remember that in the listed company environment you should be prepared to disclose the benchmarking process in the remuneration report and to justify any salary increases outside the 'norm'. Investors are increasingly looking for comfort that the senior executives are not being treated in a significantly different way from the wider employee population.

Salary differentials

A useful way of crosschecking salary levels is to look at the salary differentials between the chief executive and other main board and senior executive positions. For example, the salary of the finance director is typically between 55% and 70% of the salary of the CEO and the salary of other main board directors typically a little lower at between 50% and 65% of the salary of the chief executive. This will vary between companies but if the differential is outside of this range it should be clear as to why this is, as this may suggest a level of internal inequity which needs to be addressed.

An exception to this can be found in smaller Alternative Investment Market (AIM) listed companies, and companies preparing to float. Here the salary of the finance director is likely to be closer to that of the CEO, typically between 60% and 80%. It may be that this reflects the importance of this role in the run-up to flotation, suggesting that the role may have a greater influence on strategy than in more established companies. It is also possible that the higher ratio may be more related to the salary of the CEO; where the CEO is one of the founders, or has been there a long time, and holds significant equity in the company, the salary may be low in comparison with other companies of a similar size and complexity.

Pension

For decades there have been tax advantages to encourage companies and individuals to save for retirement. Typically this has been full, immediate tax-relief on employer and employee contributions to recognised pension plans and a tax-favoured environment for the accumulating savings. On reaching retirement the individual could elect to draw a tax-free lump sum in cash and then receive a pension for the remainder of his/her life. The tax advantage and social expectation led many companies to establish pension plans for their workforce.

Pension provision can take a variety of forms but the most common traditional pension arrangement has been a final salary defined benefit pension promise, with executives typically being members of these company pension plans, albeit at a more generous rate of pension accrual. A defined benefit pension plan is effectively a 'promise' on the part of the employer to pay an income in retirement, usually linked to pre-retirement earnings. The most widespread defined benefit plan is a commitment to pay a pension based on final salary (often defined as the average salary over a period prior to retirement). Executive directors have usually participated in the pension plan made available to the wider workforce, albeit other employees typically have earned pension at a rate of 1/60th or 1/80th of final salary for each year of employment whereas executives may accrue pension at 1/45th or, most commonly, 1/30th of final salary for each year of service.

The cost of pensions has risen over the years. In the early days, employees may have joined the workforce as early as at fifteen years old and been eligible to retire as late as at sixty-five. This could have given them easily over forty years to 'save' for the pension. Given the shorter life expectancy it is entirely possible that the 'average' employee could have contributed to the pension scheme for two or three times as long as he/she received a pension.

One of the major causes of pension deficit has been an increase in longevity. The average lifespan in the UK is now 76.6[1] for a man and 81.0 for a woman and so the cost of funding this benefit has increased dramatically. However, deficits have also grown as a result of a number of other factors including:

- lower-than-expected investment returns (the high investment returns of the 1990s saw many companies taking 'pension holidays' on the advice of their actuaries);
- a move to lower-risk investment strategies (lower-risk investments, e.g. bonds and gilts, typically offer lower returns than equities);
- an increasing number of pension funds are 'mature' and so have an increasing number of members in receipt of pensions compared with working members making contributions to the pension scheme;
- government solvency regulations impose a levy on pension funds and have also encouraged companies to reduce the exposure to higher-yield, but riskier, investments.

Employers' contributions are based on actuarial estimates of what is required to meet the pension 'promise'. In recent years, pension schemes have run up huge deficits and companies have become increasingly concerned about affordability. Many of these plans have now been closed to new entrants and it is now more common, within the private sector at least, for new appointments to be offered participation in a defined contribution plan.

A defined contribution plan is sometimes known as a money purchase plan. A level of contribution from the employer and the employee is established and the final benefit is determined not by reference to final earnings but by the amount of contributions made and the investment return achieved over the period until retirement. In practice the pensions arising

---

[1] Office for National Statistics – life tables 2003–05

from such plans are less valuable and less 'guaranteed' than those from defined benefit plans.

Other variants to defined benefit plans include career average salary plans and cash balance plans. Career average salary plans are not new, but are not common in the UK. However, a few companies have introduced these plans in recent years and they may be an attractive option for a company that does not want to discontinue the defined benefit approach entirely but wants to make pension costs more predictable and less of an open-ended commitment. They are often referred to as career average revalued earnings (CARE) plans. Average salary pensions are based on the average of an employee's earnings over their career rather than the final salary. The pension is usually defined as a fraction (e.g. 1/60) of average salary for each year of service. The scheme revalues each year's earnings to take account of inflation. This may be based on an average earnings measure or a retail prices index.

Cash balance plans look more like money purchase arrangements but the rate of investment return is more certain than could be obtained by the individual electing to invest independently and is 'guaranteed' by the company – for example it might be based on the retail prices index subject to a cap. This protects the employee against the much more volatile investment risk of the stock market that is typical of a 'normal' money purchase defined contribution arrangement.

Prior to the recent pensions legislation contained in the Finance Act 2004 (see below) which came into effect in April 2006 and which has greatly simplified future pension provision, there were eight tax-driven pension regimes, which has given rise to a variety of policies between and within companies. The legislation which has had the most significant impact on pension arrangements in recent years was the 1989 earnings cap which restricted the pension that could be provided from a tax-approved scheme for anyone joining a plan after 1989. Initially this only affected the most senior executives moving between employers and then only if the pensionable salary exceeded the cap which was initially set at £60,000. One-off arrangements started to appear as executive directors demanded an equivalent package from a new employer so that they would be no worse off than if they had not been capped. The cap has only increased with inflation, and salary inflation, particularly at senior levels, has outpaced general price inflation. In 2002/3 the cap was £97,200, in 2003/4 it was £99,000, for 2004/5 it was £102,000, and for 2005/6 it was £105,600. Over the same period, the salary of an executive director in a listed company has increased at a rate of around twice the increase in the cap, thereby catching more and more employees who have changed jobs or joined the workforce since 1989 and forcing employers to develop alternatives on a more systematic basis. Funded unapproved arrangements (FURBS) became commonplace and other ways of dealing with the cap include salary supplements, contributions to personal pension plans or unapproved unfunded arrangements (UURBS). There is currently a

Figure 4.7 *Pension value by FTSE index*

	Value of defined benefit plan including top up and above 1989 earnings cap provision % of salary p.a.			Value of defined contribution plan or pension allowance % of salary p.a.		
	Q1	M	Q3	Q1	M	Q3
FTSE 100	30%	41%	55%	20%	25%	30%
FTSE 250	15%	29%	42%	9%	17%	25%
FTSE SmallCap	16%	28%	41%	10%	14%	19%

wide range of practice and, even within the same company, executive directors may have very different arrangements. Where FURBS, salary supplements or contributions to personal plans are used, typically contributions of between 20% and 45% of the salary **above** the cap will be made.

Before the 1989 earnings cap began to take effect, directors within any one company, and to an extent across different companies, would typically have received a similar level of pension benefit and therefore it was not really necessary to include the value of the pension when benchmarking remuneration. As companies have introduced different practices to deal with the earnings cap this has become more of an issue, and as companies have started closing defined benefit plans and introducing defined contribution plans there becomes a much more significant difference in the value of the pension between senior executives in different companies, and even within the same company. Figure 4.7 illustrates the difference in the value. Our research suggests that even within the same company the value of the pension can typically range in value terms from 20% of salary to over 80% of salary.

It might be expected then that, where the pension provision in a company, or for an individual, is generous, this may be compensated for by a lower salary, or by lower incentive awards. Our research does not support this theory. This may be because including the value of the pension, and therefore benchmarking the total remuneration, has been put in the 'too difficult' box because of the problems in valuing the pension provided under a defined benefit plan and the variety of ways this can be done, all with advantages and disadvantages. Alternatively, it may be that the value of a defined benefit promise is simply too expensive to replicate and an acceptable balance has been struck at a lower level.

Previous changes to pensions legislation have always applied only to new scheme joiners, which avoids individuals losing out but increases complexity. As indicated earlier, prior to the new pension legislation contained in the Finance Act 2004 there were eight different pension regimes. The new regime replaced all of the existing regimes and therefore makes the rules more straightforward but does mean that some individuals may be worse off. The new rules provide one overall funding limit for each individual, the 'lifetime limit'. This is the total amount that an individual can accumulate through a 'registered', or what would have previously been called an 'approved' plan. Annual contributions to plans are unrestricted, irrespective of earnings, but tax relief is limited to the lower of an annual limit or relevant earnings for the year. These two limits increase each year as follows:

Lifetime allowance		Annual allowance	
2006/7	£1.5 million	2006/7	£215,000
2007/8	£1.6 million	2007/8	£225,000
2008/9	£1.65 million	2008/9	£235,000
2009/10	£1.75 million	2009/10	£245,000
2010/11	£1.8 million	2010/11	£255,000

After 2011 they will be subject to periodic review.

The changes apply to individuals who retired on or after 6 April 2006 (A-Day) and the key features are:

- Where a pension fund has a value at retirement in excess of the lifetime allowance, a recovery charge will apply. If the excess is taken as a pension, the charge is 25%. The pension income paid out of the remaining 75% is taxed at the individual's marginal income tax rate. A higher-rate tax payer will therefore pay 40% on the 75% used to fund a pension, which, in addition to the 25% charge, makes an overall tax rate of 55%. If the excess is taken as a lump sum, the charge is 55% in all cases.
- Where contributions to defined contribution plans or increases in benefits in defined benefit plans are in excess of the annual allowance a charge of 40% will be made.
- All schemes will be able to pay a tax-free lump sum of 25% of the value of the pension rights, subject to the lifetime allowance.

Testing benefits against the lifetime allowance
The recovery charge taxes the benefit of tax-free returns in excess of the lifetime limit within a registered scheme. The calculation of the value of the fund will depend on whether the pension scheme is defined benefit or defined contribution. If the scheme is defined contribution, the calculation is broadly equal to the value of the fund. If the scheme is a defined benefit scheme the value is calculated by multiplying the pension accrued by 20. Therefore anyone expecting a pension in excess of £75,000 a year will be caught by the lifetime allowance charge. This would equate to a senior executive with long service in a final salary scheme providing two thirds of salary on a salary of £112,500.

Testing benefits against the annual allowance
The annual allowance is designed to protect against large payments being made into a registered scheme in any given year. In the year of retirement, the annual allowance will not apply.

For defined contribution schemes, the annual allowance will apply to contributions paid into the fund each tax year. For defined benefit schemes, the annual allowance will be tested against the increase in the accrued pension each year multiplied by ten. Exceeding the annual allowance will often mean a tax charge applies both when contributions go into a plan and when benefits are taken out.

Unregistered arrangements

The new regime for registered schemes will not prevent unregistered arrangements from continuing, but these will no longer attract tax breaks. However, from April 2006, contributions to FURBS will neither be taxable on the employee nor tax deductible for the employer. Instead, tax will be payable by employees on taking benefits, at which time employers will receive their tax deduction. From April 2004 tax on gains, and from 2006 tax on income within FURBS will no longer benefit from reduced tax rates; instead, they will pay tax at the trust rate (32.5% for dividend income, 40% for other income and capital gains).

Transitional arrangements

Transitional arrangements provide a degree of protection for pension rights built up before A-Day.

There are two alternatives to allow employees to protect the benefits they have accrued to date. The choice of protection method will be based on individual circumstances but it will be possible to register for both where benefits exceed the lifetime allowance at A-Day.

Primary Protection – a member registers the capital value of their pre-A-Day pension rights expressed as a percentage of the lifetime allowance (it must be more than 100%). On retirement, the recovery charge is only paid on pension funds where the value exceeds this percentage of the lifetime allowance at retirement. The lifetime allowance increases from £1.5 million in 2006/7 to £1.8 million in 2010/11, providing an annual increase of nearly 5%. Benefit increases would therefore be subject to the recovery charge on amounts in excess of this level.

Enhanced Protection – pre-A-Day pension rights are totally ring-fenced. The employee must cease active membership of all registered schemes from A-Day, although defined benefits can continue to grow by reference to future pay increases and defined contribution plans may continue to receive investment returns within limits. This route is available to members with benefits both above and below the lifetime allowance at April 2006. The protection ceases if active membership resumes in any registered scheme. Where enhanced protection is lost, primary protection may apply if registered.

There is still some uncertainty about the arrangements companies are putting in place to deal with the 2006 legislative changes but a number of trends are apparent. Many, if not most, companies will not make any change at all. Where unfunded promises to provide pensions above the 1989 cap have been used, this will typically continue, although it will be possible to provide more of the pension through the approved, or registered, plan. Where companies have provided cash supplements, or FURBS, above the 1989 earnings cap most will maintain a notional earnings cap based on the 1989 cap and continue with the cash supplement. However, payments into FURBS are likely to cease and be replaced by cash supplements paid directly to the individual so that immediate tax relief is available. Where individuals have a pension in excess of the lifetime allowance many companies provide the opportunity for the executive to opt out of the plan and take a cash allowance instead. This allowance is likely to be in the region of 25% to 30% of salary.

On the face of it, it appears that the new legislation will have little impact. However, this may be masking what is really happening since it is almost certain that, in the process of addressing the implications of the changes, the value of existing arrangements will have become far more apparent than was previously the case. And future arrangements are likely to be more transparent and therefore will allow easier comparison between individuals and companies. It seems likely that many more companies will want to factor the pension provision into the total remuneration calculations in the future and their shareholders will certainly expect clarity of disclosure.

Shareholders will expect similar clarity and transparency and have indicated their concerns regarding unexpected additional pension costs – for example the right to receive a non-actuarially reduced pension from an age earlier than retirement age can significantly increase the capital value of the pension.

Current pension provision

It is worth noting that the number of executive directors participating in defined benefit plans has fallen dramatically over the past few years, primarily due to the increase in the cost of pension provision and to some extent due to the change in legislation. At the time of writing, just over half the directors in FTSE 100 companies participate in a defined benefit plan, compared to over three quarters three years ago. Fewer directors in FTSE 250 companies participate in defined benefit plans but this has also decreased from over 50% in 2004 to just over 40% currently.

Of course, many of these individuals will have been employed by the company for a number of years and will therefore continue in existing pension arrangements. The number of companies who would offer defined benefit pension provision to newly appointed directors is much lower. Less than a third of FTSE 100 companies and less than a quarter of FTSE 250 companies would offer defined benefit provision to a new appointment and this trend is likely to continue.

Other benefits and perquisites

Benefits are rarely a major source of competitive advantage and rarely do they reach financial values that are likely to attract attention. However, they can be an important hygiene factor that, if missing, would be a source of considerable irritation for the individual. Equally they can be the source of critical comment by shareholders and the media if they are seen to be over-generous or inappropriate. Accordingly, senior executives will normally be entitled to receive other benefits and perquisites on a similar basis to other employees. In some cases the benefit may be enhanced for more senior employees. This may include financial advice, medical and dental insurance, long-term ill-health insurance, and the provision of a car or car allowances, and may include specific payments for relocation such as housing allowances, children's schooling, etc. Chapter 1 addresses some of the issues around these additional benefits when hiring a senior executive.

Providing a particular benefit can serve a number of purposes. In some cases – life insurance, for example – the provision is standard market practice and is to an extent tax-effective. In other cases, providing a benefit may also be seen as a way of alleviating risk; for example, ensuring that employees who are required to drive are driving a car which is fully serviced provides the employer with some confidence that the car is safe; providing medical insurance helps to keep employees healthy and allows those requiring medical treatment to arrange treatment quickly and at more convenient times; providing assistance to complete tax returns avoids any possibility of tax issues arising. Benefits may also serve to alleviate worry and distraction; this may be particularly important for expatriates where issues such as travel back to the home country, accommodation and children's education may be a concern.

We would suggest that, unless it is clear that the provision of a benefit serves one of these purposes, then it is worth questioning whether it is necessary. Equally, it is important to be aware of market practice in benefit provision for senior executives. If the expected benefits are not provided the company may need to adjust other elements of the package to take this into account and the compensatory cost may not align with the financial cost of providing the benefit – for example, corporate sponsored group life insurance is typically simpler and cheaper than individually sourced insurance.

These benefits are not discussed in further detail in this chapter given that for the most part their value is typically a relatively small proportion of the package.

Variable elements of remuneration

An increasing proportion of the senior executive remuneration package is dependent on performance. The balance of the fixed and variable elements is discussed below, but first it is important to examine the elements that make up the variable part of the package in more detail. These can be broken down into those which are short-term in nature, i.e. linked to performance over a period of twelve months (occasionally less), and those which are linked to longer-term performance, typically over a period of three to five years. The factor differentiating these plans is the period over which performance is measured rather than simply the period of payment. Many companies that operate an annual bonus plan defer some of the award for a number of years, as an aid to retention and to align the interests of the executive director with those of shareholders by holding the deferred amount in company shares and thereby building a shareholding. However, the size of the award is determined by short-term performance and we would suggest that this plan is essentially a short-term plan. There are a growing number of deferred bonus plans which contain an element of performance-based matching and so they are based on both short- and long-term performance. The initial award is based on short-term performance in the base year, but the extent to which a matching award is earned is based on performance over a longer period.

Annual bonus

The annual bonus, or annual incentive, plan is an accepted part of the package for senior executives. The fact that short-term plans may be called bonus or incentive plans illustrates the lack of clarity that sometimes exists as to whether these plans award a bonus for achievement of performance targets, or incentivise participants to improve performance. These are not necessarily the same thing, although the end result may be the same, and clarity about the purpose should drive the design and implementation of the plan. For simplicity we refer to these plans as annual bonus plans.

Executive directors participate in an annual bonus plan in all but a very small number of FTSE 350 companies. In 2007 only four FTSE 350 companies did not operate a bonus plan for executive directors. Plans are slightly less prevalent in smaller listed companies but our research suggests that the majority of directors in FTSE SmallCap companies are likely to participate in an annual bonus plan. Our research into companies floating on the Stock Exchange and AIM during 2005 indicated that almost three quarters of these companies had an annual bonus plan in place at the time of flotation. Interestingly a broader study by Incomes Data Services of SmallCap and AIM listed companies suggests that typically a much smaller number of AIM companies, around 40%, operate an annual bonus plan.

Analyses of the design of annual bonus plans over recent years demonstrate that the level of potential bonus is increasing (see Figure 4.10) and also that the level of bonus being paid out is also increasing significantly, with fewer senior executives receiving no bonus each year. This suggests that companies have either been generally performing well or that performance targets are becoming easier. There is a danger that the link between

Figure 4.8 *Balanced scorecard*

The balanced scorecard was developed in the early 1990s by Dr Robert Kaplan and Dr David Norton. It was developed in response to the recognition of the weaknesses of previous management approaches and provides clarity as to what companies should measure in order to 'balance' the financial perspective. It provides a structured way of linking the performance measures with the strategy and is based on four elements:

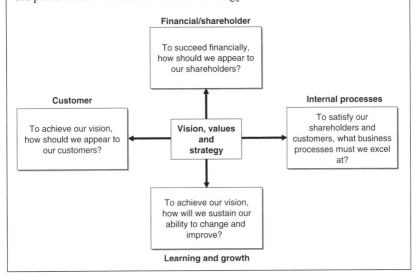

performance and award becomes weaker over time and that the bonus is increasingly seen as a 'guaranteed' element of the package. Given the size of the potential awards, listed companies should expect that shareholders will challenge plans where the link between awards and the actual level of performance achieved is not sufficiently demonstrated.

Annual bonus plans have typically been based on profit measures but we are now starting to see more companies adopting a broader approach, linking the annual bonus to the company's stated key performance indicators, including such things as health and safety, customer service, environmental targets. This may be based on a 'balanced scorecard' approach (see Figure 4.8). Plans will also often incorporate some element of personal performance. With a variety of measures, it may be more likely that at least one element of the bonus will pay out but it will also be harder to meet all performance targets and achieve maximum awards.

A weighting can be assigned to each element. For example, the financial element may be worth 50% of the total bonus, the customer element and the learning and growth element may be worth 10% of the total each, with 30% of the bonus dependent on internal processes. The weighting may vary for different groups of participants so that, for example, the financial element may have more weighting for senior executives. For each element, specific objectives are identified and the key performance indicators and the specific targets are determined. More complex plans may include specific weightings for each target.

Typically the structure of the plan will be the same for each of the senior executives but the potential awards that may be made will sometimes vary, and in some cases the performance targets may be specific to the position. Figure 4.9 illustrates the most common performance measures in place in FTSE 350 companies.

The potential awards have been steadily increasing over the past five years. Figure 4.10 illustrates how the maximum bonus has increased for FTSE 250, FTSE 100 and the top 30 UK companies over the past five years.

Although historical data is not available for smaller companies our research suggests that currently the median maximum bonus opportunity in FTSE SmallCap companies is around 75% of salary.

Given the size of these potential awards it is important to understand what the plan is intending to achieve. Only a few years ago the standard bonus opportunity for a medium-sized company was no more than 50% of salary, and typically an executive might expect to receive 70% to 80% of this amount. In many companies the bonus was an expected part of the package; at least part, if not all, of the bonus would have been regarded almost as 'guaranteed' by the participant. In many ways these plans would be seen as a reward rather than an incentive to improve performance.

The size of the potential award has now more than doubled and the bonus is an increasingly large part of the package. However, an analysis of the actual level of payout in FTSE 350 companies in 2006 indicates that an executive might still reasonably expect to receive around 80% of the maximum award. Over 75% of participants in these plans received more than half the maximum award. Figure 4.11 attempts to illustrate the link between annual performance and the level of bonus paid.

Given the range of performance measures used in these plans it is not a simple matter to analyse this link. For practical reasons it is only possible to look at the financial measures. All companies use at least one financial measure and our research suggests that in most cases this accounts for at least 75% of the total bonus. Different companies use different financial measures but as profit is most commonly used we have compared operating profit growth with the proportion of the maximum bonus that was paid out during the year. We have ranked the 2006 performance of each company in order to see whether the performance falls above or below median. We have then grouped the companies into three board industry groups and calculated the median bonus payment, as a percentage of the maximum that could be paid for companies where the overall performance rating is below the median (measured relative to companies in the same business sector),

Figure 4.9 *Most common annual bonus performance measures in FTSE 350 companies*

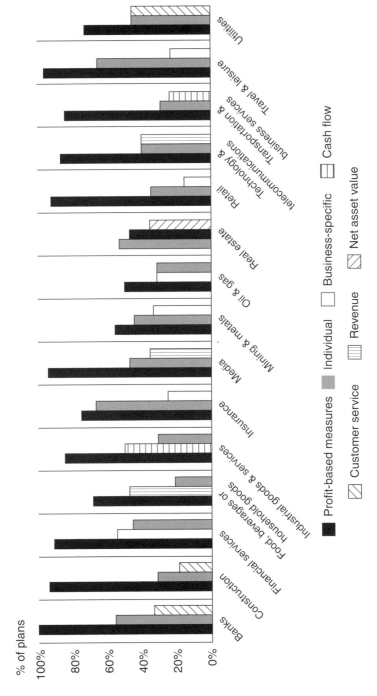

Figure 4.10 *Median maximum bonus opportunity – % of salary p.a.*

Year	FTSE 250 companies	FTSE 100 companies	Top 30 companies
2002	60%	75%	100%
2003	60%	95%	115%
2004	75%	100%	125%
2005	100%	100%	150%
2006	100%	115%	150%
2007	100%	130%	150%

and for companies where the overall performance rating is above the median.

This clearly does not give the whole picture but does suggest that the level of bonus paid increases with the level of performance attained. But the analysis suggests that this correlation is perhaps not as strong as might be expected.

It is therefore unsurprising that investors have been focusing their attention on the annual bonus plan. The ABI guidelines on executive remuneration state that:

> Annual bonuses should be demonstrably related to performance. Both individual and corporate performance targets are relevant and should be tailored to the requirements of the business and reviewed regularly to ensure they remain appropriate. Where consideration of commercial confidentiality may prevent a fuller disclosure of specific short term targets at the start of the performance period, shareholders expect to be informed about the main performance parameters, both corporate and personal, for the financial year being reported on. Following payment of the bonus, shareholders will expect to see a full analysis in the Remuneration Report of the extent to which the relevant targets were actually met. Maximum participation levels should be disclosed, and any increases in the maximum from one year to the next should be explicitly justified. Shareholders will expect increases to be subject to correspondingly more stretching performance.

Remuneration committees must address the issue of what the bonus is intended to achieve and ensure that appropriate measures and targets are in place. This raises a number of issues and questions.

- What are we paying for? What are the appropriate performance measures? Should these be the same for each senior executive? Should the measures be purely financial and/or should they include other business and personal objectives?
- What is success? Should the targets be based on budget, business expectations, absolute performance targets, improvement against last year, and/or performance relative to other companies?

Figure 4.11 *Median bonus paid (as % of maximum) in relation to level of performance achieved*

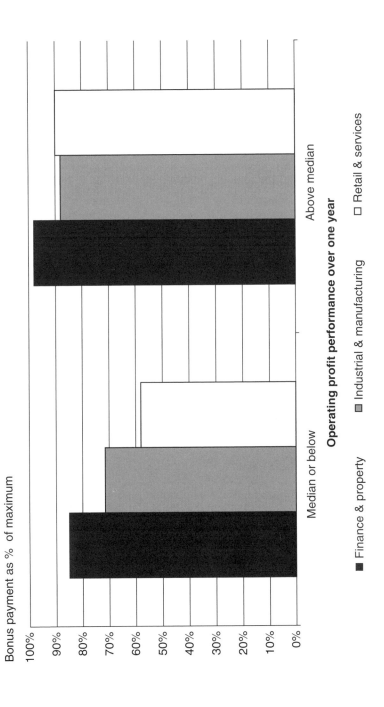

Bonus payment as % of maximum

Operating profit performance over one year

■ Finance & property   ▨ Industrial & manufacturing   □ Retail & services

- The definition of 'target' varies between companies. Typically, companies state that 50% of the maximum bonus will be paid for meeting performance targets, with the maximum requiring more stretching performance. But how can the degree of stretch in the targets be compared across companies? Most companies set the target at a level that is perceived to be reasonably stretching but not out of reach, but in some companies achievement of target performance will require something special.
- How formulaic should the level of actual payment be? Should there be any element of discretion in the plan? Shareholders are concerned about the use of discretion fearing that this allows payments to be made even when performance targets have not been met. However, it can also be used to ensure that payments that may be triggered by the application of the performance measurement 'formula' are merited. Some companies have compromised by setting principles and guidelines as to when, how and to what extent adjustments will be made.
- What is the appropriate level of bonus? It is relatively easy to obtain market data about bonus potential and it may be appropriate to benchmark these in a similar way to benchmarking the salary. However, once the data have been obtained there are a number of issues that need to be addressed in order to arrive at an appropriate relationship between the size of the award and the level of performance.
- Should the award be capped? Shareholders are generally uncomfortable with uncapped bonuses and therefore the arguments for an uncapped plan should be carefully considered and the measures of performance carefully calibrated with financial performance.
- There is likely to be a cultural element in the bonus payment. In some companies it may be accepted that the bonus plan may pay out in full or may pay nothing and this actually happens in practice. In other companies there is little chance of no bonus being paid, and there may be equally little chance of the maximum being paid, i.e. in practice awards are likely to be around target level. In the case of the former, it appears that there is a stronger link between pay and performance but the latter may be more appropriate in certain situations. What is important is that the remuneration committee is aware of the situation and makes appropriate adjustments to salary and bonus potentials to ensure that this is perceived as fair by the participants and shareholders.

Most companies use the annual business plan / budget as the basis for setting the performance targets; typically this is developed by the executives and not by the non-executive directors. But the remuneration committee needs to probe these numbers and ensure that the targets are appropriate and are sufficiently stretching. A bonus plan which either never pays out or pays out at, or near, maximum every year should sound warning bells.

Annual bonus deferral and co-investment plans

Deferred bonus plans have been around for many years but have become very common in larger listed companies. The plans vary significantly in structure but at the most basic level pay part of the bonus earned in the form of deferred shares. These usually vest after three years, although this may vary from one to four years. Typically the plan is structured so that a proportion of the bonus earned is paid in deferred shares, but it is becoming increasingly common for plans to require any bonus earned in excess of a stated percentage of salary to be paid in deferred shares. This is often the case where the maximum bonus potential has been increased, with the amount of the increase in the bonus being paid in deferred shares.

The main aim of a bonus deferral plan is usually either retention, because the delivery of shares is conditional upon remaining in employment, or to encourage share ownership and alignment of executives' interests with shareholders by holding the deferred amount in shares. Bonus deferral can also form part of the longer-term performance framework thereby providing variation and flexibility in the long-term elements of an executive directors' remuneration package.

Plans can be structured so that it is a requirement that part, or all, of the bonus is paid in deferred shares (compulsory deferral), or a participant may be given the choice of investing part, or all, of the bonus (voluntary deferral). Some plans may combine an element of compulsory and voluntary deferral. The plan can also be structured, depending on the purpose, so that the deferred shares would be forfeit if the participant left before the end of the deferral period (typically where the deferral is compulsory and where the primary aim of the plan is retention), or so that the shares would be released in the event of the participant leaving before the end of the deferral period (typically where the plan is voluntary and where the primary aim of the plan is to encourage share ownership and alignment with shareholder interests). For obvious reasons, shares are rarely delivered early in the event of voluntary departure!

When designing a bonus plan which involves an element of share investment, it is important to consider the purpose of the plan and to select a combination of voluntary/compulsory deferral and vesting conditions which are consistent with the commercial needs.

Figure 4.12 illustrates how many of these plans are currently in place and how this has changed over the past three years.

Many of the plans are used as an alternative longer-term performance vehicle and include a 'matching' award of shares which vests at the end of the deferred period. Where this is the case, the deferral of the bonus is often a voluntary option rather than a requirement. These plans award additional shares at the end of the deferral period if performance targets have

Figure 4.12 *Percentage of companies with deferred bonus plans in place*

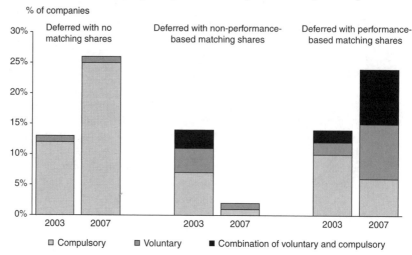

been met over the period. Three examples of the way these plans work are given in Figure 4.13.

The deferral period is usually three years, although shorter periods may be more appropriate for specific retention issues, and longer periods may be used where the plan includes performance-related matching awards and a longer performance period would be more appropriate. To encourage share ownership, the plan may increase the level of matching the longer the deferral.

The matching shares will typically be awarded on the basis of one matching share for every two deferred shares, one matching share for each deferred share or two matching shares for each deferred share. The level of matching will depend on the current bonus potential, whether or not performance conditions are attached and whether the plan is the sole long-term performance vehicle.

Until quite recently it was not uncommon for matching shares to vest simply if the participant remained in employment. From a shareholder perspective this was no different to increasing the bonus potential and, due to the pressure applied, it is now usual for the vesting of matching shares to be dependent on the performance of the company over the deferred period.

This means either that bonuses that were previously paid partly in cash and partly in simple deferred shares have become large cash bonuses or that a performance element has been added to the match.

When considering the introduction of a deferred bonus plan, these are the key questions that need be addressed:

- Is the aim of the plan to encourage retention and share ownership? If this is the case then simply paying a part of the bonus in deferred shares may achieve this aim.

Figure 4.13 *Examples of deferred bonus plans*

Example 1 – a plan which is aimed primarily at retention. Of the annual bonus earned, 50% is in the form of deferred shares. Deferred shares are subject to a restricted period of three years from the date of grant. If the participant ceases employment other than as a 'good leaver', the award lapses.

Example 2 – a plan which rewards longer-term performance and encourages share ownership and alignment with shareholder interests. A participant may invest up to 100% of the annual bonus earned in shares, which must be retained for three years. At the end of three years a matching award of shares of the same value as the invested shares will be made, dependent on performance. At the target level of performance, 10% of this matching award will vest with the full match only vesting if more stretching performance targets are met. The matching award is forfeited if the participant leaves the company or if the invested shares are disposed of before the end of the three-year period.

Example 3 – a plan which is intended to be the sole longer-term performance plan. Of the annual bonus earned, 50% is granted in the form of deferred shares. Deferred shares are subject to a restricted period of three years. A matching award of shares will be made, dependent on performance over the restricted period. For target performance, one share for every deferred share will vest. The maximum number of matching shares that may be awarded is three for every deferred share. The deferred shares vest if the participant leaves the company before the end of the restricted period but the matching award lapses unless the remuneration committee decides otherwise.

- Is the plan part of a wider policy of linking remuneration and longer-term performance? In this case a performance-linked match may be appropriate. This will allow flexibility in the value of the longer-term incentives by reference to annual performance.
- What proportion of the bonus should be deferred? If the participant is required to defer part of the bonus, the requirement is likely to be no more than 50% of bonus earned. If the deferral is voluntary, many companies allow the participant to defer up to 100% of the bonus if they wish. Some plans may require a portion of the bonus to be deferred and allow participants to defer the remainder if they choose. The plan can also be used flexibly throughout the organisation with senior executives required to defer part of the bonus and employees below this level offered the opportunity to defer if they wish.
- What ratio of matching shares should be awarded? This will depend on the nature of the plan: whether this is the primary long-term plan

or whether this is part of a suite of plans. It will also depend on the size of the potential bonus, the size of other long-term awards and the overall level of total remuneration. And it will depend on the degree of stretch in the performance conditions attached.

- What performance conditions should be attached? This will again depend on whether this is the sole long-term vehicle and, if not, how it fits with the other plans available. Some companies choose to use the same performance conditions for all long-term plans but it is more common to use different measures. For example the matching bonus plan may be in addition to a performance share plan (PSP) where the vesting of the shares is dependent on a relative measure, such as total shareholder return (TSR) relative to a comparator group of companies. Therefore, it may be appropriate for the matching bonus shares to be dependent on a financial performance measure, such as earnings per share which is a fundamental financial performance indicator.

Voluntary bonus deferral plans are often called co-investment plans but there are other types of co-investment plans which are not tied to bonus awards and allow a senior executive to invest their own money, usually up to a specified percentage of salary, in company shares, receiving matching shares in a similar way to that described above.

A relatively small number of companies use these plans on a more entrepreneurial basis, in order to mirror more effectively the buyout / venture capital environment.

This structure can be used to promote a culture of high levels of share ownership and to support more entrepreneurial behaviour, as in the Leadership Equity Acquisition Plan (LEAP) operated by WPP. As shown in Figure 4.14, the plan requires a substantial investment from the individual but provides the opportunity to make significant rewards if performance conditions are met.

Long-term incentive plans

Share ownership plans can be used to bridge the separation between ownership (in the hands of shareholders) and control (in the hands of management). When significant share ownership opportunities are provided, employees are treated more like entrepreneurs, with a stake in the success of the company in return for sharing the risks. Individuals are encouraged to think like owners, and share ownership can therefore be a foundation for long-term thinking. Share plans will usually include the senior executives but may extend beyond the top team and may reach throughout the organisation.

In terms of the design of the plans, these broadly fall into two categories, although there are a variety of structures within these two types of plans: options, which give the participant the opportunity to share in the

Figure 4.14 *WPP's LEAP plan*

LEAP

A participant must commit investment shares in order to qualify for matching shares. Executive directors other than the CEO may invest up to a maximum of 400% of annual target earnings (salary plus 50% bonus) over the five-year life of the plan. The CEO was able to invest $10m in the first year and $2m in each subsequent year of the plan. Normally the performance period will be five years. Matching shares are awarded based on TSR performance relative to other companies in the global communications industry. The number of matching shares is calculated by the relative return achieved by WPP, when compared against comparator companies: in particular, performance is calibrated by the extent to which WPP exceeds the next-ranked company. Normally 1.5 matching shares will be awarded for median performance, rising to 5 matching shares for first or second position in the comparator group.

future growth in value of the company above today's price, and performance share plans, which typically provide the participant with the opportunity to earn a number of stock in the company based on performance. These two plan types have very different dynamics. Phantom option plans or stock appreciation rights (SARs) typically have similar features to share option plans and can be managed so that they feel like share plans or can be operated as deferred cash bonus arrangements. Some of the arguments for and against the use of these plans can be seen in Figure 4.15.

Typically an award under a PSP is a specified number of shares designated at the outset and the proportion that vests depends on achievement of performance criteria. There are a small number of companies who operate long-term plans which have some of the same features as a performance share plan but where the award is made at the end of the performance period rather than at the start of the period. The award may be made in cash or shares but the key difference is that it is not impacted by the share price movement over the performance period.

It is worth noting that a number of companies have introduced long-term plans which allow awards to be made in any combination of options, SARs or performance shares, giving the company complete flexibility to use the plan in the most effective way in any given year. This approach will need a 'currency' converter in order to ensure that there is consistency between the expected value of awards made in options or shares. This structure provides full flexibility but care is needed if the company switches from one form to another on a regular basis. Executives often do not focus on the detail of plans and so any switching designed to encourage behaviour will need thorough communication if the commercial objective is to be achieved.

85

Figure 4.15 *Share option plans vs performance share plans*

Share options	Performance shares
For	**For**
• Simple and transparent	• The reward is closely linked to the chosen performance matrix
• Reward only when shareholders have seen the share price rise	• By paying in shares there is a link between remuneration and share price performance
• Link remuneration to share price performance	• Awards have an inherent value – they do not go underwater
• Well understood, embedded in market place	• Not as dilutive
• Emotional attachment of employees	• IFRS 2 impact can be less
• Deliver rewards for little cash cost	• Many investors prefer share awards to options
Against	
• Dilutive	**Against**
• Geared rewards can be volatile and unpredictable	• Inherent value of awards means awards have value even if shareholders have lost money
• If share price falls no value delivered, irrespective of performance	• Perceived complexity of plans
• Highly susceptible to market conditions	• Performance conditions may be insufficiently stretching
• Over-pay in a bull market and under pay in a bear market	

Share option plans

Share option plans offer a flexible means of giving certain selected employees the right to buy shares at a price determined when the option is granted. Share option plans can be approved by HM Revenue & Customs and receive favourable tax and national insurance treatment. The maximum market value of shares under option in an approved plan is limited to £30,000 per employee. This does not include options that have already been exercised or that have lapsed. Companies usually operate an approved share option plan in conjunction with an unapproved, or discretionary, plan which does not receive favourable tax treatment. See Figure 4.18 – 'Tax treatment and legal and regulatory issues of share option plans' – below.

Share option plans were traditionally the standard long-term plan in publicly listed companies. They offer a simple link between the interests of shareholders and participants; executives only make money if shareholders have seen the share price rise. For decades they were the instrument of choice to align the interests of shareholders with those of executive directors and employees. They have been an important part of US executive reward for many years and their use in UK companies dramatically increased in the 1980s with the introduction of Inland Revenue Approved Plans in 1984. In the 1980s approved share options (capped at shares with a grant value of four times annual earnings at any one time) became almost universal because they provided an interest in shares taxable as capital rather than income. With income taxed at 60% and capital gains tax payable at 30% there was a powerful tax incentive to adopt these plans. The tax advantages were gradually reduced as the tax rates harmonised more closely and approved options are now limited to shares with a market value at grant of £30,000.

Even when the tax advantages were reduced, the granting of share options remained widespread and still had the advantage of not giving rise to an accounting charge. This changed in 2005 (see Figure 4.16) and since that time the option plan has been in rapid decline, at least in the bigger companies. But other factors have contributed to the decline of the option plan. One of the key issues has been the somewhat tenuous link between performance and reward. Participants in option plans can enjoy significant gains when stock markets are performing well, irrespective of whether there has been any real improvement in company performance. Conversely participants may see no gain during a period of poor market performance, even where the company itself has performed well in comparison with its competitors.

Shareholders have encouraged design changes to address some of these issues:

- making smaller grants of options on a regular basis, rather than one-off large awards, which lessens the impact of a high or low share price at the date of grant and helps avoid windfall gains or large numbers of underwater options;
- including a performance target which must be met before options vest, which can avoid gains being made where this is due simply to stock market rather than company performance.

Executive directors only participate in a share option plan in less than a quarter of FTSE 350 companies, although some companies will use the share option plan as the main long-term vehicle for senior managers. Share option plans still remain popular in SmallCap, AIM companies and companies coming to the market, with around three quarters of these companies still using option plans. However, our research suggests that this too is changing: over two thirds of long-term plans introduced recently by FTSE SmallCap companies were performance share plans rather than share option plans.

It is worth noting, however, that many companies are retaining a share option plan even if they do not currently intend to use it. This provides flexibility in structuring the remuneration package in specific circumstances such as recruitment, or where there are retention issues.

In FTSE 350 companies the typical share option plan is now structured in the following way.

- Annual grants of options with a disclosed individual annual grant limit.
- Vesting dependent on performance, typically scaled so that a proportion vests for a threshold performance target, with full vesting requiring more stretching performance.
- Performance measured over a fixed three-year period, usually from the date of grant.

Figure 4.16 *Accounting for share-based payments*

The company is required to recognise an accounting expense for the 'fair value' of any share-based payments, in the profit and loss account. This expense is spread over the expected life of the award, typically the vesting/performance period.[1] Share-based payments include any awards that provide the delivery of shares or a cash amount which is linked to the share price, including free share awards, share options and phantom option awards.

The starting point for estimating the 'fair value' of a share award is the market value of the shares on the date of grant.[2] Where market prices are not available, for example for unlisted companies, a standard recognised valuation technique should be used to estimate the price 'in an arm's length transaction between knowledgeable, willing parties'. The valuation technique should be consistent with generally accepted valuation methodologies for pricing financial instruments, and should incorporate all factors and assumptions that knowledgeable, willing market participants would consider in setting the price. Valuation methodologies that are mentioned in the standard include using the share price of similar listed entities, or using a net asset or earnings basis. The fair value of share options should be estimated using an option pricing model such as a Black-Scholes or a binomial model. The option pricing model that is used should take into account the exercise price and current share price, expected share price volatility, expected dividends, the expected life of the option and the risk-free interest rate. If the company is unlisted at the time options are granted, the current share price and expected share price volatility should be estimated using an established valuation methodology (as outlined above).

If vesting of the share-based payment is dependent on performance, the type of measure used will affect the accounting treatment of the awards.

If vesting is dependent on non-market-based performance measures, such as EPS, the final expense recognised will be based on the number of shares that actually vest. In the first year the company makes an assessment of the likelihood of meeting the performance condition and estimates the number of shares that will eventually vest.

However, if the performance measures are market-based, such as share price or TSR, then the probability of meeting the performance target must be taken into account when determining the fair value of the award. The more demanding the relative performance measure, the lower the fair value. No subsequent adjustments will be made to reflect actual performance achieved. In particular, no adjustment would be made if the performance conditions are not met and the awards lapse.

[1] The accounting treatment for share awards and share options for listed companies is set
     out in International Financial Reporting Standard 20 – Share-based Payment ('FRS 20')
     and International Financial Reporting Standard 2 ('IFRS 2'), which is effective for all
     accounting periods commencing on or after 1 January 2005 and applies to all share-based
     payments granted on or after 7 November 2002. The accounting treatment for share
     awards and share options for private UK companies is set out in FRS 20 which is identical
     to IFRS 2 and applies for accounting periods commencing on or after 1 January 2006.
[2] This may be adjusted to take account of the terms of the share award such as
     non-entitlement to dividends.

Up until comparatively recently the plan would have required the performance target to be met over any three consecutive years over the life of the plan. Moving to a fixed performance period clearly reduces the probability of meeting the performance target and initially companies moved away from 'rolling re-testing' (i.e. any three consecutive years) to a regime which allowed for performance to be re-tested over the initial three-year period extended over a further one or two years, i.e. after three, four and five years from grant. Few plans now allow for any re-testing of performance after the three-year period, with options lapsing if the targets are not met.

- Flexibility to settle the option exercise in equity settled share appreciation rights (ESARs), which delivers shares equal to the gain that would have been made on the exercise of the option (see Figure 4.17). This can reduce dilution once the option is exercised as fewer shares are needed but it should be noted that, from an investor point of view, the number of shares should be counted in full on grant (treated as a normal share option) and then reduced on settlement.

Smaller companies will usually incorporate an individual grant limit and a fixed performance period but will sometimes not include scaled vesting targets and will instead use a 'cliff vesting' approach with all options vesting once a specified performance target is met.

For companies operating internationally, particularly where there is a predominance of senior executives based in the USA, options are sometimes granted below board level with no performance conditions and with vesting earlier than three years, as is more common in US-style plans (for example vesting monthly over thirty-six months). Investors may accept this where there is a clear business need but are unlikely to be happy where executive directors are eligible to participate in the plan.

Share option plans can also be used in private companies, and are popular in start-up companies that intend to become publicly traded. A minority interest in a private company often has a low valuation because there is limited marketability, the ownership percentage does not give control or influence and there may be little or no dividend. Accordingly, there is often a substantial increase in value following the flotation. In small

---

Figure 4.17 *Example of how equity settled share appreciation rights work*

- An employee has an option to acquire 1,000 shares with an exercise price of £1.75 per share
- The total exercise price is therefore £1,750
- The employee exercises the option when the share price is £4.30 per share
- With a conventional option the company issues 1,000 shares to the employee and the employee immediately sells 407 shares to pay the exercise price, i.e. 407 shares 'wasted'
- The employee has therefore made a gain of £2,550

If the options are settled in the form of equity settled SARs, the company issues 593 shares to the employee, equal in value to the £2,550 gain but reduces dilution by 40%.

---

companies like these, which may be cash poor and unable to pay high salaries or cash bonuses, share options offer significant wealth creation opportunities for employees if the business succeeds. Pre-initial public offering (IPO) options can often be granted with an exercise price which is a 'market price' but which may be significantly lower than the float price if they are granted more than six to twelve months prior to flotation, before the 'float premium' is recognised. The exercise of the options can be made conditional on the flotation which avoids the practical challenges of share ownership in a private company. Vesting can be phased over a number of years following admission if a further retention element is required. It is also common for newly floated companies to grant options at, or immediately following, flotation with an exercise price equal to the float price, which have no performance conditions and which vest earlier than the usual three years. Incoming investors accept the arrangements operating prior to and at the point of flotation; however, shareholders will expect ongoing grants of options to conform to the guidelines for listed companies.

Share options are not as common in private companies that intend to remain private but many private companies do use them for key employees. As there is no public market, it will be necessary to create an internal market which may be simply that the company repurchases the shares. In established private companies there may be a true internal market where shares are traded between employees on a regular basis.

When considering whether to replace a share option plan, to amend an existing plan to bring it into line with best practice, or to introduce a new plan, the following key questions should be addressed:

- Is a share option plan the most effective way of incentivising employees and aligning interests of employees and shareholders?

Figure 4.18 *Tax treatment and legal and regulatory issues of share option plans*

Tax implications for the employee

Approved plan – no income tax or National Insurance Contributions (NIC) liability arises on exercise unless the option is exercised within three years of grant. If an income tax charge does arise this will be payable through PAYE if the shares are 'readily convertible assets' (which typically means that arrangements are in place which enable the employee to convert the shares into cash – e.g. the shares are listed on a stock exchange – but may include where the shares are in a subsidiary of an unlisted company). In such cases NIC is also due on the gain.

Unapproved plan – income tax is generally payable when the option is exercised, based on the value of the shares less the exercise price. In addition, if the shares are readily convertible assets (which typically means that arrangements are in place which enable the employee to convert the shares into cash – e.g. the shares are listed on a stock exchange – but includes where the shares are in a subsidiary of an unlisted company), NIC is also due on the gain.

NIC is payable at 11% where total earnings are below the upper earnings limit (£2,795 per month for 2006/7). There is also 1% employee's NIC on all earnings above the upper earnings limit.

A capital gains tax (CGT) charge arises on any subsequent growth in value of the shares after exercise when the shares are disposed of (which may be mitigated by an employee's annual CGT exemption and capital losses).

Tax implications for the employer

If the shares are readily convertible assets (see above), the employer is required to operate 'Pay As You Earn' (PAYE), and employer's National Insurance is payable at 12.8% (for 2006/7) on any gain realised by the employee on the exercise of the option.

There is no maximum earnings limit for employers' NIC. However, for share options granted on or after 6 April 1999 where no gain has yet arisen:

- an employer and employee may come to an agreement by which the employee undertakes to fund all or part of the employer's NIC; and
- the employee may offset any NIC paid under such an agreement against the income tax liability arising on the option gain.

There are strict time limits within which any income tax due under PAYE must be paid to Her Majesty's Revenue & Customs and

Figure 4.18 *continued*

recovered from the employee. Failure to meet these time limits may result in additional income tax, penalties and interest.

The employer is entitled to an automatic corporation tax deduction when the option is exercised, subject to satisfaction of certain conditions regarding the employer and the shares acquired. The deduction is equal to the amount of the employee's gain. This applies for all accounting periods beginning on or after 1 January 2003.

Legal and regulatory issues

No significant legal issues arise from the introduction of a share option plan, although shareholder approval at a general meeting is generally required for listed companies.

Enterprise management incentive plans (EMI)

The EMI is intended to help smaller companies with potential for growth to recruit and retain high-calibre employees, and to reward employees for taking a risk by investing their time and skills in helping small companies achieve their potential.

Main features of the plan:

- The total value of shares in respect of which unexercised EMI options exist must not exceed £3 million (by reference to the market value of the shares at the date of grant of the EMI options).
- The value of shares in respect of which an employee may hold EMI options must not exceed £100,000 (again, by reference to the market value of the shares at the date of grant). Approved Company Share Option Plan (CSOP) options (granted in respect of the employee's employment with the same group) count towards this £100,000 limit.
- EMI options can be offered by trading companies (or holding companies of trading groups) which are not under the control of another company and which have gross assets not exceeding £30 million. There are various other important qualifying tests concerning matters such as the nature of the trade carried out, which the relevant group must also satisfy.
- Qualifying options can only be granted to employees:
  - who work at least twenty-five hours per week for the group; or
  - 75% of working time for the group

  and own less than 30% of the company.

The EMI does not require the prior approval of the HMRC (although the HMRC will give an advance ruling (on provision of the relevant facts) on whether a company is qualified under the EMI legislation to grant EMI options).

HMRC must be notified of the grant of EMI options within ninety-two days thereafter (and options will not qualify as EMI options if this notification requirement is not complied with).

Tax implications for the employee

No income tax or NIC liability on exercise of options unless the option is:

*   granted at a discount;
*   exercised more than forty days after a disqualifying event;
*   exercised more than ten years after the date of grant.

Gains made on the subsequent sale of the shares are subject to CGT, although this may be mitigated by the employees' annual CGT exemption.

Tax implications for the employer

There is no charge to the employer's NIC and no requirement to operate PAYE on the grant or exercise of the option (provided that the conditions referred to above are satisfied). A corporate tax deduction will not be available for the cost of setting up the plan.

SAYE plans

Sharesave plans (or Save-As-You-Earn – 'SAYE') are HMRC approved all-employee share option plans that receive favourable tax and national insurance treatment.

Key features

*   Share options must be offered to all employees who have more than five years' service and on similar terms.
*   Options can be offered which can be exercised three, five or seven years from grant, although few companies offer seven-year options.
*   The exercise price can be set at a discount of up to 20% of the market value of the shares on grant.
*   Employees enter into a savings contract with a bank or building society and use the funds to pay the exercise price of the option. The amount saved is between £5 and £250 per month and interest is received in the form of a tax-free bonus at the end of the savings contract.
*   No income tax or NIC liability should arise on grant or exercise.
*   If the employee does not want to exercise their option (for example if it is underwater), then they are able to take the proceeds of their savings account including the tax free-bonus.

Figure 4.18 *continued*

- Options normally lapse on leaving employment (other than in compassionate circumstances) or if the employee ends the savings contract. In addition, options can generally be exercised early in the event of a takeover, reconstruction or winding-up of the company.

Tax implications for the employee

No income tax or NIC liability generally arises on grant or exercise.

Where tax is payable it is collected through self-assessment, not via PAYE. Gains made on the subsequent sale of the shares are subject to CGT, although this may be mitigated by the employee's annual CGT exemption.

Tax implications for the employer

There is no charge to the employer's NIC and no requirement to operate PAYE on the grant or exercise of the option.

The employer is entitled to an automatic corporation tax deduction when the option is exercised, subject to satisfaction of certain conditions regarding the employer and the shares acquired. The deduction will be equal to the amount of the employee's gain. This applies for all accounting periods beginning on or after 1 January 2003.

Share Incentive Plans

Share Incentive Plans (SIPs) provide a unique opportunity for employees to purchase shares out of gross income and to receive awards of shares on a tax-free basis.

A SIP is an umbrella scheme which operates on an all-employee basis. Under a SIP, employees can be given shares (Free Shares), can be given the opportunity to purchase shares (Partnership Shares) and can be offered the opportunity to receive extra shares (Matching Shares) for each Partnership Share purchased.

Key features

- A SIP operates in conjunction with a special UK resident trust which holds the shares while they remain subject to the SIP.
- Free and Matching Shares must normally remain in the SIP for a minimum of three years (the 'Holding Period') and can be forfeited if the employee leaves within three years of the award (the 'Forfeiture Period'). Matching Shares can also be forfeited if the associated Partnership Shares are withdrawn.

- Partnership Shares can be withdrawn at any time and are not subject to a Holding Period or Forfeiture Period.
- Maximum tax efficiencies are achieved if the shares are held in the SIP for five years from the award.
- When income tax is due on Free, Matching and Partnership Shares, PAYE and NIC will normally be due.

Free Shares

- Up to £3,000 of Free Shares can be awarded to an employee each tax year.
- Awards must be made to employees on the same terms (e.g. a flat award, or by reference to salary or length of service).
- The award can also be based on objective performance criteria.
- The Holding Period must be between three and five years.
- Free Shares cannot be taken out of the SIP during the Holding Period unless the employee leaves.
- Bad leavers can be made to forfeit their Free Shares.
- The Forfeiture Period must be no more than three years.

Tax treatment for employees

- No income tax or NIC on award.
- If shares are held in the SIP for five years there is no income tax.
- Good leavers pay no income tax on the shares leaving the SIP.
- If shares are taken out within three years of award, the employee will pay income tax on their value at removal. If shares are withdrawn between three and five years of award, income tax is due on the lesser of the initial market value of the shares and the market value of the shares when withdrawn.

Partnership Shares

- Partnership shares are bought out of pre-tax salary. A maximum of £1,500 (or 10% of salary, if less) of salary can be allocated for the purchase of Partnership Shares in any tax year.
- The company can determine if shares are to be bought with each deduction from salary or the deductions are saved up over an 'Accumulation Period' and shares purchased at the end.
- No Holding or Forfeiture Period.

Tax treatment for employees

- No income tax or NIC on award.
- If held in the SIP for five years, there is no income tax.

Figure 4.18 *continued*

- Good leavers pay no income tax on the shares leaving the SIP.
- If the shares are taken out between three and five years, the employee will pay income tax on the lesser of the salary used to buy the shares and the market value of the shares at the time they are removed from the plan.
- If the shares are taken out within three years, the employee will pay income tax on the market value of the shares at the time they are removed from the plan.

Matching Shares

- Additional shares awarded on the same basis to all employees in a ratio of up to two Matching Shares for each Partnership Share purchased.
- Holding Period must be between three and five years.
- Cannot be taken out of the SIP during the Holding Period unless the employee leaves.
- Bad leavers can be made to forfeit their Matching Shares.
- Forfeiture Period must be no more than three years.
- Can also be forfeited if the corresponding Partnership Shares are withdrawn within three years of purchase.

Tax treatment for employees

- The income tax and CGT treatment of Matching Shares for employees is the same as for Free Shares.

Tax-free re-investment of dividends

- Up to £1,500 of cash dividends on plan shares per year can be re-invested tax-free in 'Dividend Shares' which must have a three-year Holding Period.

Tax treatment for employees

- No income tax or NIC on award.
- No PAYE or NIC on withdrawal.
- No income tax if held within the SIP for three years.
- If withdrawn within three years, income tax on original value of cash dividend received.

- Does the share option plan offer 'value for money'?
- What is the appropriate annual grant size?
- Which employees should participate?
- What are the right performance measures and targets? Should the plan allow all options to vest if the performance targets are met or

should the plan have scaled vesting according to the level of performance? Should this be the same for all employees?

Performance share plans

Performance share plans started to appear in the mid 1990s, introduced by companies such as Reuters, and more particularly from 1995 when the report of a study group chaired by Sir Richard Greenbury was published. The study group was set up in response to public and shareholder concerns about the pay and other remuneration of company directors in the UK. The report was written following a strong bull market and after a period of significant privatisation of businesses. The report suggested that the use of share options, for the reasons given above, should be weighed against the use of other forms of long-term incentive plan.

Since then performance share plans have increased in popularity and are currently used by over 80% of FTSE 350 companies. In many companies only the executive directors and the senior executive team will participate in these plans. There are fewer plans in smaller companies but over two thirds of FTSE SmallCap companies operate a performance share plan.

Performance plans award a number of whole shares for nominal or no cost, provided certain corporate performance conditions are met. Typically the plan will incorporate a limit, usually expressed as a percentage of salary, on the number of shares that may be awarded to any individual. The number of shares ultimately released to the participant is based on the company's performance over a pre-determined period and is usually subject to the participant remaining in employment.

The plan can be structured in a number of ways: as nil-cost options, as a promise to receive shares in the future, or as restricted shares with a risk of forfeiture. Nil-cost options give the individual the right to call for the shares once any performance conditions have been satisfied and the necessary time period has elapsed. When restricted shares are awarded, the employee owns the shares from the start of the plan, and there may be issues for the company associated with retrieving the shares in the event that performance conditions are not met, or the participant leaves.

Where the individual holds restricted shares, they receive the dividends paid on the shares during the restricted performance period. Where the awards are made as nil-cost options or as a promise to receive shares in the future, it is becoming good practice to make dividend equivalent awards in respect of the number of shares vesting at the end of the performance period. These may be paid in cash or shares.

Unlike market value options, performance shares always have an intrinsic value and therefore it is generally accepted that these plans will have tougher performance conditions than share option plans. When these plans first appeared, they nearly always used TSR measured relative to a group of comparator companies, as this was the recommendation made in

Figure 4.19 *Typical annual performance share award*

	FTSE SmallCap	FTSE 250	FTSE 100	Top 30 UK companies
Upper quartile	100%	150%	200%	300%
Median	100%	100%	150%	245%
Lower quartile	75%	100%	100%	150%

the Greenbury Report. This is still the most common measure, but plans have evolved over the years with many more plans using a combination of measures and more companies starting to use bespoke measures which are considered more appropriate to the circumstances of the company.

Figure 4.19 shows the typical face value of a performance share award in FTSE 350 companies. This is usually stated as a percentage of salary.

The key questions to ask when introducing a performance share plan include:

- What is the appropriate annual grant size?
- Which employees should participate? Is this the right way of incentivising all senior employees or would this plan be more appropriate for the board only, with a simple share option plan being more appropriate to other senior employees?
- What are the right performance measures and targets?
- Should performance be measured relative to other companies? And, if so, what comparator group should be used?
- What level of vesting should occur for target performance and what level of performance should be required for full vesting?

The design features of a performance share plan may be replicated in long-term cash plans with the only difference being that the award will be paid out at the end of the performance period and, the eventual payout, which may be in cash or shares, will not be influenced by the movement in share price over the period. If one of the aims of the plan is to create alignment of interest between participants and shareholders, this clearly will not have the same effect, but for non-quoted companies this can be an effective alternative structure.

Performance measures

The choice of measures

In this section we look at some of the more common performance measures, how they are calculated and some of the advantages and disadvantages of using them to measure performance in incentive plans. We then go on to examine TSR and EPS in more detail.

Figure 4.20 *Tax and accounting treatment and legal and regulatory issues of performance share plans*

Tax treatment – employee

No income tax or NIC liability usually arises on the grant of an award to an employee under the plan. However, with certain structures, it is possible for the employee and employer to elect jointly to be taxed when the award is made.

Income tax is generally payable when the shares are transferred, based on the value of the shares at transfer less any amount paid by the employee. In addition, if the shares are readily convertible assets (which typically means that arrangements are in place which enable the employee to convert the shares into cash, e.g. the shares are listed on a stock exchange), NIC are also due on the gain.

A CGT charge arises on any subsequent growth in value on disposal of the shares (which may be mitigated by an employee's annual CGT exemption and capital losses).

Tax treatment – employer

If the shares are readily convertible assets (see above), employer's National Insurance is payable when the shares are transferred on the value of the shares at that time, less any amount paid by the employee. In addition, the employer is required to operate PAYE on the transfer of the shares.

Provided certain conditions are met, the employer will be entitled to a corporate tax deduction equal to the taxable gain made by the employee on transfer of the shares.

Accounting treatment

For accounting periods that started on or after 1 January 2005, companies are required to recognise a charge in their profit and loss account in relation to share-based payments. The charge is based on the fair value of the underlying share at the date of grant and is spread over the vesting period of the award.

An accepted model (such as Black-Scholes or Binomial) should be used to determine the fair value of a share-based payment which is driven by the following inputs: volatility, share price on grant, dividend yield, the life of the award, risk-free rate and the amount, if any, the employee is required to pay for the award. Adjustments should be made for lapse rates.

The way in which share-based payments are expensed depends on the type of performance condition(s) applicable to the award. If performance conditions are non-market based (i.e. not connected to the

Figure 4.20 *continued*

company's share price), the fair value will not take account of the existence of performance conditions and the total amount expensed by the end of the period will reflect the proportion of the award that ultimately vests. If, on the other hand, the performance condition is market-based (i.e. connected to the share price), the fair value determined at the grant date takes account of the existence of the performance condition (i.e. it is discounted to reflect the probability of performance conditions being satisfied). The corollary of this is that no adjustments are made at the end of the vesting period to reflect actual vesting (i.e. a charge is incurred irrespective of the extent to which the award vests).

Legal and regulatory issues

No significant legal issues arise from the introduction of a performance share plan, although shareholder approval at a general meeting is generally required for listed companies. Guidelines of institutional investor bodies such as the ABI recommend that performance conditions should be 'challenging' and should:

- relate to overall corporate performance;
- demonstrate the achievement of a level of performance which is demanding in the context of the prospects of the company and the prevailing economic environment; and
- be disclosed and transparent.

In relation to the latter, the Directors' Remuneration Report Regulations require companies to include a policy statement with details of performance measures used in any long-term incentive arrangements. Companies implementing performance share plans should therefore consider:

- What performance measure(s) should most appropriately be used?
- Are any elements of the performance measurement commercially sensitive? If so, how will this be handled?
- Is there a clear methodology for assessing whether the performance conditions are met?
- Is there a clear rationale behind the choice of comparator companies against which performance is measured, and a methodology for dealing with changes in the group?

Total shareholder return (TSR)

TSR measures the growth in share price together with dividends reinvested and provides an external market view of the company's success. TSR is usually measured against a group of relevant comparator companies with vesting dependent on the ranked position against those companies. A typical vesting schedule would have minimum vesting (e.g. 25% of the award) for median TSR ranking, rising on a straight line basis to maximum vesting for at least an upper quartile rank position.

Earnings per share (EPS)

EPS is calculated as earnings divided by the weighted average number of shares in the year of measurement and is disclosed at the bottom of the income statement in the financial statements.

Basic EPS includes all items of profit and loss in the year. It can therefore be an erratic measure of performance because it includes large one-off and unusual non-recurring items, and other non-operational expenses. For the purposes of obtaining a performance measure, it is common practice to use a 'normalised' EPS figure which makes adjustments for factors such as one-off and unusual items and is therefore a more stable and more meaningful basis for comparison year on year.

Typically, performance will be based on the growth in EPS over a three-year period. The target is usually set by reference to the RPI so that only 'real' growth is measured. There will usually be a level of threshold vesting which will occur for growth in excess of RPI + x%, on a sliding scale to full vesting for growth in excess of RPI + y%.

Economic profit

Economic profit is net operating profit less a charge for the capital used in the business. The charge for capital can be calculated as:

Capital employed (average during the period) × Weighted average cost of capital (WACC)

The WACC represents the average return required by all investors in the company.

Economic profit is the absolute amount of profit made during a financial period over and above that which is required to satisfy all investors in the company at their required rates of return. It can be thought of as the 'value added' profit.

Return on capital employed (ROCE)

ROCE is calculated as profit before interest and tax (PBIT) divided by the average capital employed during the period. The capital employed represents the debt and equity resources available to the company.

The key difference compared to profit measures (such as EPS) is that profit measures represent a growth in absolute profit, while ROCE represents profits achieved relative to the company's assets. ROCE measures the capital efficiency with which profit is generated. The measure is most often used in capital intensive businesses.

As a performance condition, the company would typically be required

Figure 4.21 *Advantages and disadvantages of different performance measures*

	Capital focused measures	Strategic measures	Share price based measures	Revenue based measures	Profit based measures	Cashflow based measures
Advantages	Provide a strong link to shareholder value creation	Strategic milestone measures can be (internally) transparent indicators of individual performance, e.g. logistics measures and product availability. Provide a link to the business plan and strategy	Strongest link to value creation and highly transparent	May be perceived as more directly under management control In some sectors are seen as an important measure of performance	More directly under management control. Relatively well understood by investors (particularly margin) and common as a measure in short-term incentive plans and in longer-term plans through EPS	Provide a good indication of ability to cover financing costs and overall health of the business
Disadvantages	May be most suitable for capital driven companies, as opposed to those driven by revenues/ earnings	Inherently subjective and can be open to objections that they lack (external) transparency. If decisions on whether they have been met are perceived to be arbitrary by participants the measure may be devalued	Do not necessarily reflect actual performance of management Share price performance already inherent, given form of award Share price reflects market perception of expected performance so may not be a good indicator of performance to date	May raise questions about how performance is measured May be considered too remote from ultimate delivery of value	Can be perceived as too narrow (e.g. relative to capital focused measures) Differences between accounting treatments can make inter-company comparisons problematic Adjustments can make some analysts distrustful of the measure and IAS complicates interpretation	Adjustments can make some analysts distrustful of the measure

Figure 4.22 *Advantages and disadvantages of TSR*

Advantages	Disadvantages
• Simple concept	• Subject to influences outside the company's control. For example, in a small comparator group, consolidation in a sector can result in bid premium influencing the TSR of the comparator companies and unfairly penalising the company being measured
• The performance of the company is measured by the external market, which is arguably more robust than an internal measure	
• Favoured by institutional shareholders and ultimately aligned with shareholders	• Participants may feel that they are not sufficiently able to influence the outcome
• Targets do not need to be set; they are set externally by the market	• TSR results may not always appear to reflect adequately the underlying performance of the company over the short term
	• Performance is dependent on the selected base starting point

Figure 4.23 *Advantages and disadvantages of EPS*

Advantages	Disadvantages
• Simple and understood by participants, analysts and shareholders	• Can encourage a short-term outlook
	• Ignores cost of capital associated with the company
• Transparent and based on published, audited information	• Only transparent if any normalising adjustments are fully disclosed
• Generally acceptable to shareholders	• Earnings growth can be 'bought' via acquisitions

to achieve an average ROCE, over the period, of x% for minimum vesting, with a more stretching target set for maximum vesting.

Return on equity (ROE)

ROE is calculated as profit after tax (PAT) divided by the average equity during the period. The key difference compared to ROCE is that ROE only measures the return to shareholders rather than the return to all providers of capital to the company.

As a performance condition, the company would typically be required to achieve an average ROE, over the period, of x%.

ROE has broadly the same advantages and disadvantages as ROCE, with the additional comments in figure 4.26.

Measuring TSR relative to a comparator group

One of the key decisions when using TSR is what comparator group to use to measure performance. The comparator group used to benchmark

Figure 4.24 *Advantages and disadvantages of economic profit*

Advantages

- Economic profit is the only measure which takes into account the return which is implicitly required by investors in the company and is therefore fully aligned with investors

- Focuses on profitable growth and capital efficiency

- An absolute value (rather than a percentage), therefore rewards the size of the profits achieved

Disadvantages

- Volatility makes long-term target setting difficult

- Difficult to set inputs for the calculation (such as the exact value of WACC)

- Complex to calculate, understand and communicate for both participants and shareholders

- May encourage the wrong behaviours if measured over short periods, such as underinvestment (i.e. to keep capital employed as low as possible)

- Can be volatile from year to year

- Unlike market measures (TSR), it does not capture any 'forward-looking' performance

Figure 4.25 *Advantages and disadvantages of ROCE*

Advantages

- Simple concept to understand and easy to calculate directly from the financial statements

- Rewards efficient profit generation

Disadvantages

- Only transparent if any adjustments (e.g. to capital employed) are fully disclosed

- May encourage the wrong behaviours, such as underinvestment (i.e. to keep capital employed as low as possible), or shrinking the business

remuneration may not be the appropriate comparator group against which to measure company performance.

When performance plans were first introduced it was common practice to measure TSR relative to the constituent companies of a relevant market capitalisation based index, for example the FTSE 100 or FTSE 250. There has been a trend towards using a more bespoke group over the past few years, with the majority of companies using either the constituents of a FTSE sector index or a bespoke group of comparator companies, frequently with an international component. The use of an industry-based comparator group seeks to remove sector-specific trends and so removes the opportunity to reward or penalise the management simply for operating in a particular sector – for example, around the year 2000 we experienced the 'dotcom' boom and in recent years mining and natural resource companies have performed well against the wider market.

One of the disadvantages of TSR, as stated above, is that it may not necessarily reflect the company's underlying financial performance, and a

Figure 4.26 *Advantages and disadvantages of ROE*

Advantages	Disadvantages
• Could be considered to be more aligned to shareholders than ROCE	• Does not take into account the debt resources of the company and may, therefore, incentivise the company to 'gear up' beyond an optimal point

number of shareholders prefer a TSR-based incentive plan to include a measure of financial performance, often EPS, incorporated so that none of the award will vest, irrespective of TSR performance, unless there has been an improvement in underlying financial performance.

The choice of comparator companies can have a significant impact on the likelihood and level of awards vesting and it may be helpful to take this into account when looking at how stretching the conditions are. The spread of TSR performance varies significantly by sector as would be expected, but what may come as more of a surprise is that it also varies by company size. A larger company using a comparator group which includes predominantly smaller companies may be perceived to be making the targets easier; however, Figure 4.27 shows that in fact larger companies may find it harder to achieve the upper quartile position against a comparator group of predominantly smaller companies. The chart illustrates this point, looking at the TSR between 2004 and 2007 for constituents of the FTSE 350 at the beginning of the period.

Compiling an appropriate group of companies against which to measure TSR which will be seen as fair by both participants and shareholders is likely to be quite difficult. Our analysis suggests that at the very least you will need to consider the type of business and the size of the comparable companies.

A further consideration when choosing the comparator group is how you will handle the inevitable changes to the group which will occur through mergers, de-mergers, takeovers, etc. Our research suggests that there is high probability that one or more of the constituents of a comparator group will delist during a typical performance period. This will impact on the resultant TSR ranking. For example, if the TSR of the companies delisting were typically below median then this would make the TSR targets harder to achieve. There are a number of approaches that can be adopted to deal with companies delisting and these include:

- Remove the delisted company from the comparator group and measure the TSR relative to the remaining companies. Our example above suggests that this may have unforeseen consequences on the end ranking.
- Measure the TSR of the delisted company in the usual way up to the date of delisting and include this in the final ranking.

105

Figure 4.27 *Three-year TSR performance*

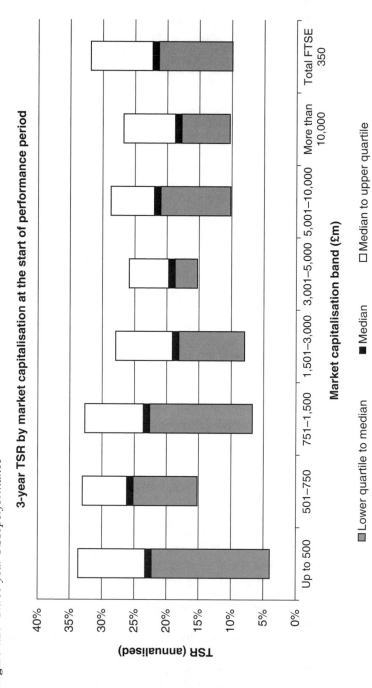

3-year TSR by market capitalisation at the start of performance period

Market capitalisation band (£m)

■ Lower quartile to median ■ Median □ Median to upper quartile

Source: Datastream

- If the company is acquired by another listed company then, from the date of acquisition, the TSR of the company concerned could be considered the same as that of the acquiring company.
- From the date of the delisting, the TSR of the company concerned could be re-invested into a 'risk-free' security.
- From the date of the delisting, the TSR of the company concerned could be re-invested into a specified index.
- From the date of the delisting, the TSR of the company concerned could be re-invested into 'synthetic stock', such as the average TSR of the remaining comparator companies or a sector-based group of companies.
- Replace the comparator company with a substitute company which is then measured over the full period.

The approach selected will depend on the timing of the delisting and the reason the company ceased to be listed.

Probability of meeting TSR targets

Another factor to be borne in mind is that it may become increasingly difficult to maintain an upper quartile TSR position. Figure 4.28 illustrates, for companies in either the upper quartile or lower quartile in the two preceding three-year periods, the probability of achieving first, second, third or fourth quartile position in the current three-year period.

For a company previously in the upper quartile, based on this analysis, the likelihood of achieving upper quartile position in the current period is around 17%, compared to those previously in the lower quartile who have a 32% probability of being in the upper quartile.

For a previously upper quartile performing company, based on this analysis, there is a 40% chance of being above median in the current period compared with a 58% chance for companies previously in the lower quartile.

Index-based TSR+2 approach

An alternative approach to ranking TSR within a comparator group is to create a comparator group index and measure TSR relative to the index. This approach takes the 'average' TSR performance of a number of companies, typically those in a comparator group or an industry sector, to create a synthetic index. The TSR performance of the company is then measured against this index and vesting is dependent on the extent to which the company out-performs the index.

Typically, where the index approach is used, a proportion of the award will vest for matching the index with full vesting requiring the company to exceed the index by a specified percentage which is set at the start of the performance period.

Figure 4.28 *Probability of achieving TSR growth based on TSR performance in the previous two three-year periods*

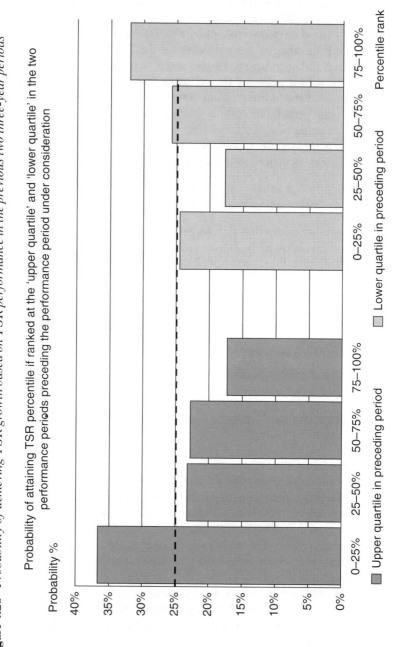

Probability of attaining TSR percentile if ranked at the 'upper quartile' and 'lower quartile' in the two performance periods preceding the performance period under consideration

Probability %

40%

35%

30%

25%

20%

15%

10%

5%

0%

0–25%   25–50%   50–75%   75–100%   0–25%   25–50%   50–75%   75–100%

Percentile rank

■ Upper quartile in preceding period   ■ Lower quartile in preceding period

Source: Datastream

Figure 4.29 *Advantages and disadvantages of index TSR*

Advantages

- Avoids disproportionate changes in vesting from only small changes in TSR performance, as can occur with using the rank-based approach when the companies are closely clustered together

- Useful where the desired comparator group consists of a small number of good comparators and vesting is even more sensitive to small changes in TSR

- Incorporates the TSR performance of the whole comparator group, rather than being based just on specific companies around the median and upper quartile positions

- Absolute performance is taken into account as it is not sufficient to 'only just' out-perform a comparator company

Disadvantages

- Comparator companies which perform very well or very badly may weight the performance of the index to such an extent that the final vesting result is not reflective of the relative performance of the company against the comparator group

- There is a requirement to determine the percentage by which the index must be out-performed in order to vest since there is no 'market practice' figure as to what this should be and it will vary for each comparator group

Figure 4.29 provides some of the potential advantages and disadvantages of this approach.

The key challenge in using this approach is setting the appropriate targets required for minimum and maximum vesting. A useful way of looking at this is to consider the level of out-performance of the index which would deliver an equivalent level of stretch to that of the rank-based approach, thereby providing reassurance that the targets are appropriately stretching, robust and defensible to shareholders.

In a typical plan using a rank-based approach, threshold vesting would occur for median performance and maximum vesting would occur for at least upper quartile performance. It is possible to plot the TSR performance of the index against both the median and upper quartile performance of the comparator group over a period of time as illustrated in Figure 4.30. This will help inform the decision on the level of out-performance of the index which would broadly equate to an upper quartile position.

Figure 4.31 shows, for each business sector, the difference between the index and the median, and, in the second column, the percentage by which the upper quartile exceeds the index. These figures are based on monthly averages over a ten-year period.

This analysis suggests that equalling the index, in most sectors, is harder than achieving the median of the ranked companies. The percentage by which the upper quartile ranked TSR exceeds the index varies significantly by sector. In order to determine an appropriate target for maximum vesting it would clearly be necessary to undertake more specific research into the appropriate comparator companies, the appropriate period over which to analyse the data and other relevant factors.

Figure 4.30 *Index TSR vs median and upper quartile*

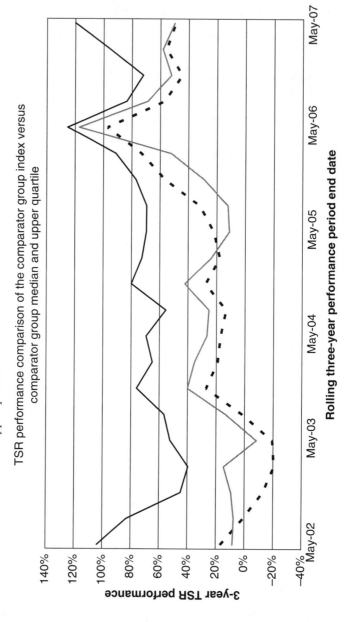

TSR performance comparison of the comparator group index versus comparator group median and upper quartile

Source: Datastream

Figure 4.31 *TSR index compared to median and upper quartile by business sector*

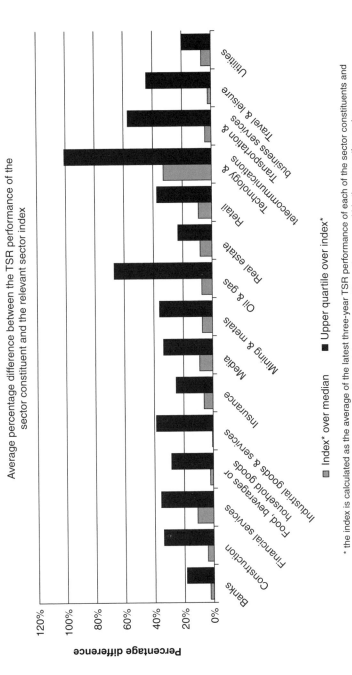

Average percentage difference between the TSR performance of the sector constituent and the relevant sector index

Percentage difference

120%
100%
80%
60%
40%
20%
0%

Banks
Construction
Financial services
Food, beverages or household goods
Industrial goods & services
Insurance
Media
Mining & metals
Oil & gas
Real estate
Retail
Technology & telecommunications
Transportation & business services
Travel & leisure
Utilities

■ Index* over median   ■ Upper quartile over index*

* the index is calculated as the average of the latest three-year TSR performance of each of the sector constituents and this is then measured relative to the median and the upper quartile performance within the respective sector

Source: Datastream

Other decisions that affect the calculation of TSR

If TSR is to be used as one of the main measures, a number of other decisions will need to be made in calculating the TSR and these should be documented to avoid any misunderstanding. These include:

- When should the dividends be re-invested, on the ex-dividend date or the payment date?
- Should the dividends be invested gross or net of tax (and is the answer different if comparators are not UK listed)?
- Over what period should TSR be averaged at the start and end of the performance period? This can vary from two weeks to one year but is more typically over one, or three, months.
- Should the calculations be carried out in local currency or in a common currency?

Setting EPS targets

While EPS is not commonly used as the main performance measure in performance share plans, many companies incorporate an element of EPS measurement. EPS is still the most common measure in share option plans.

EPS growth is typically measured relative to the retail price index (RPI) although some companies use an absolute EPS target. It is rarely measured relative to a comparator group. The EPS targets for share option plans have changed significantly over the last few years. It was previously common for all options granted to vest if a single specified EPS growth target was achieved over **any** three-year period during the life of the option. This is usually known as 'rolling re-testing'. The target would typically have been growth equal to or greater than RPI + 2% per annum. Our research indicates that the majority of companies would achieve this target over at least one three-year period over the life of the option, and so it would be reasonable to conclude that it was not a stretching performance measure for most companies. Consequently, shareholders started to apply pressure in a number of areas. One was to encourage companies to make the target more stretching, to perhaps RPI + 3% or even 4% per annum. Even then our research indicates that most companies would achieve this over the life of the option.

Alongside investor pressure to grant options on a phased basis rather than in large blocks, pressure also mounted to measure performance over a fixed three-year period from grant. This represented a significant change since it is clearly much harder to meet the target over a single period than the under rolling re-testing method where there were effectively eight chances of meeting the target during the ten-year life of the option. Companies therefore typically allowed some form of opportunity for performance re-testing over a further number of years, often fixing the base year by reference to the grant date so that performance would be measured over three years, then over four years and, typically, over five years. Shareholders have voiced strong concern over the use of re-testing provisions of any kind and these too have now almost disappeared. This means that performance is now typically measured over a single three-year period, and if the test is not satisfied the option lapses and cannot be exercised. This has had a significant impact on the gains made on these plans.

The next area of investor pressure was for scaled vesting where, rather than a single performance hurdle which would result in all, or none, of the options vesting, only a proportion would vest for achieving a threshold target with more stretching performance required for all the options to vest.

During 2006 there was a strong emergence of EPS as a performance factor in plans which use more than one performance measure.

Where EPS is used in combination with other measures it will typically be on a scaled basis. This should not be confused with those plans which use EPS as a minimum performance hurdle (an 'underpin'), most commonly where TSR is the primary measure, and this will normally be a simple threshold target that must be met before any of the award can vest, irrespective of the TSR performance. This is usually to ensure that the TSR performance is consistent with the company's underlying financial performance.

Probability of meeting EPS targets

The process of setting the EPS target is different from that adopted for TSR since this is an internal measure and looking at general market practice is of less value, although looking at how companies in the same business sector are performing may be helpful. It will be necessary to model past EPS performance over a number of years and to look at growth forecasts to identify appropriate threshold and stretch performance levels.

It is interesting to look at the probability of meeting EPS targets based on previous performance in the same way as with TSR to see if the same pattern occurs. Based on EPS data for FTSE 350 companies for three-year periods over the past five years, we have calculated that, on average, around 60% of companies are likely to meet an RPI + 3% target at least once over a three-year period.

Figure 4.32 looks at those companies which met this target over one three-year period, over two three-year periods and over three three-year periods. The first set of columns looks at each of the last three three-year periods and demonstrates that, in the most recent period, two thirds of companies met the target. In the previous three-year period, 62% of companies met the target, and two periods prior to that only 51% of companies met the target.

The second set of columns looks at companies meeting the target in two consecutive three-year periods. We can see that, in the most recent two periods in a row, 45% of companies met the target; in the previous two

113

Figure 4.32 *Probability of meeting EPS targets*

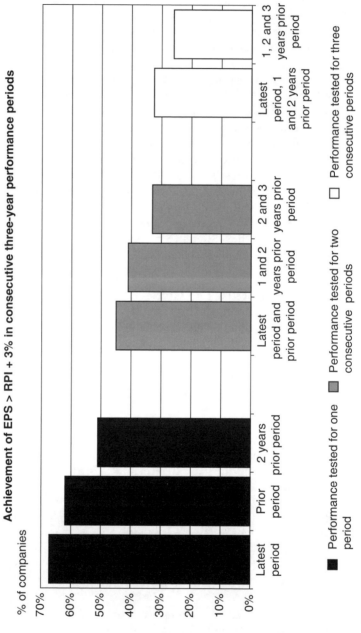

Achievement of EPS > RPI + 3% in consecutive three-year performance periods

% of companies

■ Performance tested for one period

▨ Performance tested for two consecutive periods

▨ Performance tested for three consecutive periods

□ Performance tested for three consecutive periods

Source: Datastream

periods, 41% of companies met the target; and in the two periods prior to that, only 33%. It it clear therefore that the likelihood of meeting the target for two consecutive periods is considerably less than meeting it over one period only.

The third set of columns looks at those companies meeting the target three years in three consecutive three-year periods. The first column looks at the current and previous two periods, when 33% of companies achieved the target, and the second column looks at the previous three periods when only 26% of companies met the target. This suggests that, on average, there is only around a 30% chance of meeting the target for three consecutive periods.

It may also be useful to look at market practice to ensure that intended targets are not out of line.

In share option plans which use EPS as the main performance measure and where the vesting of options is scaled depending on the level of performance, the threshold target is for EPS growth to exceed RPI by 3% per annum in over 60% of plans. In over 40% of plans the threshold target is higher than this, typically RPI + 4% or 5% per annum. At the threshold level it is usual for between a third and half of the award to vest.

In such plans, the target required for full vesting ranges from RPI + 5% per annum to RPI + over 10% per annum, as can be seen in Figure 4.33.

In performance share plans, EPS targets are more stretching as participants are awarded the value of the whole share rather than the potential growth in value of the share. As would be expected, the target EPS growth ranges vary considerably from company to company. If there is such a thing as a 'typical range' it would be for minimum vesting to require EPS growth of at least RPI + 4% per annum and maximum vesting to occur for EPS growth of at least RPI + 10% per annum.

In around 40% of plans the threshold EPS target is growth of at least RPI + 3% with around a quarter requiring threshold performance in excess of RPI + 5% per annum. At the threshold level it is usual for around 25% of the award to vest.

The target required for full vesting ranges from RPI + 4% per annum to over RPI + 15% per annum, as can be seen in Figure 4.34.

Although market data provide context, a robust target setting approach will require a comprehensive review of a number of reference points which reflect a range of internal and external historical performance and future expectations. This will inform and support the remuneration committee but of course will not replace the need for judgment by the committee. Figure 4.35 illustrates how a target setting approach might look.

Figure 4.36 shows an example of how these reference points could look in practice, providing a logical and robust framework for making a decision on the most appropriate targets.

Figure 4.33 *EPS vesting targets in share option plans*

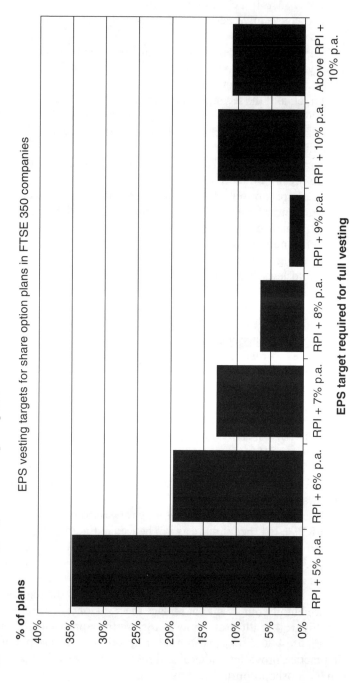

EPS vesting targets for share option plans in FTSE 350 companies

% of plans

40%

35%

30%

25%

20%

15%

10%

5%

0%

RPI + 5% p.a.   RPI + 6% p.a.   RPI + 7% p.a.   RPI + 8% p.a.   RPI + 9% p.a.   RPI + 10% p.a.   Above RPI + 10% p.a.

EPS target required for full vesting

Source: Datastream

Figure 4.34 *EPS vesting targets in performance share plans*

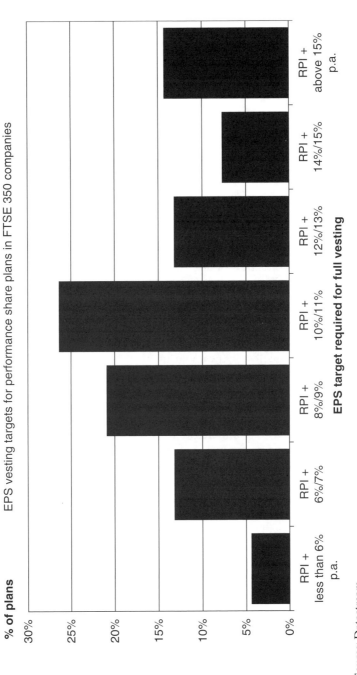

% of plans

EPS vesting targets for performance share plans in FTSE 350 companies

EPS target required for full vesting

Source: Datastream

Figure 4.35 *Example of a target-setting approach*

EPS adjustments for International Accounting Standards
The introduction of International Accounting Standards (IAS) marks a very significant change in the calculation of EPS for most UK listed companies. The changes include:

- 'Marking-to-market' of most financial instruments.
- No systematic amortisation of goodwill. Instead goodwill is tested annually for any impairment.
- P&L charges for share-based payments.
- Capitalisation of certain R&D expenditure.

The introduction of IAS will generally lead to more volatile EPS figures year on year, and therefore the practice of using 'normalised' EPS for the purpose of performance measurement is likely to continue. However, the change to IAS means that most companies will need to consider carefully their current definition of 'normalisation' and what normalisation will mean in practice going forward.

There is no standard definition of normalisation and most investment analysts will have their own 'house' methodology. For the purpose of share incentive performance measurement, many companies have in the past interpreted normalised EPS as being basic EPS excluding exceptional items. Under IAS, the concept of 'exceptional' items does not exist. However, there remains the requirement that some items are disclosed separately by virtue of their size and incidence.

Market practice for defining EPS for the purpose of performance measurement may emerge but until then companies using EPS in incentive plans will need to look carefully at the normalising adjustments that are made and may find that shareholders are taking a close interest.

Figure 4.36 *Example of target-setting approach*

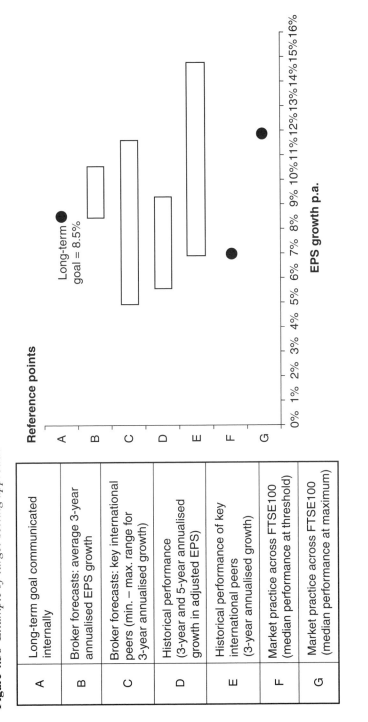

A	Long-term goal communicated internally
B	Broker forecasts: average 3-year annualised EPS growth
C	Broker forecasts: key international peers (min. – max. range for 3-year annualised growth)
D	Historical performance (3-year and 5-year annualised growth in adjusted EPS)
E	Historical performance of key international peers (3-year annualised growth)
F	Market practice across FTSE100 (median performance at threshold)
G	Market practice across FTSE100 (median performance at maximum)

Reference points

A   Long-term
       goal = 8.5%

B

C

D

E

F

G

0% 1% 2% 3% 4% 5% 6% 7% 8% 9% 10%11%12%13%14%15%16%

EPS growth p.a.

Vesting levels

Is there any indication that bigger awards require more stretching performance? We would suggest that there should be a relationship between the performance target and the size of reward and our research suggests that this is indeed the case.

Typically, plans using TSR as a performance measure have required upper quartile performance of the comparator group for awards to vest in full. In recent years this has started to change, with many plans now requiring performance above the upper quartile, typically upper quintile or upper decile, for the award to vest in full.

Figure 4.37 looks at whether there is a link between the size of the award and the level of performance required to achieve this. It is important to remember that there are many other factors influencing the degree of stretch in the performance measures, such as the type and number of companies in the comparator group, along with the current level of performance. This will also impact on the decision on what level of performance should be reasonably required for full vesting.

However, Figure 4.37 does demonstrate that larger awards often require more stretching performance targets to be achieved in order for the full award to vest. This is important to note when comparing market practice between companies, where it may be more appropriate to look at the level of award that would vest for upper quartile performance in order to compare like with like.

Where the size of the award is below median market practice, only a fifth of plans require performance above upper quartile for full vesting to occur. Where the size of the award is between median and upper quartile, around a third of plans require performance above the upper quartile. Where the size of the award is in the top quarter of market practice, almost two thirds of plans require performance above the upper quartile for full vesting.

Figure 4.37 *Relationship between size of award and level of TSR performance required for vesting*

Relative TSR performance required for full vesting	Level of maximum award within the FTSE 350		
	Below the median	Between the median and upper quartile	Above the upper quartile
Above 90th percentile	2%	0%	26%
90th percentile	5%	15%	32%
Between 76th and 89th percentile	15%	20%	5%
75th percentile	78%	65%	37%

Figure 4.38 *Relationship between size of award and level of EPS performance required for vesting*

	Level of maximum award within the FTSE 350	
EPS target	**Below the median**	**Above the median**
Above RPI + 15% p.a.	9%	24%
Between RPI + 12% and RPI + 15% p.a.	15%	11%
Between RPI + 10% and RPI + 12% p.a.	9%	18%
Between RPI + 8% and RPI + 10% p.a.	48%	24%
Between RPI + 6% and RPI + 8% p.a.	15%	18%
Below RPI + 6% p.a.	4%	5%

Figure 4.38 analyses the level of award in relationship to the EPS targets in the same way. There is not such a strong relationship between the size of the award and the level of EPS performance required, as clearly the degree to which the EPS targets reflect stretching performance is more specific to the particular circumstances of the company. However, there is still some indication that plans with award levels above the median of market practice tend to require a higher level of EPS growth for full vesting than those with lower levels of award. Where the size of the award is below median only a third of plans require EPS growth in excess of RPI + 10% per annum. Where the size of the award is above median over half the plans require EPS growth at this level.

Director shareholding requirements

It is now considered good practice to encourage senior executives to build up a significant shareholding in the company. This is strongly supported by shareholders as it provides a clear alignment which is greater than the linkage provided by options which offer the asymmetric risk of future incentives failing to vest. It can be achieved by using bonus deferral plans, or by adding a further retention period once shares have vested in a long-term plan. But many larger quoted companies now have a specified share-holding that executives are expected to maintain. Figure 4.39 illustrates how the number of companies with shareholding requirements in place has increased over the past five years. The shareholding will typically be specified as a percentage of salary and executives will normally be given a period of time over which to build this up, or may be expected to retain a certain percentage of shares vesting in incentive plans until the sharehold-ing is achieved. Further incentive awards may be reduced if the sharehold-ing is not achieved. In FTSE 100 companies, a shareholding of twice salary or more would not be unusual.

Figure 4.39 *Shareholding requirements*

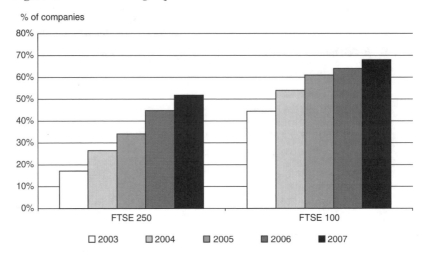

% of companies

Legend: □ 2003   □ 2004   ■ 2005   ■ 2006   ■ 2007

(Categories: FTSE 250, FTSE 100)

Equity dilution

It is particularly important to note, for quoted companies, that there are guidelines laid down by institutional shareholders on the overall number of newly issued shares that may be made available through share plans. These guidelines aim to limit the dilution of shareholdings of ordinary shareholders. The guidelines are not mandatory, but unjustified departures from them are unlikely to be supported by shareholders and there has been a history of shareholders 'enforcing' these guidelines.

The balance of the package

How the individual elements are put together into a package is a critical step. Few companies have the luxury of setting a pay policy from scratch, and in most companies elements of the policy will be reviewed separately. Many companies may not be aware of the balance between fixed and variable pay, and just as importantly, the balance of short- and long-term awards. Certainly, as we have previously discussed, the pension will often have been excluded from any analysis of the total package, which would cause the 'fixed' element to be understated.

For quoted companies, the introduction of the Directors' Remuneration Report Regulations has created a focus on this balance, as there is now a requirement for companies to explain the relative importance of those elements of the package which are, and are not, related to performance.

There is no perfect balance of fixed and variable. This must be looked at in the context of the individual company and in some businesses it will be more appropriate for a larger proportion of the package to be

Figure 4.40 *Equity dilution*

Institutional guidelines set out dilution limits for employee share plans for quoted companies.

Share plans are normally subject to an overriding limit restricting the number of newly issued shares that can be placed under option, or otherwise issued, to 10% of the company's share capital in any ten-year period. In calculating this amount, awards or options which may be satisfied using new issue shares granted under other share plans must be taken into account.

The guidelines normally also limit further the number of newly issued shares that a company can issue under a discretionary, or executive, plan to 5% in any ten-year period. This may be increased to 10% where very demanding performance criteria are set. The overriding limit for all share plans would still apply. The limits apply to newly issued shares only, not plans that operate over shares purchased in the market.

The limits are calculated on a rolling basis, and whenever a new award is made companies have to calculate how many shares have been placed under awards granted in the preceding ten years which have either been satisfied or may be satisfied by the issue of shares. Lapses due to participants leaving or the failure of performance conditions are taken out of account as are awards that have expired unexercised. The calculation of the limit itself must also be checked – it is increased by any issue of shares whether by rights or bonus issue or a share placing for cash, although in the case of the first two these would normally also have some (if not an identical) impact on the number of shares under outstanding awards. Cancellation of shares reduces the limit.

In order to minimise the number of shares required to satisfy options granted under a share option plan companies are increasingly introducing provisions to enable the company to deliver fewer shares on the exercise of the option.

This is achieved by removing the necessity for the participant to pay the option exercise price in order to acquire shares. The value of shares that is delivered is equal to the gross gain the participant would have made on sale of all the shares following exercise of the option (effectively a cashless exercise without the need to involve a third party such as a stockbroker).

Such a change does not impact on the tax position of the participant or the company. Similarly the accounting treatment for the company is not affected. Therefore these arrangements (commonly referred to as equity settled stock appreciation rights) are very attractive for many companies.

Figure 4.40 *continued*

Treasury shares

Since 1 December 2003 UK companies have been able to buy shares and hold them in their own name as treasury shares without the need to cancel those shares. Many companies who have held shareholder meetings since that date have sought authority to buy and hold shares in this manner, often with the intention of using this power to acquire shares to satisfy share-based incentives, as an alternative to acquiring and holding shares in an employee benefit trust (EBT).

However, from a headroom perspective, whilst these shares have been purchased from the open market in a similar manner to shares held in an EBT, Institutional Shareholders recommend that they are treated as though they were cancelled and then re-issued at a later stage. This means that, whilst held in treasury, they will reduce the available headroom for a company (the 10% and 5% limits will be calculated using a lower number of 'shares in issue') and shares supplied to satisfy the awards will count against the headroom limit.

performance-related. The remuneration package needs to meet a spectrum of employees' needs and aspirations. Parts of the package provide different things: security, sense of participation, incentive to stay, reward, motivation. The mix of the package will therefore be different for different companies, for different groups of staff within a company and at different stages of a company's development.

Where remuneration is linked to performance, then consideration should be given to whether this is appropriately weighted towards short-term targets or long-term performance. This is particularly important given that many companies have been moving away from share options towards other types of plan, potential awards under annual bonus plans have been increasing, and there has been a significant increase in the number of deferred bonus matching plans. If the weighting between short- and long-term performance changes, shareholders will expect to see the rationale behind this decision.

Figures 4.41 to 4.44 on the following pages show the composition of the package for executive directors of FTSE 350 companies in two different performance scenarios. The first is based on the achievement of on-target performance and the second based on the maximum awards that would be earned if the 'stretch' targets were fully met. We have looked at companies by size (as measured by market capitalisation) and by business sector.

There is a clear difference by company size, with a greater proportion of the package at risk in the larger companies for both on-target and

Figure 4.41 *Composition of package for on-target performance by market capitalisation*

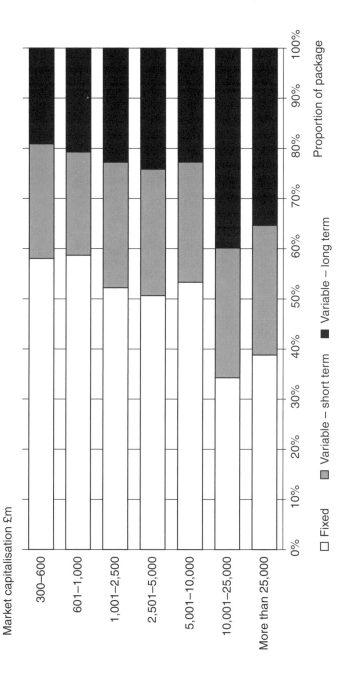

Market capitalisation £m

☐ Fixed ▨ Variable – short term ■ Variable – long term

Figure 4.42 *Composition of package for stretch performance by market capitalisation*

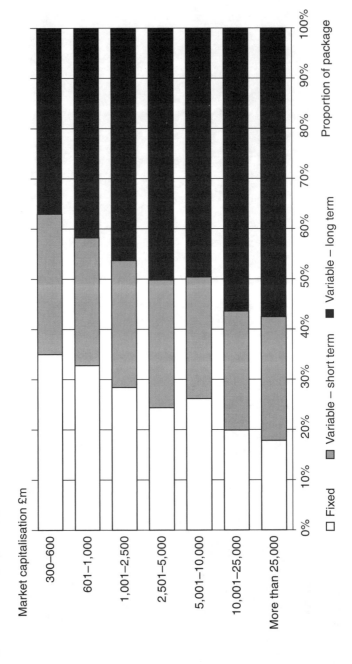

Figure 4.43 *Composition of package for on-target performance by business sector*

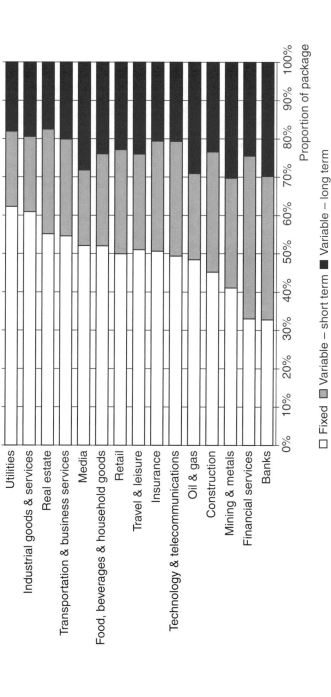

□ Fixed ▨ Variable – short term ■ Variable – long term

Figure 4.44 *Composition of package for stretch performance by business sector*

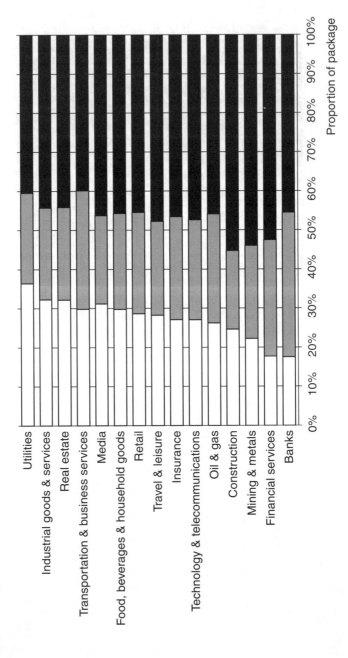

Proportion of package

☐ Fixed ☐ Variable – short term ■ Variable – long term

maximum performance. There is also some indication that the package is weighted towards the longer term in larger companies but there is not a high correlation with company size.

As we have already suggested, the weighting between fixed and variable and between short- and long-term performance is more likely to be influenced by industry. The banks and financial services sector have the highest proportion of the package at risk – just under two thirds of the package is at risk for on-target and around 80% of the package where the maximum awards are earned. In contrast, utilities, transportation and business services, industrial goods and services and real estate companies have the lowest proportion of the package at risk, around a third at risk for on-target and around two thirds where the maximum awards are earned.

There is a great variation in the balance of short and long term by industry sector.

Pulling it all together

For a number of years, compensation specialists have talked about taking a 'total remuneration' approach. Our experience suggests that, while there has undoubtedly been an increase in the number of companies where all aspects of the remuneration package are benchmarked on a regular basis, there is not yet much evidence of a 'total remuneration approach' to benchmarking. In its purest form, this would mean using a benchmarking exercise to identify an appropriate market level of total remuneration for a given individual, identify an appropriate balance between the fixed and variable elements, and then identify an appropriate balance between short- and long-term elements. It would then be possible to work backwards to identify the value of each individual element. An individual may be given some flexibility in how the fixed element is paid by allowing them to choose whether to take this all in salary, or to combine elements of salary, pension and other benefits.

Some companies have adopted a flexible benefits approach. This typically identifies a 'benefits' pot of money for each individual and allows individuals to choose from a menu of benefit options up to the annual value allowed. However, this rarely includes pensions and is not usually linked to the salary of the individual, other than in the sense of a generic 'grade' to which salaries and the level of benefit allowance may be linked. Therefore, different grades of employee may have different benefits allowances but this allowance will not change depending on whether the salary of the individual is above or below market practice for the role. And few companies allow individuals to choose how the fixed remuneration is paid.

Benchmarking total remuneration requires valuing not only the benefits, but also the incentive and share awards. Chapter 3 explores the different methods that can be applied to value these awards and it is clear that it is difficult, if not almost impossible, to calculate a precisely accurate value which is comparable across different companies with different types of plan in place. This makes benchmarking total remuneration very complex unless practical compromises are made. Pragmatism is the only viable approach.

For most companies, different elements of the package will have evolved at different times and there will rarely be an opportunity to develop a complete remuneration policy from scratch. It therefore makes sense to adopt a pragmatic and reasonable approach to benchmarking total remuneration, which could usefully be based around the following framework.

- Undertake a regular, robust salary benchmarking exercise. Salary is the driver of many other elements of the package and therefore should be positioned carefully. Ensure the comparator companies are appropriate and where possible use two or three different sources of data in order to arrive at a fair and reasonable 'competitive range'.
- Ensure other benefits and pension provision are broadly in line with comparator companies. For most benefits it should be sufficient to look at how prevalent the provision of a particular benefit is and make a judgment as to whether your level of provision is above or below market practice. Where the pension provision is of a defined contribution nature, there is a reasonable amount of good data available and it will be relatively easy to benchmark the company contribution quite accurately. Where the pension provision is of a defined benefit nature there are ways, outlined in Chapter 3, of assessing the annual value of the benefit, albeit this may be a more expensive and time-consuming exercise. However, it will not always be necessary to take an in-depth approach. It may be sufficient to make an assessment of whether the pension provision is significantly above or below the market, and, where this is the case, it may suggest that salaries should be positioned below or above the desired market position.
- Benchmark the annual bonus potential against comparator companies. It is difficult to benchmark the level of stretch in the performance targets of plans in other companies. However, it is possible to use the market data to inform a judgment about the level of award and the probability of achieving the targets. Ensure that market data are comparable in respect of how deferred bonus arrangements have been treated.
- Benchmark the long-term award potential in a similar way.
- Look at the 'shape' of the package in terms of the balance of fixed and variable, and, within the variable element, the balance of short and long term, and ensure that this is appropriate for the industry and culture of the company.
- Ensure that the variable elements are:
    - based on measures which support the business strategy and which reward the right behaviours;

- based on targets that are set appropriately with the right degree of stretch;
  - that the form of the award is the most effective, both in terms of tax and accounting treatment and in terms of the perceived value by the participant.
- Finally undertake a valuation of total remuneration. It may not be necessary to do this every year; once every two or three years may be sufficient. For this purpose the projected value method may provide the most effective way of looking at the values. The purpose of this is to confirm that the total remuneration is at an appropriate level against other comparator companies, both at target performance and assuming the incentive plans payout at maximum. It may, of course, highlight any issues that could have been overlooked and identify any major gaps in the package, or where remuneration is above typical market levels.

The next chapter looks at how the design of the remuneration package fits into the wider context of the business.

5

Supporting the business strategy

CAROL ARROWSMITH

This chapter explores in more detail the wider corporate context in which any individual reward package must be designed. The remuneration structure will always be a function of the individual circumstances of a particular company and will depend on the origins and history of the business, the ownership characteristics, sector and many other elements. However, there are some useful principles that may guide the choices and direction of pay for particular circumstances. These are summarised in Figure 5.1.

The rest of this chapter looks at each of these situations in more detail.

Start up and initial public offering (IPO)

A start-up company is likely to be a combination of new money and new management. The company is born out of an idea of the founder, or founders, who then have to find investors willing to fund the development of the idea into a business proposition. Biotech companies, for example, were founded predominantly by entrepreneurial scientists who had to raise funds to commercialise research. The main characteristics of a start-up company are:

- entrepreneurial;
- the founders are critical to the success of the company;
- cash resources are needed for investment in the business proposition;
- there is a finite supply of capital;
- there is commonly a finite period before sale or flotation is planned.

The source of executive talent may be academia, other start-ups, or from mature businesses. The company is likely to be run, initially, by the founders. There is unlikely to be a hierarchical organisational structure, roles are likely to be fluid and pay will be negotiated on an individual basis, with limited remuneration policy or structure to speak of.

Start-ups offer the founders the opportunity to make millions but equally to risk losing everything. Typical start-up companies are highly geared, which leverages the equity return because any volatility in performance (for example profit after financing costs) is typically attributed to a small number of shareholders. Good performance therefore creates more value for equity shareholders. This is illustrated in Figure 5.2 which shows

Figure 5.1 *Matching reward elements to circumstances: illustrations*

	Start up	IPO	Growth	Mature	Realignment	Turnaround
Salary	Lower Supply driven	Low to median Market driven	Median to high Market driven with significant premium for key roles and experience	Median Internal relativity framework with market input	Median to high Market driven Significant premium for key roles and experience	High Market driven with significant premium for key roles and experience
Benefits	Few or none	Basic benefits – defined contribution pension, medical insurance and car	More established benefits often flexible	Full range of established benefits, often defined benefit pension	Full range, some flexibility	Full range of established benefits, often defined benefit pension, some flexibility
Incentives	Limited annual bonus High potential LTIP value – typically large option grants, no performance conditions	Median annual bonus High potential LTIP value vesting on float High potential value ongoing LTIP with performance conditions	High potential annual bonus with deferral to aid retention High potential value LTIP with stretching performance targets	Median bonus All-employee share ownership plans Median LTIP for senior executives only	Median annual bonus Initial high value LTIP	High value medium-term incentive plan replaces existing incentive plans
Corporate values	Innovative Entrepreneurial High growth	Innovative Entrepreneurial High growth	Innovative Customer/service orientated High growth	Efficiency Customer/service orientated Steady growth	Entrepreneurial High growth	Focus on core business Customer/service orientated High growth
Culture	Flexible Informal Dynamic	Flexible Informal Dynamic	Flexible Dynamic	Fairness Respect Loyalty	Team based Dynamic	Team based Respect Loyalty

Figure 5.2 *How gearing impacts returns*

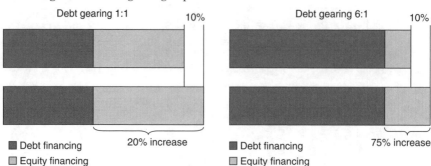

the impact of a 10% increase in enterprise value on equity shareholder returns under two different debt gearing scenarios.

Founder directors typically draw modest salaries and have very little in the way of other benefits, or pension provision. Given the size of their shareholdings and the potential wealth creation this provides, they will often not receive any other incentive awards or participate in any incentive share plans. Their interest will be in the form of a direct shareholding.

It may become necessary to recruit an executive into a start-up company (for example, it is quite common for a start-up company to have no finance director initially, but as the company moves towards flotation it will become necessary to recruit someone into this role). At this point, having some knowledge of market rates will be helpful; it may not be possible to pay salaries much higher than the lower end of the market-competitive range but in order to attract someone of the right calibre it may not be appropriate to offer a salary much below this. It is not common to offer any additional fixed remuneration or significant cash bonus at this stage.

The key element of the package for a senior executive recruited into a start-up company is usually share options. Traditionally share options were 'free' for the company but now the fair value of share options and share awards must be charged to the profit and loss account. However, minority interests in a private company are usually low in value due to the lack of liquidity and the limited influence over dividend payments. This may offer the opportunity to provide significant value even using the relatively modest tax-favoured option opportunity of EMI or COSOP (see Chapter 4). Where options are granted over shares in a private company, the exercise price will also be low, based on the private company share valuation. If the company subsequently floats, assuming the options were granted sufficiently in advance of the flotation, gains can be significant, given that the exercise price is likely to be much lower than the value of shares when listed.

Because of the low initial value, it is difficult to assess the monetary value of share option grants made to senior executives in private companies and therefore it is not realistic to compare this with executives in quoted companies. In order to determine the appropriate grant size, it is more helpful to consider the proportion of the business the company is willing to share and the potential values that may be realised at exit. Our research into the level of share options held by main board directors in companies coming to the market suggests that, typically, an individual executive director is likely to have been granted between 0.5% and 2% of share capital in options.

Private companies

In private companies that intend to remain private, the remuneration structure is likely to be different. These companies may be family owned or controlled and in these situations the senior executives will often have no ownership interest as this can create complexity and tension with family owners. The challenge for family-owned businesses is passing on the ownership across generations. Some family-controlled businesses retain the family stake over generations but many find the next generation less interested in retaining a concentrated investment and so there is pressure to sell. Where the executives are not interested in becoming owners, this may result in a decision to sell to a third party on the open market, but a number of well-established companies operate a blend of family ownership and employee ownership and utilise a trust to 'warehouse' the shares to maintain a dynamic internal market. In these cases executives can be rewarded through share plans providing them with the opportunity to build value slowly over time. The incentives are limited by the level of demand in the internal market and the funding appetite of the sponsoring company. It is possible, however, to create a successful combination of family and employee ownership.

Levels of cash remuneration in family-owned businesses will typically be on the low side relative to comparable roles in the public market, but there are often other factors which may be attractive, such as the general working environment and the culture and, for this reason, staff turnover can often be seen to be quite low.

Other long-term private company ownership structures include a consortium of professional owners who supply the investment capital over the medium/long term, or businesses with a common interest, for example joint venture partners.

In these cases, share ownership is rarely offered to the executives unless there is an exit planned. Otherwise, the executives could inadvertently be provided with a small stake which holds the balance of power between the joint venture partners.

Unsurprisingly, privately held companies most commonly choose to reward senior executives in cash. Below is an illustration of how a long-term cash incentive plan might work in a private company.

135

IPO

At IPO the company will be entering the quoted company environment and it is important to ensure that decisions relating to remuneration taken prior to the IPO will support the business going forward. The future remuneration structure may not always be sufficiently focused on by sponsors but will convey important messages to possible investors.

There is a risk that decisions are made which subsequently need to be unwound when it is recognised that they do not support the business strategy in a quoted environment. Factors which could lead to such decisions include:

- Lack of management experience of the dynamics of remuneration in a more mature company. Expectations may be driven by the heavy management equity base frequently found in private companies with

---

Figure 5.3 Example of pool-based long-term cash incentive plan

As mentioned above, in private companies there may be little appetite for shareholders to provide equity-based incentives. Therefore, the objective of this plan is for shareholders to provide the participant with a 'quasi-equity' stake in the future value of the business. This will allow the participant to build up wealth, but only if sustainable long-term shareholder value is created.

This plan would typically be based on the achievement of a certain level of financial (e.g. profit) performance. Performance above the minimum level then provides funds for a cash pool for payments under the plan. This is to ensure that the plan is in essence 'self-financing' – i.e. it will only result in payouts if there are available profits.

However, the performance must be sustainable in the long term and a simple profit pool may create damaging short-termism. For example, if a large amount of profit is produced and 'loaded' into one particular year, to the detriment of next year's profits, executives could benefit at the expense of the company. Accordingly, the pool should be built up and spread over a number of years and so a dip in performance could consequently reduce the size of the incentive pool for distribution in the next year.

The diagram below illustrates an example of this structure. It is assumed that one third of the cumulative pool is delivered to participants each year, with the remaining two thirds being carried forward to form part of the pool for the following year. One third of the 'final' pool under the plan is paid out immediately, with the remaining two thirds being paid out in a year's time.

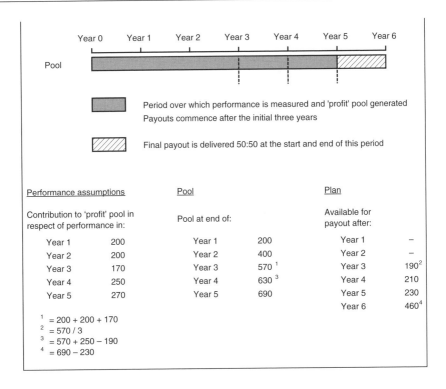

Year 0   Year 1   Year 2   Year 3   Year 4   Year 5   Year 6

Pool

Period over which performance is measured and 'profit' pool generated
Payouts commence after the initial three years

Final payout is delivered 50:50 at the start and end of this period

Performance assumptions		Pool		Plan	
Contribution to 'profit' pool in respect of performance in:		Pool at end of:		Available for payout after:	
Year 1	200	Year 1	200	Year 1	–
Year 2	200	Year 2	400	Year 2	–
Year 3	170	Year 3	570 [1]	Year 3	190 [2]
Year 4	250	Year 4	630 [3]	Year 4	210
Year 5	270	Year 5	690	Year 5	230
				Year 6	460 [4]

[1] = 200 + 200 + 170
[2] = 570 / 3
[3] = 570 + 250 – 190
[4] = 690 – 230

specific business targets often based on an exit strategy such as a flotation. Quoted companies do not typically deliver the same growth in value as can be delivered through the transition from private to publicly quoted company.

- Some executives will be able to realise significant sums as a result of the vesting of their pre-float incentives, which may distort the expectations of their packages post-listing. The gains may also give rise to retention issues.
- The non-executive directors populating the remuneration committee will often be recruited shortly before the listing occurs and will therefore not have had time to develop a full understanding of the company, its management structure and specific features of the company's operation relevant to the development of a coherent remuneration policy.
- The development of the remuneration policy is often left until late in the flotation process when the attention of the company is on achieving flotation so that insufficient regard is given to remuneration.

The flotation should give the company an opportunity for further growth and development and the scope to recruit more top talent. The development of a suitable reward structure will be an essential tool in cementing both the existing team and newly recruited talent. However, the packages, particularly the performance-driven elements, will not only be influenced by the expectations and reaction of the participants but now also be scrutinised by outside investors.

Given these factors, it is essential for companies and their advisors to have a full understanding of the dynamics of different forms of remuneration, the common practice of new listed companies and the reasons for choosing the forms of plan and their commercial features.

The remuneration packages of senior executives in newly floated companies are typically structured in the following way:

- Salaries are set at broadly comparable levels to those in other similar-sized quoted companies, although the salary for the CEO may be lower where he or she is one of the founder members of the company.
- The maximum potential annual bonus is typically 50% of salary which again is comparable with the general market of similar-sized companies. Performance measures are chosen by reference to the strategic goals of the company and the commitments made to new investing shareholders.
- Most senior executives are eligible to participate in a long-term plan. Traditionally this has been a share option plan which provides for the grant of market value options. Limited grants are typically made to those individuals who are critical to the future of the newly floated business but who were not founder shareholders. More recently, companies are equally likely to award a variable number of whole shares subject to future corporate performance to that focused pool of individuals.
- Most senior executives are eligible for some form of pension provision. This is often a pension allowance or participation in a defined contribution plan. It is very unlikely that a defined benefit plan will be provided. The typical level of employer contribution is 10% to 15% of salary, which again is broadly comparable to the market.
- There are few other benefits typically provided, other than medical insurance which is quite common. It is not uncommon for an executive to receive a car allowance, although it is relatively uncommon to be provided with a company car.
- Although almost all companies have implemented some form of share plan at the time of flotation, the number of companies doing so prior to the flotation is quite variable. Figure 5.4 illustrates the types of plan that a company may want to consider in the run-up to flotation and what these plans can be expected to achieve.

Rapid growth

In a period of rapid growth a company will usually be recruiting a large number of employees and may also be looking to grow by acquisition,

Figure 5.4 *Long-term incentive arrangements to meet different commercial objectives*

Objective	Possible long-term incentive arrangements

Retention and motivation of key executives pre-flotation	• Approved Enterprise Management Incentive plan (EMI) adopted pre-flotation to take advantage of tax treatment
	• Approved and unapproved executive share option plan adopted pre-flotation
	  – exercise conditional on flotation
	  – options lapse if the employee leaves prior to flotation
	• Long-term incentive plans such as restricted share plans (RSPs) and performance share plans (PSPs) where vesting of awards is conditional on float
	• Flotation bonus

Recruitment of new key executives in the run-up to flotation	• Share options, long-term incentive awards granted on joining the company some time prior to float so that key executives will be attracted by the package due to the prospect of future growth in value of shares. Options and awards only become exercisable / vest if the float takes place
Retention and motivation of executives post-float	• Further executive options with exercise price based on offer price • Use of a long-term incentive plan adopted at float for delivery of free shares • Performance targets for options and share awards to assist in aligning the interests of the executive with those of the business • Vesting period of three to five years for options or awards
Ensuring all employees are motivated towards the flotation and are rewarded for a successful float	• Approved savings-related share option plan (SAYE) – adopted at flotation • Share incentive plan (SIP) – adopted at flotation • Employee share offer on flotation allowing all employees the opportunity to acquire shares in the business at the offer price, or at a discount • Approved executive share option plan operated on an all-employee basis adopted pre- or at flotation

which will create issues around integrating remuneration structures. At this stage in the life cycle, the company will be starting to implement more formal remuneration structures and internal relativities will be starting to become a consideration, although it is likely that salaries will be predominantly market driven with premiums for key roles and experience.

As the remuneration strategy is being developed, it is worth remembering that while the company is planning on significant growth the remuneration package may need to be flexible to allow for recruitment, to deal with retention issues and to help with the integration of acquired companies.

In order to facilitate rapid recruitment of key talent, salaries may be above median, with incentives focused on the longer term rather than short-term bonuses. As well as being based on corporate financial measures, a significant proportion of the annual bonus is likely to be linked to specific objectives which may be on an individual basis. Long-term incentive awards are likely to be high and it may be appropriate to include an element of outperformance of a comparator group of companies or an index to reflect the growth aims.

The key challenge may be balancing the need to provide sufficient security to newly hired talent with the responsibility to ensure that high rewards are only earned if the ambitious growth is delivered.

Some companies manage to achieve the Holy Grail of delivering rapid growth over many years (e.g. Microsoft) and are able to recruit and retain talent through the use of simple share options which could build substantial wealth over time. However, few companies manage this level of sustained excellence and often the rapid growth is designed to build (or rebuild) fortunes over a relatively confined period. This can lend itself to 'one-off' arrangements with stretching goals.

Figure 5.5 *PartyGaming*

PartyGaming, established in 1997, became the world's largest on-line gaming company. It set itself the aim of being 'the world's number one gaming company, with the most trusted brands, innovative technology and outstanding customer service'.

The key strategies were set as:

- Grow the poker business by developing the brand credentials, particularly outside North America
- Expand internationally, targeting territories where there has been recent growth in broadband internet penetration and acceptance of e-commerce retail. Multi-lingual and multi-currency versions of games are being developed to broaden appeal
- Develop excellent customer service which is considered a key competitive advantage and critical for attracting new customers and retaining existing customers. Committ to broadening the range of payment options
- Keep at the forefront of technology
- Offer a diverse and comprehensive portfolio of games
- Look to acquire or invest in complementary businesses and new games
- Explore use of technology channels

The remuneration policy was designed to support a 'fast-moving competitive environment' and is intended to appeal to 'entrepreneurial and innovative executives'.

Mature and growing companies

The majority of FTSE 100 and FTSE 250 companies can be classified as mature and growing companies. Investors demand continuously improving financial returns from these companies and these returns can be generated by operational efficiency savings or by growing the business through organic growth or acquisition.

For larger companies, the common issues around motivating executive directors to grow the business and rewarding the growth are driven not only by the underlying financial performance but also by the level of scrutiny by shareholders.

Shareholders have encouraged companies to shift from share options which provided exposure to share price performance over a ten-year period to performance share plans which deliver shares based on performance over three-year periods. The regular cycles of awards made each year and tested once only at the end of the performance period fit well with a world focusing on continuous improvement. Until recently, these plans followed the preferences of the majority of shareholders and so performance was assessed by measuring the relative returns delivered to shareholders over each three-year period. This cyclical structure is consistent with the continued pressure to improve the business on behalf of shareholders.

Many companies now use additional measures. The choice will depend on how the company seeks to improve its fortunes, including: improving operational efficiency through cost saving, improving the use of assets, reducing capital costs, or expanding through increasing revenues, profits or margins.

Cost saving

For many companies the opportunity to grow their business substantially is contingent on generating sufficient cash to fund the expansion. Remuneration structures can be used to support the drive for cost savings and cash generation. In particular, it is often the case that the annual bonus targets will be set around operational efficiency measures such as margin improvement, identified cost savings and cash flow. More sophisticated

---

Figure 5.6 *Pilkington*

Pilkington identified that it needed to generate cash in order to fund further international expansion and so introduced a long-term incentive plan which explicitly targeted the generation of cash over successive three-year periods. The plan operated successfully for several cycles and provided Pilkington with the cash to fund business development, reduce pension fund deficits and reduce overall gearing.

---

operational drivers can include economic profit targets for generating improved economic profit. This can be set for each individual business unit to reward subsidiary company executives for the parsimonious use of corporate capital and also improving profits.

Although operational efficiency is a never-ending goal, most companies give it primary focus when times are difficult, using incentives to drive behaviours during specific periods of change and then making a switch to improve returns through expansion.

Organic growth

Organic growth opportunities commonly arise where a business has a successful model and expands that model into new markets or new applications. For example, a retail chain may open further stores in different parts of the country, may venture into international markets or reach its customers using different channels, whereas a manufacturing business may seek to market its products to other customers and look for new and fresh applications of their product.

It is important to identify clearly the key measures of success. The criteria used to measure successful growth and the setting of appropriate targets can be quite business-specific. For example, a manufacturing company looking to expand may focus on return on capital. The capital invested in the factory will remain broadly the same as the throughput increases. There will be a small increase in working capital as more raw material may be needed to produce the greater output, and more stock may need to be held to supply customer orders, but overall this should lead directly to an increased return on capital.

On the other hand, an expanding retailer using return on capital as a measure of success may discourage the expansion of the business through the opening of new stores unless newly invested capital is excluded or different targets are set for the mature and developing areas of the business. This is because new stores will typically consume sizeable amounts of capital for a period of time before generating a return. In these circumstances, some companies elect to measure growth using simple direct financial measures such as sales or earnings before interest, taxes, depreciation and amortisation (EBITDA). Single simple measures provide a clear line of sight and are valuable particularly when there are many participants in the incentive plan. However, simple measures are more readily abused. For example, EBITDA in the current year can be increased by deferring the advertising spend which could lead to depressed sales in successive periods, and sales can be generated by cutting prices to levels that are uneconomic. Accordingly, some companies try to balance the incentive framework by blending measures into a more sophisticated matrix, for example earnings per share and return on capital employed (ROCE), profit and sales margin and cash flow.

142

Shareholders will commonly seek some assurance that financial performance will genuinely lead to improved returns for them. Accordingly, many of the longer-term incentives (which account for a large proportion of the executive package) will be linked to share price performance. This was an important factor in the use of share options historically, where the assumption was that the growth would be reflected by a rise in share price. However, shareholders have more recently discouraged companies from using share options, concerned that the share price may also rise as a result of general market buoyancy.

Growth by acquisition

Many large companies have built their existing businesses through a combination of organic growth and acquisition. Until comparatively recently, most FTSE 100 companies saw their future as an independent company and as predator rather than prey. However, in recent years, the appetite for acquisition of major UK companies has grown by leaps and bounds. It was almost unthinkable for a FTSE 100 company to be subject to a takeover bid and acquired by private equity or foreign owners. However, 2006 saw the acquisition of P&O, BAA and O2 and it is no longer unusual for UK plcs to be taken into foreign ownership. No company in the FTSE 100 can afford to be complacent in the face of the potential risk of a bidder being prepared to put more money on the table than the current market capital of the company.

However, on the assumption that the business strategy is to grow by acquisition, it is important to recognise the impact this will have on rewards.

- The performance measures that are in place for the annual and the long-term incentives for the current management will need to be robust and capable of accommodating an acquisition.
- It is important to establish clarity on how the acquisition will impact rewards; the structure of an acquisition will have a material impact on how awards are treated and companies generally need to be vigilant and aware of the law of unforeseen consequences. Business combinations are typically structured to minimise the tax payable on acquisition of the business. In particular, although Company A may in truth be acquiring Company B and the management of Company A will continue to run the newly enlarged enterprise, it may be that for technical reasons (including tax consequences or regulatory issues) the deal is structured so that a new holding company, Company C, is established, which acquires both Company A and Company B. Alternatively, Company B may be used as the holding company for Company A. Indeed, some business combinations can produce complex corporate trails, as can be seen in Figure 5.7

Figure 5.7

Granada plc and Compass plc embarked on a complex corporate recombination which involved the merger of Granada and Compass to form Granada Compass plc. This company then owned the catering business of Compass, the hotel and catering businesses of Granada and the media business of Granada. The media business of Granada was then spun out independently to form Granada Media plc later, which acquired Carlton plc to form ITV, leaving behind the combination of hotel and catering businesses. The hotel businesses were then sold on to other owners leaving the combined and newly named Compass owning its original catering businesses and those of the Granada empire.

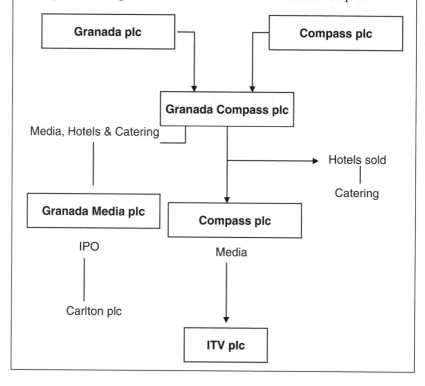

Complex transactions such as these bring with them a number of challenges: firstly, and in many ways most simply, the structure of each stage of the deal will determine which share plans are eligible for vesting. For example, if Companies A and B merge by scheme of arrangement so that they are both effectively acquired by Company C then both A and B employees will typically receive shares prorated for performance to the point of transactions; and Company C will then need to establish plans for all employees in line with the new strategy. However, if the merger is achieved by A acquiring B or vice versa, one set of employees will see some/all of their share awards eligible for vesting and the employees of the acquiring company will typically not have had any awards vest. Indeed, in the absence of an adjustment to the performance outline, it is entirely probable that the share award will be *less* likely to become exercisable because the integrative costs arising as a result of the acquisition may reduce financial performance in the immediate future and the TSR may become less volatile. Accordingly, the performance conditions attached to the outstanding awards will need to be adjusted.

There are a number of things that can be done in preparation to make the integration of two remuneration structures easier. These include:

- Reviewing the change of control clauses in share plans to check what happens in the event of a transaction, identify the flexibility and potential for use of discretion and determine how the performance conditions are to be measured.
- In some rare cases it is possible to force 'rollover', i.e. the exchange of share awards in the old companies, for share awards in the new company which vest over the original timescale. More commonly, the remuneration committee can decide the extent to which the existing performance conditions have been satisfied and whether to apply strict prorating of the award for the proportions of the performance period completed to the date when contract passes.
- Check if there are any special provisions in service contracts that will need to be considered.

  Many executives in countries like the USA have service contracts that provide for individual rights to share awards and may also provide for the individual to trigger a change of contract clause which may include 'golden parachute' terms, i.e. highly favourable termination payments. These contract terms are much rarer in the UK but individual executives who have been hired into companies in challenging circumstances may have individual rights and the recent proliferation of 'one-off' plans may also have led to unconventional terms triggered by a change of contract.
- Identify any potential retention issues, recognising that there will be some insecurity about jobs and concern about the difference in cultures.
- Individual deals may be necessary and the head hunters recognise this is fertile territory.

Impact of acquisitions

Shareholders will be concerned that new acquisitions should support the business development that leads to long-term shareholder value; that

145

acquisitions should be value-accretive (there is some evidence that many large acquisitions may be value-destructive) and that executives should not make windfall gains simply from completing a transaction.

A company that expects to grow by acquisition therefore needs to review performance measures:

- Are the selected measures likely to encourage acquisitions?
- Are there inherent risks in the measures, such that they need to be changed or safeguards need to be applied?

  (For example, incentives based on EPS may encourage acquisition of businesses which add to short-term profitability, where it may be more advisable to acquire a business which has longer-term profit opportunity but is dilutive in the short term. Incentives based on financial measures (EPS, ROCE, ROE, economic profit, etc.) need to have the flexibility to adjust for acquisitions to ensure that remuneration aligns with business strategy over and beyond the acquisition timescale.

Setting the targets

Increasingly, companies are seeking to drive superior performance by using more carefully targeted incentives, and in a large and diverse business this may involve setting very different targets for each significant business unit. For example, a growing financial services business will commonly be made up of a number of distinct and separate businesses. Although they all work together under a common brand and they may share customers, IT systems, risk management processes and other common features, they will also operate in substantially different market places in terms of their talent. The need to recruit and retain high-calibre individuals will necessitate radically different pay structures and performance measures.

For example, within the retail banking business, a modest margin needs to be generated from the efficient processing of the massive numbers of transactions on behalf of millions of customers and so success may be measured using efficiency measures. On the other hand the private wealth management business needs access to a multitude of investment skills, portfolio management, estate and inheritance planning and many other individuals with technical skills, and will need to create profitable business within the context of high levels of compliance with the relevant regulatory regimes.

Alternatively, for companies seeking to grow in the private equity part of business, the ability to attract sums into private equity deals requires highly knowledgeable and talented individuals who can maximise the returns on investments, which may take the form of equity together with mezzanine debt or senior debt, in selected business investment opportunities. The timescales for measuring success may need to be longer and there will be greater emphasis on the use of invested funds. The individuals who raise and invest funds are allocated a 'carried interest' in the fund, which gives them the right to participate in the profits made by it when the investments are realised. It is not unusual for carried interest to generate no value for a number of years, but it may then deliver large amounts five to ten years from when the funds were raised.

When a private equity fund acquires a company, the executives within the portfolio company are incentivised to deliver value in the interests of shareholders (the fund managers) and so, typically, they will purchase some of the equity in a highly geared structure. The equity will grow rapidly if the business succeeds and particularly as debt is reduced. The management can sell their shares when investors sell and so there is strong alignment of interest. The structure has proved highly attractive over recent years as there have been copious quantities of cheap debt and a ready secondary market able and willing to acquire businesses. During 2007, the uncertainty in the debt market reduced the more highly leveraged structures. Indeed, some of the private equity funds are also targeting businesses they intend to hold well beyond the traditional three to seven years of a 'classic' private equity deal, and are now turning their attention to incentive structures consistent with their longer-term investment goals.

The basis for motivating each of these pools of talent is very different.

Companies that seek to grow through acquisition need to examine their remuneration framework to ascertain whether:

- there is appropriate flexibility in the calculation of performance to encourage acquisition but not to trigger inappropriate expansion (for example a bonus which rewards EPS performance may encourage management to purchase incremental profits for a price which damages longer-term shareholder value, simply because it offers an annual increase in earnings);
- the incentives can be modified to ensure that the structure of the deal can be optimised for the benefit of shareholders without unduly rewarding (or penalising) executives (for example an EPS performance condition may encourage an increase in debt to fund an acquisition rather than an issue of new shares).

Many companies prefer to avoid the complexity of multiple target setting for individual businesses, but, as the value of incentives rises and the complexity of businesses continues to increase, we anticipate that more companies will seek to drive performance more effectively through the use of more tailored and focused incentives.

To the extent to which mature companies use efficiency measures alongside the share-based measures, it is important to ensure that the company has a clear perspective on how those measures will operate and how they will deal with changing circumstances and changing accounting policies and regulation.

Shareholders have developed a degree of suspicion over the years regarding flexibility in presenting accounting numbers which are managed to maximum effect. Major UK companies are subject to extensive scrutiny of their remuneration, and shareholders demand that companies and their remuneration committees have a clear and transparent process for dealing with adjustments to accounting numbers.

Over recent years, companies have wrestled with the switch from UK GAAP to International Accounting Standards and there have been some fundamental changes, particularly regarding the accounting for pensions and share incentives themselves. These have had important consequences for the way performance is measured in remuneration, and companies will be well served if they devote appreciable time to identifying which elements (if any) should be excluded.

Many remuneration committees neglect this level of detail until such time as the final calculation of an incentive plan is called into question. At that point, the wisdom of hindsight rarely illuminates the outcome; rather there is the risk of unnecessary tension between executive and non-executive directors. Shareholder aggravation can be avoided if the remuneration committee sets out the principles for any adjustment against which any changed circumstance will be evaluated. For example, when using EPS it is generally wise to recognise that the measure may need some modification to take account of material acquisitions and/or disposals. However, it is rarely desirable for the targets to be reset and recalibrated on a regular basis to accommodate changing economic circumstances and unforeseen expenditure.

In order to facilitate and motivate growth, remuneration packages should generally be more highly geared in expanding companies than those in slow-growth businesses. There is more opportunity for the executives to win and to share in the growth in value of the business. It is important to adopt arrangements which are scalable and can accommodate growth in the number of people who may need to be included in the incentive plans. Over time, this can be a particular problem for smaller companies, who often start by allocating incentives to individuals as a percentage of the capital or the profits, only to find that early joiners have too much and there is too little to offer new talent.

Larger, mature businesses

Setting targets in this environment should be relatively straightforward as companies will have well-established tools to predict the growth in business and to identify the expectations of shareholders. Target setting within these parameters, whilst not trouble free, is considerably easier than in many other business circumstances.

Remuneration in these companies is typically of the 'steady as we go' variety. In other words, it is rare for it to be necessary to make awards other than on a regular annual cycle, with annual bonuses based on established parameters with only the growth targets being modified from year to year. Longer-term incentives will also typically be using well-established performance measures, and awards will be made annually and vest over three to four years.

Mergers, de-mergers and acquisitions – the threat from private equity

Is private equity a threat? There has been much speculation in the media concerning the trend for private-equity-funded firms to attract top management from the quoted sector. There are certainly some high-profile instances of this happening. The UK quoted sector holds a pool of top international managerial talent who are attractive targets to private-equity-funded companies. The compensation packages offered can be attractive to executives considering their next move.

Another area where private equity may be an increasing threat is that of acquisitions. Private equity houses move quickly and are often more skilled in using the capital markets and in the tactics of bids and auctions. Corporates pursuing growth by acquisition may find themselves at a disadvantage. Private equity has been the most successful investment medium of the last decade, whereas many acquisitions destroy value in the acquiring company. Clearly, it is much easier to buy a single business and improve it than to buy a business and then try to integrate it into a large existing company with different working practices, accounting systems, cultures and business philosophy. So how do corporates compete?

In remuneration terms, the most striking difference between remuneration in private-equity-funded companies and the listed sector is the approach to incentivisation. In private equity, management incentives are simple, focusing on achieving the required internal rate of return and value at exit. In the corporate world, incentives have to fit within the wider remuneration structure and are influenced by other needs and aims of the company such as retention, alignment with shareholders, market practice and internal equity.

Can quoted companies learn from private equity? Clearly, the two worlds are different. In private equity, there is generally a simple timescale – from acquisition to the exit event. This is typically a period of not more than five years. In the corporate world, shareholders acquire shares every day and there are likely to be numerous exit events depending on when individual shareholders seek to realise their investment by selling their shares. The potential rewards in private equity may be higher but the risks in terms of personal investment and job security are often greater. Traditionally, the corporate world was seen as a safer environment with fewer direct demands from a focused group of shareholders and the benefit of long career expectations and a generous retirement plan based on two thirds of final pay. The two thirds of final salary pension is rapidly disappearing, the career

149

expectations may be less certain, and there is far more scrutiny of executives running public companies than there has ever been. So what can quoted companies learn from the way incentive plans work in private-equity-funded companies? The key to this is simplicity. Focus on what success looks like and then focus the rewards on those responsible for delivering the success.

In an acquisition situation, this may mean that the senior management of the acquisition do not participate in the long-term arrangements of the new parent company with performance based on broad-based measures such as TSR or EPS, but instead participate in a plan which focuses on the performance of the acquired business alone. The plan should also focus on a timescale which is relevant for delivering value in the business following the deal, which may not be the usual three-year performance period seen in corporate incentive plans. Where performance is not delivered, management should not get an incentive payment. The incentives should be focused on those who actually have the power to make the deal work.

Another situation where this approach may be appropriate is where the company refocuses the existing business. An example of this is Cable & Wireless plc, whose incentive plan was designed to support the separation of the business into two operationally independent entities. These are called 'UK' and 'International'. All shared services were devolved to the businesses with a very limited number of activities – those concerned with running a quoted company – retained centrally.

In essence the plan works in the following way: the remuneration committee fixed the base value of the businesses at the start date (the aggregate of the base values will not be less than the average market capitalisation of the company during the month prior to the start date). The valuation of the businesses is subject to guidelines and involves a five-stage process. A notional balance sheet is drawn up for each business, which is designed to encourage the minimum use of cash and drive the speed at which they achieve self-sufficiency. The balance sheet allocates the market value of the company at the start date between equity, senior debt, junior debt and interest-bearing payment in kind (PIK). The value of each business is then adjusted over the performance period. The adjustment reflects any increase in investment notionally made in the business and any cash treated as returned by the business. The adjusted base cost is then increased by the notional weighted cost of the capital of the business.

For example, the base value of one of the businesses is assumed to be £1.9bn, and at the end of the performance period grows to £3bn. Assuming a cost-of-capital hurdle of 8.3% per annum, the adjusted base cost of the business will be £2.61bn. The value created will therefore be around £386 million and the value of the pool will therefore be £38.6 million.

The CEO of each business will receive 20% of the pool subject to an overall limit of £20m for each director (or £10m if there is a vesting event within twelve months of the start date; note: this cap was removed at the

2007 Annual General Meeting (AGM)). A vesting event would be a takeover of the company, a sale of either or both of the businesses, or a de-merger of the businesses.

This plan borrows from the private equity model in that it is based on a simple concept of delivering a share in the absolute increase in value of the business above a hurdle value to meet the prior claims of other capital providers, and has complete clarity about what constitutes good performance. It focuses the senior executives on each specific business and delivers potentially high rewards if outstanding performance is achieved.

However, the plan also includes features which will provide comfort to shareholders. The remuneration committee will only approve payments if it is satisfied that there has been an underlying improvement in the performance of the business over the specified period. There will be no payments unless TSR is positive. Awards can be scaled back if the remuneration committee considers that the price of the company's shares in the valuation period has been materially affected by non-disclosable inside information or by any breach of regulatory requirements relating to the disclosure of information.

In conjunction with the introduction of the cash LTIP, other elements of the remuneration package have also been reviewed, resulting in salaries being frozen for three years and a reduction in the annual bonus potential. Participants in the new LTIP will not participate in any other long-term plans.

This plan generated significant press comment and mixed reactions from shareholders when it was introduced. However, at the 2006 AGM a poll was taken on all resolutions. The remuneration report received a 98% vote for and the plan received an 86% vote for, although if the abstentions were included this would fall to 79%.

A word of caution should be included at this point. We would strongly advocate that remuneration be structured in a way that the company believes best supports the business strategy and this may mean, as in the Cable & Wireless example, implementing quite innovative structures. In our view, a company should not be afraid to be different. However, for a quoted company it is important to remember that longer-term plans will need prior shareholder approval, and it is essential to have a clear rationale and be able to demonstrate that the structure has been well thought through and tested before a radical proposal will be approved. Above all, it needs careful communication and a commitment to open dialogue with shareholders.

Turnaround

In a turnaround situation the company may seek to replicate some of the same characteristics as are appropriate for a private equity type deal – in particular, the unambiguous focus on performance over a specific time period and the desire to foster an ownership culture so that management

151

and shareholders share the same goals. It is important to focus on the drivers of success and to ensure that the remuneration structure incentivises those leading the recovery. One such plan is the 2005 plan adopted by the leading food retailer J Sainsbury plc. The group had experienced a number of years of declining relative performance and had recruited a new senior management team. It was identified that the seeds of recovery lay in driving performance improvement across the business, and therefore widespread involvement was a key requirement.

Figure 5.8 Sainsbury

In 2004 Sainsbury's laid out plans to 'Make Sainsbury's Great Again'– this was a three-year programme designed to grow sales by £2.5bn and return Sainsbury's to sustainable growth in both sales and profitability. Sales were seen as the purest measure of customer satisfaction. The vision was about 'delivering great quality food at fair prices'. The recovery plan was about fixing the basics, which covers everything from supply chain to technology infrastructure. A clear road map had been developed to get Sainsbury's to where it aims to be. The most important change was building the leadership team. The long-term incentive plan was specifically designed to incentivise senior management to deliver the sales-led recovery. The company undertook extensive consultation with major shareholders, the ABI and NAPF and the plan is closely aligned with UK best practice.

In order to incentivise the senior management team to deliver the recovery, a long-term plan was developed and implemented in 2005. The circular to shareholders states that:

> The underlying principle of the Plan is to reward strong growth in sales and profitability. The Plan is a one-off self-funded incentive arrangement covering a four-year period. The Plan is intended to introduce an ownership culture for the new management team, incentivising those who will be responsible for leading and implementing the recovery. Over 1,000 colleagues will participate in the Plan, from the Chief Executive through to supermarket store managers, focussed on identical targets. The level of awards are scaled according to seniority. In addition, there is an opportunity for executive directors and eligible Operating Board members to make a personal investment of up to 50% of salary in the Plan.

In the year of operation, no other long-term awards were to be made. In addition, participants must surrender existing options. A core award of shares with a value of 100% of salary were to be made to the chief executive, 80% of salary to other executive directors, and 50% of salary to departmental directors. Awards, expressed as a number of shares, were also to be made to senior managers, supermarket store managers and managers at equivalent grade.

A multiplier is applied to the award based on sales growth and EPS growth over the four-year period. The circular goes on to say that 'The targets mirror milestones in the recovery plan and are stretching in the context of market expectations. The relevant performance multiplier, which is on a sliding scale up to a maximum of five times, will be calculated and applied to both the core award and the personal investment.'

The maximum award requires sales growth of £2.5 billion and compound annual growth in EPS of at least 21% per annum. No vesting will occur for sales growth of less than £1 billion and compound annual growth in EPS of less than 5% per annum. Up to half of the award can vest at the end of year 3 if accelerated performance targets have been met.

Conclusion

Designing appropriate incentive plans is a complex and subtle process; careful consideration of the needs of the business must shape and direct the remuneration committee's deliberations. The committee needs to:

- select appropriate performance measures;
- set suitably challenging performance targets;
- measure success over reasonable timescales (too short and success may not be established; too long and there may be no motivational impact); and
- involve the right people (incentives may be a market-competitive necessity but they can also influence behaviour and should be extended to those capable of taking the necessary steps to deliver change).

If plans are properly designed to support the commercial needs of the business, they will inevitably be dynamic, challenging and sometimes unconventional. Shareholders have a keen interest in supporting arrangements which drive value creation, and remuneration committees need to engage in effective dialogue to build understanding and support for any new proposals.

6

Reporting and explaining the deal

ANGUS MAITLAND AND ISOBEL SHARP

Communicating remuneration policy

ANGUS MAITLAND

On 20 November 1994 the business section of *The Sunday Times* published an exclusive lead entitled 'British Gas Pioneers Huge Executive Pay Shake Up.[1] The paper described the British Gas move as 'the biggest shake up of executive pay in UK corporate history' and noted that the new system would involve unprecedented levels of remuneration disclosure, scrapping of annual bonuses and automatic share option grants, the reduction in rolling contracts from three years to two, and a long-term share option scheme tied to growth in shareholder value. With what was shortly to prove a nice sense of irony, an industry commentator was quoted in the piece as saying: 'this kind of sensitivity to shareholders is the way the market is going. Things are not going to stop with two-year rolling contracts.'

Linked to the piece was an editorial: 'British Gas leads way to open management'. It described the company, then with a market capitalisation in excess of £13 billion with pre-tax profits of £1.3 billion, as 'conservative and monopolistic' and said that its directors had recognised that 'such a stance was unsustainable'. And, on the pay system, it said that British Gas's initiative was the most radical attempt at that time to reconcile the interests of executives and shareholders.

That was Sunday. By Monday, British Gas was in crisis. Cartoons of rather plump cats with cigars and bowls of cream filled the front pages of the tabloids, and the broadsheets shrieked in indignation. British Gas's chief executive, starting a fortnight's holiday, came under siege at his home and was filmed taking tea with his media tormentors.

The bad publicity persisted until the boil was, to some extent, lanced by a virtuoso performance by the chairman at the following year's AGM. The AGM itself lasted six hours; featured London's future mayor as a spokesman for a New-York-based fund management group with Celtic sympathies, complaining about religious discrimination at British Gas's

---

[1] Andrew Lorenz, 'British Gas Pioneers Huge Executive Pay Shake Up', *The Sunday Times*, 20 November 1994.

Ballymena power station; and included a live pig shipped in by the Telecommunications Workers' Union in one of their employer's vehicles. Extraordinary stuff.

Remuneration rows did not, of course, start with the 1994 British Gas crisis. In BT's annual report for the year to 31 March 1991 it emerged that its chairman received a 43% pay rise (which the media compared to an increase of only 14% in pre-tax profits) and a controversial bonus of £150,000. The crisis was somewhat defused when it emerged that the bonus found its way to charity. Even the governor of the Bank of England was, in the words of Andrew Alexander, then City Editor of the *Mail*, 'plain daft enough' to call for pay restraint while receiving a large rise himself.[2]

The major problem the privatised utilities faced, of course, was that they had, by and large, emerged from monopolistic, or near monopolistic, positions enjoying a relatively comfortable life; and executive directors were, not surprisingly, poorly paid in comparison with their private sector counterparts.

As the chairman of British Gas observed in those fateful days in 1994, with the advent of competition and the demands for continually improved performance from the City, higher-calibre executive directors were required and these could not be recruited if remuneration packages were seriously uncompetitive.

A decade of pay turmoil

There is no doubt that the British Gas remuneration crisis represented a watershed in the recent history of board pay. It was followed in January 1995 by the Confederation of British Industry (CBI) setting up the Greenbury Committee[3] to come up with a new Code of Practice on Board Pay. The overheated political atmosphere in which it operated was hardly conducive to clear-headed thinking, but the committee was seen to have done a good job in tough circumstances and to a very tight timescale.

As the decade progressed, the question of pay became intertwined with corporate failures, such as Worldcom, Marconi and Enron. And regulation built on itself, culminating in the first AGM votes on remuneration reports in the UK in the 2003 reporting season.

Since 1997, many famous corporate names have been embroiled in pay rows. Some, like GSK, at the time of writing the only FTSE 100 company to have its remuneration report voted down, successfully navigated the storm and emerged with reputation intact. Others were less fortunate. What made the difference? And why do companies continually find themselves in

---

[2] Andrew Alexander, 'How to Curb Greed in the Boardroom', *Daily Mail*, 27 June 1991.
[3] Directors' remuneration – report of a study group chaired by Sir Richard Greenbury, 17 July 1995.

difficulty in the first place? Quite often pay crises can arise from short-term market imperfection. A company needs to replace its CEO. Available candidates are in short supply and quite happy where they are at the time. So they have to be offered a handsome package to move, which can create a ratchet effect. In markets served by small numbers of large corporations, such as oil and pharmaceuticals, remuneration committees have to keep a close eye on the pay levels of competitors. A step change in one can often lead to a 'me too' reaction in another, with little thought as to the consequences in terms of shareholder reaction.

It is also possible for the crisis to stem from the inward-looking nature of some boards. What may look to the remuneration committee like a justified bonus to a CEO can look like an unnecessary bonus, for simply doing the job the CEO is paid to do, to external commentators and shareholders.

It may seem puzzling why some of the crises we have seen in remuneration policy have come to pass without the board in general, or the remuneration committee in particular, foreseeing them. As one FTSE 100 chairman famously remarked about the furious reaction to his special bonus: 'They told me it would be fine. Then the roof fell in. And when I looked over my shoulder there was no-one there!' Clearly the remuneration committee in question had simply run for cover.

Much of the problem stems from pay policies which are formed (often with remuneration consultants' advice) and executed with no thought given to external perception. And the latter is often irrational. As has happened on many occasions, pressure groups and commentators faced with the hard logic of a well-argued remuneration case respond by simply saying: 'It's too much.'

Despite the numerous examples of wholly avoidable pay crises, it is unlikely that they will decrease in future. The corporate memory trace on pay is remarkably short lived. And some companies are likely to continue to prefer the option of risking an adverse vote on remuneration policy to consulting at an early stage and having their policy shot down or badly compromised before they can implement it.

Avoiding crisis

Are pay rows really corporate crises? In the case of British Gas the answer was certainly 'yes'. It had all the ingredients, well reflected in the barometer of its share price performance. In other cases, rows turn out to be 'issues' rather than 'crises'. However, the communications planning and response tend to be similar for either. The difference is the scale of the tremors which run through the corporation.

So, getting into crisis is not difficult. It can happen with quite extraordinary speed and, certainly in the case of British Gas, it can be wholly unexpected.

However, if a crisis is anticipated and prepared for assiduously, more often than not it can be managed.

The need to explain – the first question a remuneration committee should ask itself is: can the policy it has developed be explained relatively simply and in a way which is rational to the outsider? A way of testing this would be to ask remuneration committees to present new pay policies to external advisors with expertise on communications and perception management. If the policy cannot surmount that hurdle, it needs to be rethought.

The need to anticipate – even if a policy can be explained, that is not enough. The committee also needs to ask itself if each element of the policy passes the 'It just isn't right / it's just too much' test. Failing this test does not necessarily mean the policy or any aspect of it is wrong and must be changed. But it should be reviewed to see if, in terms of external perception, it can be improved without compromising it. And following such a review, the rogue elements need to be the focus of special attention.

The need to persuade – remuneration policy is a key element in a company's competitive armoury. If a company can persuade its shareholders to buy into a leading-edge policy, sooner or later it will attract the best of breed. So, it can be argued that if a remuneration policy does not make a company's owners sit up and take notice, it is probably not sufficiently competitive. This makes it hard to understand why, in a competitive market, so many companies pay little or no attention to building a persuasive case for their remuneration policies.

The need to plan – this is the 'how' of communications. The right messages can be counter-productive if delivered at the wrong time and in the wrong place by the wrong person. Exactly how a sensitive and complex communication will be delivered is critical to its success; and it needs a well-thought-through plan to maximise the effectiveness of delivery and to ensure elephant traps are avoided.

The need to prepare – time is never wasted in preparation. Executives who believe they are on top of a particular brief often are not. An unanticipated question provoking a half-baked answer can bring the communications edifice down around an executive's feet. Presentation rehearsals and robust question-and-answer (Q&A) sessions are a must.

Elements of a successful remuneration communication strategy

On 17 May 2004 William Claxton Smith of Insight, the fund management division of HBOS, was quoted in the *Financial Times*[4] as saying that 'GSK had made huge efforts to communicate with shareholders [on its revised

---

[4] Sundeep Tucker, 'GSK Rebuilds Confidence After Pay Set Back', *Financial Times*, 17 May 2004.

remuneration policy] and "that should be recognised by all investors" '. On the same day, shareholders voted through GSK's remuneration report at the company's AGM. Thus ended one of the most dramatic turnarounds in media and investor perception on remuneration. Claxton-Smith's comment reflected only one part of a strategy that took around a year to develop and execute.

Successful communications strategies on remuneration policy have a number of essential elements.

The overarching theme – this is the proposition that binds the strategy together and gives it focus and consistency. In GSK's case it was 'pay for performance and only for performance'. The new remuneration policy was then developed and communicated with that theme at its heart.

The key messages – it may be tempting for a company to dump onto the market everything it wants to say about its remuneration policy, and there is often an overcharged earnestness in communications. The result is usually to confuse rather than inform, and when commentators surface from the mass of information they are generally in a cynical frame of mind. Separating what counts and what will hit home from everything else is essential. A few succinct and memorable messages are worth more than an essay, no matter how well constructed.

The difficult questions – these are the ones most likely to be absent from the internally generated Q&A brief. Media questions on pay – relevant or not – are often unpalatable and need to be replicated in Q&A preparation and tested robustly.

The key audiences – clearly the top institutional shareholders are the priority for a company aiming to launch successfully a new or revised remuneration policy. Capture them, and forget the rest? Not quite. In the shifting mass of audiences which determine corporate reputation, it is not just a case of pushing a policy through. It is achieving that aim while not compromising, and ideally enhancing, corporate reputation. So careful attention needs to be paid to those who advise as well as those who decide: the trade associations such as the ABI; the media; the sell side; the internal audiences; customers; suppliers; and, sometimes, the public at large and the politicians.

The messenger / credibility of source – is key to communications success. A respected, persuasive, well-briefed independent chairman is worth his weight in gold on these occasions. And much the same can be said of the chair of the remuneration committee, who may, however, have a lesser role in communications. Other key players will be the head of Human Resources, the company secretary, and the heads of Media and IR and their respective advisors.

The importance of performance – financial performance, provided it is recognised in value growth, is often the determinant as to whether or not a remuneration issue becomes a crisis. However, it would be unwise to rely on performance alone. Companies with good financial records have had to change tack on pay decisions to avoid critical confrontation with institutions.

Sometimes a retrospective look at pay issues leads to the question: 'How did the board manage to get into that position in the first place?' The answer is often that the company simply did not spot a potential issue.

The kinds of decision that can contain the seeds of crisis are manifold, but there is also a repetitive pattern about some of them.

Rebasing incentive schemes – this was not unusual with share option schemes and it has continued, albeit to a lesser extent, into LTIPs. The dilemma can be appreciated. The stock market or the company's market place has done something unexpected and destroyed the basis of a carefully wrought incentive plan. It is a choice of living with one that will not deliver or rebasing it. Remuneration committees tend to head in the latter direction and into stormy waters.

Adding new schemes – experience can show that LTIPs are too long term to motivate and retain, so an annual bonus scheme is added. Or it could be that annual bonuses are seen as driving short-term decision making, so an LTIP is introduced. If either looks like delivering substantial sums to under-performers, trouble is in store.

Paying one-off bonuses – this can seem a good idea at the time when the company is on a high; but by the time it is communicated, it rapidly hits the buffers. These bonuses are often related to corporate transactions: CEOs being awarded bonuses for making what the remuneration committee believed to be a good acquisition – or a good disposal. The shareholders' view can be: 'How do I know it will create value?' or 'That's the job they are paid to do, and the normal incentives should be designed to reward that.'

Paying-out contracts – this is the infamous 'payment for failure' and in the past decade the reaction to it has sometimes been so hysterical that it has attracted the attention of and comment (or threats) from government. Here the company can find itself between a rock and a hard place. How were they to know when they hired the CEO that he would be a disaster? Without a one-year rolling contract, no-one would have taken the job. And now they have a contractual obligation to pay. This is a bad place to be when the share price is falling.

Getting timing wrong – in this category, decisions are communicated to top shareholders to help garner support – at the wrong time. For instance, a company's remuneration report is about to be voted on and the company writes to its major shareholders announcing a material change – which they may or may not like. If they don't well, they cannot vote on it. Ruffled institutional feathers are at the mild end of the spectrum. A 'no' vote on the remuneration report is at the other.

How can a company anticipate a pay storm arising from such actions?

The short answer is for the remuneration committee to present the proposal – and justify it – internally before presenting it externally, to those, including advisors, who are neither involved in the process nor beneficiaries of it.

Although pay crises can be anticipated, they cannot be predicted with certainty. Remuneration votes have been won by a few percentage points. If they had been lost, a crisis of some degree would have followed.

Having become embroiled in such a crisis, how can a company best extricate itself with minimum damage to its reputation?

Accept the decision – it is essential to accept a defeat with good grace and quickly move to the resolution phase. The genie cannot be put back into the bottle so do not try or there is a risk that the institutional attitudes will harden further.

Don't concede the argument – a defeat does not mean a company made the wrong decision. A company will need to explain cogently to the media and the market why it came to a particular decision; but this explanation might be linked to full acceptance of the majority shareholder view, and it must be followed by a commitment to engage with the shareholder base on the issue.

Listen to shareholders – a programme of meetings should be held with shareholders and their representative bodies to listen to their concerns about the company's pay policy and how they feel policy should be redesigned. It is important that the board has the last word. Pay policy is the responsibility of the board, not the shareholders.

Review pay strategy – having gathered comprehensive views from shareholders, policy must be taken apart, re-examined with these views in mind and re-assembled as a coherent package which successfully addresses shareholder concern.

Revisit the shareholder base – the new policy must be communicated comprehensively and persuasively to major shareholders. The company is unlikely to receive 100% backing; but it will know whether or not the new policy is largely right.

Keep the media informed – if the key commentators are kept abreast of the process, which may take many months, they will be in a much better position to comment sensibly on the new policy as and when it arises.

Summary

Executive remuneration has become an increasingly contentious issue during the last decade and pay issues have occasionally tipped over into full-blown corporate crises.

The pay issues which have created controversy, such as paying terminal bonuses and rebasing incentive schemes, have tended to recur and will probably continue to do so. But controversial pay issues can almost always be anticipated. And, if anticipated, with careful planning and thorough preparation they can be managed in a way which minimises damage to corporate reputation, a precious commodity which is long and hard to build and easy and fast to lose.

The key to managing them is a successful communications strategy. The communication of pay policies should have an overarching theme which binds all elements of policy together, and a few easily understood key messages of explanation. New pay polices also need to be communicated by a credible source, usually an independent chairman.

Where a company has failed to avoid a crisis, there is always a way out. It requires close consultation with major shareholders and regular communication with those who advise and influence.

Disclosing the details annually

ISOBEL SHARP

If International Financial Reporting Standards applied to UK listed groups, then the annual disclosure on executives' pay might read as follows.

> The remuneration of directors and other members of key management during the year was as follows:
>
> **Figure 6.1** *Compensation of key management personnel*
>
> | | Year ended 31/12/06 CU'000 | Year ended 31/12/05 CU'000 |
> |---|---|---|
> | Short-term benefits | 13,681 | 10,270 |
> | Post-employment benefits | 1,602 | 1,391 |
> | Other long-term benefits | 1,153 | 1,769 |
> | Share-based payments | 949 | 863 |
> | | 17,385 | 14,293 |
>
> CU = Currency unit
>
> The remuneration of directors and key executives is determined by the remuneration committee having regard to the performance of individuals and market trends.

This would be the shortest chapter in the book. But while the UK enjoyed a similarly short regime until the early 1990s, the present number of rules in this area, some of which conflict with others, ensures that this chapter will be much longer. For those who may wish to know now the answer to any question on whether something must be reported, the answer is probably 'yes'.

The 1990s

In May 1991, the Financial Reporting Council, the London Stock Exchange and the accountancy profession set up a committee under the chairmanship of Sir Adrian Cadbury. It came at a time when there had been some unexpected failures of major companies and because there had been criticism of the lack of effective board accountability on matters such as directors' pay. The committee's final report, published in December 2002, may now be seen as the snowball which started the avalanche of corporate governance disclosures which have built up over the last fifteen years. The Cadbury Report's comments on the actions to be taken in respect of disclosure of directors' pay were simply as set out in figure 6.3.

Figure 6.2 *Illustrative directors' remuneration report (DRR) extract*

Remuneration committee

The company has established a remuneration committee which is constituted in accordance with the recommendations of the Combined Code. The members of the committee during 20XX were [insert names of members] who are all independent non-executive directors and the committee is chaired by Mr _____. In addition, Mr _____ was also a member of the Committee during 20YY when the committee was considering directors' remuneration for 20XX.

None of the Committee has any personal financial interest (other than as shareholders), conflicts of interests arising from cross-directorships or day-to-day involvement in running the business. The Committee makes recommendations to the board. No director plays a part in any discussion about his or her own remuneration.

In determining the directors' remuneration for the year, the Committee consulted Mr _____ (Chief Executive) and Ms _____ (Group HR Director) about its proposals. The Committee also appointed XYZ Remuneration Consultants Limited to provide advice on structuring directors' remuneration packages. XYZ Remuneration Consultants Limited did not provide any other services to the company or group.

However, this light-touch approach was soon superseded. Earlier in this chapter we saw that British Gas and the story of the pig led to another committee being established, namely the Greenbury Committee. That committee's Code of Best Practice, which focuses solely on remuneration matters, contained forty separate recommendations.

The Stock Exchange moved swiftly to recognise the final Greenbury Report published in July 1995. With effect for accounting periods beginning on or after 31 December 1995, companies were required to comply with the Code or to explain and justify areas of non-compliance. For the first time, remuneration committees were expected to report annually to shareholders on behalf of the board.

However, before Greenbury took effect, another group had been set up. The task of this group was to review the findings of the Cadbury and Greenbury Committees. Chaired by Sir Ronald Hampel, it published its final report in January 1998, albeit with one task left undone, which was to produce a set of principles and a code which embraced the work of Cadbury, Greenbury and Hampel. This was called the Combined Code and it was issued in June 1998, fulfilling that promise. On the same day, the Stock Exchange issued Amendment 12 to the Listing Rules. That

Amendment required listed companies incorporated in the UK to include in their annual reports for years ending on or after 31 December 1998:

- a narrative statement on how the Principles in the Code had been applied; and
- a statement as to whether or not the Code provisions had been complied with throughout the accounting period.

With rules in company law on disclosure of directors' emoluments, specific requirements in the Listing Rules, and the Combined Code providing extensive recommendations in this area, it might have been thought that all the guidance that could be issued on the subject had been issued. But in 2001 the Department of Trade and Industry started consulting on whether amendments should be made to the provisions in company law. By 2002, the DTI had issued the Directors' Remuneration Report Regulations. These require quoted companies to produce a detailed annual directors' remuneration report. It also required a shareholder vote on that report, a step which the Cadbury Committee had specifically rejected only ten years earlier.

Rules and guidance

There are many sources for rules and guidance on disclosing details of directors' remuneration. These include:

- Companies Act 1985 as updated by the 2002 Directors' Remuneration Report Regulations. In particular, sections 234B and 234C cover the duty to prepare a directors' remuneration report for quoted companies and state that this must be laid before the company in general meeting. Schedule 6 of the Act discusses the disclosure of emoluments and other benefits to directors and others, setting out the separate regimes for quoted and unquoted companies;[1]
- Chapter 9 of the Listing Rules;
- the Combined Code, the most recent version of which was issued by the Financial Reporting Council in June 2006;
- the Association of British Insurers (ABI), 'Principles and guidelines on remuneration';

---

[1] For accounting periods commencing on or after 6 April 2008, the regulations relating to the disclosure of directors' remuneration are contained in Schedule 8 (Quoted Companies: Directors' Remuneration Report) to the Large and Medium-sized Companies and Groups (Accounts and Reports) Regulations 2008. The only substantive change is the addition of a new requirement to disclose how pay and employment conditions of employees in the company have been taken into account when determining directors' remuneration. However, this only applies for financial years beginning on or after 6 April 2009. Sections 420–2 of the Companies Act 2006 cover the duty to prepare a directors' remuneration report for quoted companies. The requirements of Schedule 6 of the Companies Act 1985 are contained in Schedule 5 to the Large and Medium-sized Companies and Groups (Accounts and Reports) Regulations 2008.

- the National Association of Pension Funds (NAPF) joint statement with the ABI on 'Best practice on executive contracts and severance'; and
- the CBI, 'Best practice guidelines on directors' contracts and severance'.

The purpose of this chapter is not to go through each in detail but to take a look at the main sections of the directors' remuneration report as it typically appears in the annual reports of quoted companies, to gain an insight into the expected level of disclosure.

The directors' remuneration report (DRR)

Since December 2002, quoted companies have been required by law to prepare a directors' remuneration report. A quoted company means a company whose equity share capital:

(a) has been included in the official list in accordance with the provisions of Part VI of the Financial Services and Markets Act 2000; or
(b) is officially listed in a European Economic Area State (i.e. the EU plus Norway, Iceland or Liechtenstein); or
(c) is admitted to dealing on either the New York Stock Exchange or the exchange known as NASDAQ.

Therefore AIM companies and companies which have only debt or non-equity share capital listed do not fall within the scope of the requirement.

Schedule 7A contains the requirements for the contents of DRRs. Listed companies previously prepared such reports to comply with the Listing Rules and the Combined Code. These requirements have not been withdrawn. Although compliance with Schedule 7A will meet most of the requirements of the Listing Rules, there are a few areas where the Listing Rules require additional or different disclosures. Some of these are highlighted below where relevant.

Remuneration committee

The Act does not require a company to have a remuneration committee. However, if a committee of the company's directors has considered matters relating to directors' remuneration for the relevant financial year, certain disclosures are required. If a company does not have a remuneration committee, this would be a departure from the Combined Code, which should be disclosed and explained.

The name of each director who was a member of the committee at the time when the committee was considering matters relating to directors' remuneration for the financial year should be disclosed. The wording of this requirement potentially requires information about the composition of the committee in previous years. This is because directors' remuneration is often set in advance. The equivalent requirement in the Combined Code is differently worded and appears to require the current membership of the committee. In any event, it would be helpful to explain any changes in the composition of the committee during the year and after the year end.

Disclosure is also required of the name of any person who provided advice or services to the committee that materially assisted the committee in its consideration of directors' remuneration. This requirement applies to any directors who are not members of the committee as well as to any third parties such as remuneration consultants. One of the supporting principles at B.2 in the Combined Code states that the committee should consult the chairman and/or chief executive officer.

Where such advice or services are provided by a party who is not a director, the report should state the nature of any other services that the person has provided to the company during the year and whether the person was

---

Figure 6.3 *Board remuneration*

4.40 The overriding principle in respect of board remuneration is that of openness. Shareholders are entitled to a full and clear statement of directors' present and future benefits, and of how they have been determined. WE RECOMMEND that in disclosing directors' total emoluments and those of the chairman and highest-paid UK director, separate figures should be given for their salary and performance-related elements and that the criteria on which performance is measured should be explained. Relevant information about stock options, stock appreciation rights, and pension contributions should also be given.

4.41 In addition, WE RECOMMEND that future service contracts should not exceed three years without shareholders' approval and that the Companies Act should be amended in line with this recommendation. This would strengthen shareholder control over levels of compensation for loss of office.

4.42 WE ALSO RECOMMEND that boards should appoint remuneration committees, consisting wholly or mainly of non-executive directors and chaired by a non-executive director, to recommend to the board the remuneration of the executive directors in all its forms, drawing on outside advice as necessary. Executive directors should play no part in decisions on their own remuneration. Membership of the remuneration committee should appear in the Directors' Report. Best practice in this field is set out in PRO NED's Remuneration Committee guidelines, published in 1992.

Extract from the Report of the Committee on the Financial Aspects of Corporate Governance (Cadbury Report)

appointed by the committee. This requirement is presumably intended to indicate whether there might be a conflict of interest, for example where a consultancy which is advising the committee is also receiving fees for work it is doing for the executive directors.

Remuneration policy

The report is required to contain a statement of the company's policy on directors' remuneration 'for the following financial year and for financial years subsequent to that'. The statement should therefore be forward-looking rather than referring to the policies in place during the past financial year. In particular, it must deal with each person who served as a director between the year end and the date when the report will be laid before the company in general meeting.

Schedule 7A provides a list of items that the policy should include. The statement should, in respect of each director's terms and conditions relating to remuneration, explain the relative importance of those elements which are, and those which are not, related to performance.

The report of the Greenbury Committee also included some more detailed suggestions for matters to be included within remuneration policy:

(a) the total level of remuneration;
(b) the main components and the arrangements for determining them, including the division between basic and performance-related components;
(c) the main parameters and rationale for any annual bonus schemes, including caps;
(d) how performance is measured, how rewards are related to it, how the performance measures relate to longer-term company objectives and how the company has performed over time relative to comparator companies;
(e) the company's policy on allowing executive directors to accept appointments and retain payments from sources outside the company;
(f) the company's policy on contracts of service and early termination;
(g) pension schemes for directors, including the type of scheme, the main terms and parameters, what elements of remuneration are pensionable, how the Inland Revenue pensions cap has been accommodated and whether the scheme is part of, or separate from, the main company scheme; and
(h) attention should also be drawn to any special arrangements made and any material changes introduced during the year.

Although some of these requirements have now been made law, this is still a helpful checklist of items to consider.

Figure 6.4 below illustrates this section of the DRR on remuneration policy, which, as might reasonably be expected, given that it is required to cover every element of every director's remuneration, is quite lengthy.

Figure 6.4 *Illustrative DRR extract*

Remuneration policy for the executive directors

Executive remuneration packages are prudently designed to attract, motivate and retain directors of the high calibre needed to maintain the group's position as a market leader and to reward them for enhancing value to shareholders. The performance measurement of the executive directors and key members of senior management and the determination of their annual remuneration package are undertaken by the Committee.

There are five main elements of the remuneration package for executive directors and senior management:

basic annual salary;

benefits-in-kind;

annual bonus payments which cannot exceed 40% of basic salary;

share option incentives; and

pension arrangements.

The company's policy is that a substantial proportion of the remuneration of the executive directors should be performance-related. As described below, executive directors may earn annual incentive payments of up to 40% of their basic salary together with the benefits of participation in share option schemes.

Executive directors are entitled to accept appointments outside the company providing that the chairman's permission is sought and fees in excess of £20,000 from all such appointments are accounted for to the company.

Basic salary

An executive director's basic salary is reviewed by the committee prior to the beginning of each year and when an individual changes position or responsibility. In deciding appropriate levels, the Committee considers the group as a whole and relies on objective research which gives up-to-date information on a comparator group of companies which comprises the top ten companies by capitalisation within the sector. Basic salaries were reviewed in November 20YY with increases taking effect from 1 January 20XX. They were again reviewed in November 20XX and increased by 2% from 1 January 20WW. The ten companies used in the salary reviews for 20XX and 20WW were [*give names of companies*]. Executive directors' contracts of service which include details of remuneration will be available for inspection at the Annual General Meeting.

Benefits-in-kind

The executive directors receive certain benefits-in-kind, principally a car and private medical insurance.

Annual bonus payments

The Committee establishes the objectives that must be met for each financial year if a cash bonus is to be paid. In setting appropriate bonus parameters the Committee refers to the objective research on a comparator group of companies as noted above. The Committee believes that any incentive compensation awarded should be tied to the interests of the company's shareholders and that the principal measure of those interests is total shareholder return. Account is also taken of the relative success of the different parts of the business for which the executive directors are responsible and the extent to which the strategic objectives set by the board are being met. The maximum performance-related bonus that can be paid is 40% of basic annual salary. Incentive payments for the year ended 31 December 20XX varied between 22% and 26%. This reflects the improvement of the company from being eighth to fifth within its sector in terms of total shareholder return. The strategic objectives, control system and indicators are also aligned to total shareholder return.

Share options

During the year ended 20XX, following approval at the Annual General Meeting, the company established a new share option scheme (the 20XX Share Option Scheme). The reason for the new scheme was to incentivise the executive directors and to enable them to benefit from the increased market capitalisation of the company. The Committee has responsibility for supervising the scheme and the grant of options under its terms.

The performance criterion that must be met requires the company's share price to out-perform the FTSE All Share Index over a period of three years from the date the option was granted. Thereafter the option may be exercised for the rest of its ten-year life without further test. The performance criterion, which applies to all executive directors to whom options have been granted under the scheme, was chosen because [*give reason*]. [*If not already clear, summarise the methods used in assessing whether the performance condition has been met and the reason for choosing those methods.*]

The executive directors also have options granted to them under the terms of the 1992 Share Option Scheme which is open to all employees with more than three years' service. Under that scheme, options are

Figure 6.4 *continued*

allocated to qualifying employees by reference to profit for the year and basic salary. The exercise of options granted under the 1992 Scheme is not dependent upon performance criteria. Following approval of the 20XX Share Option Scheme, the executive directors will cease to be eligible to acquire new options under the 1992 Scheme.

The exercise price of the options granted under the above schemes is equal to the market value of the company's shares at the time when the options are granted. The company also operates a SAYE Share Option Scheme for eligible employees under which options may be granted at a discount of up to 20% of market value. The executive directors are not eligible to participate in the SAYE Share Option scheme.

The company's policy is to grant options to directors at the discretion of the Committee taking into account individual performance up to a maximum of [x] times salary over a three-year period. It is the company's policy to phase the granting of share options rather than to award them in a single large block to any individual.

The company does not operate any long-term incentive schemes other than the share option schemes described above. No significant amendments are proposed to be made to the terms and conditions of any entitlement of a director to share options.

Pension arrangements

Executive directors are members of the company pension scheme. Their dependants are eligible for dependants' pensions and the payment of a lump sum in the event of death in service. The pension arrangements provide for a pension on retirement of two thirds basic annual salary after thirty years' eligible service. No other payments to directors are pensionable.

To the extent that a director's benefits from the company scheme are restricted by Inland Revenue limits, payments are made to a funded unapproved retirement benefit scheme. There are no unfunded pension promises or similar arrangements for directors.

Mr _____ does not participate in the company pension scheme and the company has agreed instead to make a contribution equivalent to 20% of his basic salary into his private pension scheme.

Directors' contracts

It is the company's policy that executive directors should have contracts with an indefinite term providing for a maximum of one year's notice. However, it may be necessary occasionally to offer longer notice periods to new directors. Where this arises, it is the company's policy to reduce the notice period to one year within [*number*] years of appointment of the director. The service contract of Mr _____, who was appointed a director in 20XX, provides for [a notice period of [*number*] years / compensation of £_____ on termination] because [*state reasons if effective notice period is over one year*]. All other executive directors have contracts which are subject to one year's notice by either party.

Mr _____ and Mr _____ who are proposed for re-election at the next AGM have service contracts which provide for a notice period of one year. Mr _____ who is also proposed for re-election, being a non-executive director, does not have a service contract.

The details of the directors' contracts are summarised in the table below.

	Date of contract	Notice period
Name of director		

[*The notice period column could be omitted if this is covered adequately in the narrative, as in the above example.*]

In the event of early termination, the directors' contracts provide for compensation up to a maximum of basic salary for the notice period.

Non-executive directors

All non-executive directors have specific terms of engagement and their remuneration is determined by the board within the limits set by the Articles of Association and based on independent surveys of fees paid to non-executive directors of similar companies. The basic fee paid to each non-executive director in the year was £ _____. The non-executives receive further fees for additional work performed for the company in respect of membership of the remuneration committee, nominations committee and audit committee. The additional fees paid during the year were at a rate of £ _____ for membership of a committee and £ _____ for chairmanship of a committee. Non-executive directors cannot participate in any of the company's share option schemes and are not eligible to join the company's pension scheme.

Performance graph

The 2002 Regulations introduced the requirement for a performance graph in the DRR. The graph essentially compares the company's performance, measured by total shareholder return (TSR), with the performance of a broad equity market index. The requirement is not linked directly to performance-related remuneration and is required irrespective of whether directors' remuneration was linked to such a performance measure.

The requirement, more exactly, is that the report should contain a line graph that shows, for each of

(a) a holding of shares of that class of the company's equity share capital which has resulted in the company meeting the definition of 'quoted company', and

(b) a hypothetical holding of shares made up of shares of the same kind and number as those underlying a broad equity market index,

a line drawn by joining up points plotted to represent, for each of the financial years in the relevant period, the TSR on that holding.

The name of the index selected for the purpose of the graph and the reasons for selecting it should be given. The 'relevant period' is defined as the five financial years ending on the balance sheet date although a shorter period is permitted where the company has not been in existence for the full five years. However, paragraph 4 of Schedule 7A does not provide an exemption in cases where the company has been in existence for five years but has not been quoted throughout that period. It would be impracticable to provide information on TSR for a period during which no market price for the shares was available. Thus, presumably a short explanation of this should suffice.

Aggregate directors' remuneration

When a company is required to prepare a DRR in accordance with Schedule 7A, it is relieved of the obligation to comply with the requirements of Part I of Schedule 6 except for paragraph 1. This paragraph requires that aggregated details of directors' remuneration should be disclosed under four headings:

(a) emoluments;
(b) gains made on exercise of share options;
(c) amounts receivable under long-term incentive schemes; and
(d) company contributions to money purchase pension schemes.

The paragraph also requires the numbers of directors to whom retirement benefits are accruing under money purchase schemes and defined benefit schemes, respectively. But in a typical DRR, this information would be in the section covering directors' pension entitlements.

In the illustration below, a line has also been included for compensation

Figure 6.5 *Illustrative DRR extract*

Performance graph
The following graph shows the company's performance, measured by TSR, compared with the performance of the FTSE All Share Index also measured by TSR. The FTSE All Share index has been selected for this comparison because it is the index used by the company for the performance criterion for the 20XX Share Option Scheme.

[Provide a brief description of the basis upon which the graph has been prepared. For example, is it based on the constituent companies in the index at a point in time or is the notional investment changed each time the index changes?]

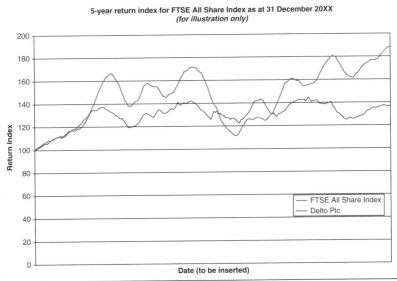

Figure 6.6 *Illustrative DRR extract*

Aggregate directors' remuneration
The total amounts for directors' remuneration were as follows:

	20XX	20YY
	£	£
Emoluments		
Compensation for loss of office		
Gains on exercise of share options		
Amounts receivable under long-term incentive schemes	————	————
Money purchase pension contributions	————	————

173

for loss of office because this is required to be shown in the table of emoluments required by Schedule 7A and an inconsistency would otherwise arise.

These details of aggregate remuneration are usually presented in the DRR to place in context the subsequent detailed disclosures. This is not, however, required and they could be given in the notes to the financial statements instead.

Directors' emoluments and compensation

For each person who served as a director of the company at any time during the year, show, in tabular form, the total amount of:

(a) salary and fees paid to or receivable by the person in respect of qualifying services;
(b) bonuses so paid or receivable;
(c) sums paid by way of expense allowance that are chargeable to UK income tax and paid to or receivable by the person in respect of qualifying services;
(d) any compensation for loss of office (or any other payments in connection with the termination of qualifying services) paid to or receivable by the person;
(e) the estimated value of any benefits received by the person otherwise than in cash that are emoluments of the person and received by the person in respect of qualifying services except where covered by other disclosure requirements. The nature of any element of the remuneration package which is not cash should be stated; and
(f) the total of (a) to (e) above.

The total of (a) to (e) for the previous financial year should also be shown for each person. This is required only for persons who were directors during the current year but it is usual to show amounts in respect of former directors in the comparative period.

The Listing Rules require disclosure of any significant payments to former directors. Payments to third parties for making available the services of a person as director should also be disclosed for each director by name. Amounts paid to or receivable by persons 'connected with' the director or companies controlled by the director are not paid to 'third parties' and should be disclosed in the table of emoluments as if they had been paid to the director.

Directors' share options

The following shows, in tabular form, the typical share option details for each person who served as a director of the company at any time during the year.

Schedule 7A does not require the gain on exercise of options in the period to be quantified for each director but ensures that sufficient information is made available for the gains to be calculated. Paragraph 1 of Schedule

Figure 6.7 *Illustrative DRR extract*

Directors' emoluments [and compensation]

Name of director	Fees/Basic salary £	Benefits in kind £	Annual bonuses £	20XX total £	20YY total £
Executive [List directors]					
Non-executive [List directors]	———	———	———	———	———
Aggregate emoluments	———	———	———	———	———
Fees to third parties	———	———	———	———	———

[If any compensation for loss of office or other payments in connection with termination have been made to persons who served as directors during the year, they must be shown in a column in this table. Details are also required to be given of any significant awards made in the year to former directors, including compensation for loss of office and pensions (although these details need not be in the table).]

Fees to third parties comprise amounts paid to *[name of third party]* under an agreement to provide the group with the services of Mr _____ . The agreement requires *[describe main terms]*.

Ms _____ waived emoluments of £_____ (20YY – £_____) and has agreed to waive future emoluments totalling £_____ in respect of services to be provided over *[specify period]*.

6 requires the aggregate gains on exercise of options for all directors to be disclosed, but not individual amounts. It is, however, regarded as good practice to disclose the gains for each director and this is illustrated above.

Long-term incentive schemes

The following should be shown, in tabular form, for each person who served as a director of the company at any time during the financial year:

(a) details of the scheme interests that the person has at the beginning of the year (or later date of appointment);
(b) details of scheme interests awarded to the person during the year;
(c) details of the scheme interests that the person has at the end of the year (or earlier date of cessation of appointment);
(d) for each such scheme interest, the end of the period over which the qualifying conditions have to be fulfilled and a description of any variations made in the terms and conditions of the scheme interests during the year; and

175

Figure 6.8 *Illustrative DRR extract*

Directors' share options

Aggregate emoluments disclosed above do not include any amounts for the value of options to acquire ordinary shares in the company granted to or held by the directors. Details of the options exercised during the year are as follows:

(a)

Name of director	Scheme	Number of options	Exercise price	Market price at exercise date	Gains on exercise 20XX	Gains on exercise 20YY
		_____	_____	_____	_____	_____
					_____	_____

Details of options for directors who served during the year are as follows:

(b)

Name of director	Scheme	1 January 20XX*	Granted	Exercised	31 December 20YY**	Exercise Price	Date from which exercisable	Expiry date
____	____	____	____	____	____	____	____	____

* or date of appointment, if later.

** or date of cessation of appointment, if earlier.

[An additional column will be required if any options have lapsed during the year. A separate line will be required for each block of options for each director. If this would lead to a statement of excessive length, a more concise disclosure, using weighted average exercise prices for each director, is permitted subject to certain constraints.]

(e) for each scheme interest that has vested in the year, the relevant details of any shares, the amount of any money and the value of any other assets that have become receivable in respect of the interest.

The details required for a scheme interest awarded in the year are the number of shares, the market price of those shares when the scheme interest was awarded and details of the qualifying conditions that are conditions with respect to performance.

The details required for a scheme interest that has vested in the year are the number of shares, the date on which the scheme interest was awarded, the market price of the shares when the scheme interest was awarded, the market price of the shares when the scheme interest vested and details of qualifying conditions that were conditions with respect to performance.

Directors' pension entitlements

The last seven or eight years have been difficult ones for pension schemes. Many employees have seen their final salary pension schemes closed and for some the promised pension has not materialised. In the meantime, directors enjoying substantial pension benefits have been the target of more public criticism, particularly when the disclosures in this area were less than transparent. Therefore, there are now extensive requirements in this area.

The following should be shown for each person who served as a director of the company at any time during the year where the person has rights under a pension scheme that is a defined benefit scheme and any of those rights are rights to which he/she has become entitled in respect of qualifying services:

(a) details of any changes during the year in the person's accrued benefits under the scheme;

(b) details of the person's accrued benefits under the scheme as at the end of the year;

(c) the transfer value, calculated in a manner consistent with 'Retirement Benefit Schemes – Transfer Values (GN 11)' published by the Institute of Actuaries and the Faculty of Actuaries and dated 6 April 2001, of the person's accrued benefits under the scheme at the end of the year;

(d) the transfer value of the person's accrued benefits under the scheme that was contained in the directors' remuneration report for the previous year or, if there was no such report or no such value was contained in that report, the transfer value (calculated in accordance with GN 11) of the person's accrued benefits under the scheme at the beginning of the year; and

(e) the amount obtained by subtracting the transfer value of the person's accrued benefits at the beginning of the year from the transfer value of the person's accrued benefits at the end of the year and then subtracting from the result of that calculation the amount of any contributions made to the scheme by the person in the year.

Although the Listing Rules contain broadly similar requirements for defined benefit pension schemes to those in Schedule 7A, two additional disclosures are required to meet in full the requirements of the Listing Rules. First, the increase in accrued pension in the year must be stated net of inflation rather than as the absolute amount of the increase. Second, the Listing Rules require the transfer value of that increase, whereas Schedule 7A requires the actual increase in transfer value (in both cases net of directors' contributions). These may be materially different because of the effect of changes in discount rates on the transfer values.

Disclosure of the increase in transfer value in the year, as required by Schedule 7A, may be confusing because transfer values are discounted

Figure 6.9 *Illustrative DRR extract*

Directors' pension entitlements

[*Number*] directors are members of the company's defined benefit pension scheme. The following directors had accrued entitlements under the schemes as follows:

(a)

	Accrued pension 31 December 20YY £	Increase in accrued pension in the year £	Accrued Pension 31 December 20XX £
Name of director	_____	_____	_____

The following table sets out the transfer value of the directors' accrued benefits under the scheme calculated in a manner consistent with 'Retirement Benefit Schemes – Transfer Values (GN 11)' published by the Institute of Actuaries and the Faculty of Actuaries.

(b)

	Transfer value 31 December 20YY £	Contributions made by the director £	Increase in transfer value in the year net of contributions £	Transfer value 31 December 20XX £
Name of director	_____	_____	_____	_____

The following additional information is given to comply with the requirements of the Listing Rules which differ in some respects from the equivalent statutory requirements.

(c)

	Increase in accrued pension in the year in excess of inflation £	Transfer value of increase in year less directors' contributions £
Name of director	_____	_____

The transfer values disclosed above do not represent a sum paid or payable to the individual director. Instead they represent a potential liability of the pension scheme.

Members of the scheme have the option to pay Additional Voluntary Contributions; neither the contributions nor the resulting benefits are included in the above tables.

[*Number*] directors are members of money purchase schemes. Contributions paid by the company in respect of such directors were as follows:

(d)

	20XX £	20YY £
Name of director	_____	_____
	_____	_____

Retirement benefits amounting to £_____ (20XX – £_____) were paid to Mr _____, a past director of the company, in excess of the benefits to which he was entitled on [the date retirement benefits first became payable to him / 31 March 1997].

amounts which depend on market conditions, so are likely to change materially from year to year, even if no additional benefits are promised in relation to services during the year. The original 1998 Combined Code stated that 'Companies may wish to make clear that the transfer value of the increase in directors' accrued pension benefits represents a liability of the company, not a sum paid or due to the individual.' However, in some cases this wording may not be correct, and the alternative wording illustrated in figure 6.9.

For each person who served as a director of the company at any time during the financial year, where the person has rights under a pension scheme that is a money purchase (defined contribution) scheme and any of those rights are rights to which he/she has become entitled in respect of qualifying services, details of any contributions to the scheme in respect of that person that are paid or payable by the company for the relevant financial year, or paid by the company in that year for another financial year, are to be disclosed.

Details are required of any retirement benefits paid to or receivable by current and past directors in excess of those to which they were entitled on the date on which the benefits first become payable or 31 March 1997, whichever is the later.

In summary

From the illustrations and discussions above, the length and complexity of the rules requiring directors' details to be disclosed annually can be judged. The UK disclosure environment is undoubtedly more onerous than in many other places. Openness and transparency are the only acceptable qualities in this area.

7

Governance of senior executive remuneration

KATHRIN KAHRASS

> The governance of the corporation is now as important in the world
> economy as the government of countries.
>
> James D. Wolfensohn, 'A Battle for Corporate Honesty',
> *The Economist: The World in 1999* (1998), p. 38

Corporate governance is commonly understood to be the system and processes by which a company is directed and is founded on virtues of accountability, integrity, transparency and fairness. It is wider than control which stands for regulation or exertion of authoritative influence, and describes a continuum – the process of exercising authority in which oversight assumes a more subtle meaning.

Whilst the concept of corporate governance is as old as the 'principal-agent problem', the term was rarely used and, arguably, understood before the 1990s. Since then, there has been much attention and focus by regulators, boards and investors alike on the way in which companies are managed and led, in an attempt to identity and codify good corporate practices and behaviours.

There is a growing body of analysis and study dedicated to illuminating the link between good corporate governance and corporate success, in the form of financial and share price performance and a company's ability to raise cheap capital. The findings of the Global Investor Opinion Survey undertaken by McKinsey in cooperation with the Global Corporate Governance Forum in 2002[1] indicate that investors consider corporate standards on a par with financial indicators when evaluating investments. In addition, an overwhelming majority of respondents indicated their willingness to pay a premium for a company with high corporate governance standards.

Based on the evidence it is not surprising that recent years have seen the launch of corporate governance indices, such as the FTSE ISS Corporate Governance Index launched in April 2005, aimed at strengthening the armoury at the disposal of the investment community for quantifying the risks associated with different investment choices. Such indices are constructed on the basis of numerous governance indicators which are

---

[1] McKinsey & Company, 'Global Investor Opinion Survey: Key Findings', July 2002.

Figure 7.1

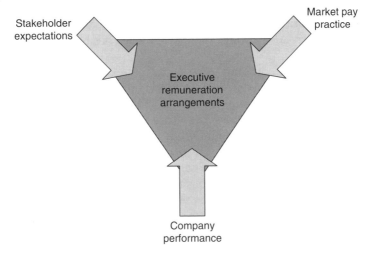

weighted based on their respective level of impact and grouped into key themes. The remuneration arrangements in place for both executives and non-executive directors tend to be one of the key themes driving a company's corporate governance score.

As noted in the Introduction to this book, whilst there is a substantial body of literature dedicated to corporate governance on a broader level, there is little around that examines from a practitioner's point of view the processes and manner by which executive reward is operated and governed. This chapter focuses on the governance of executive reward and aims to illuminate the governance framework within which remuneration committees discharge their responsibility and find the right performance measure(s) which, if met, will deliver sufficiently competitive rewards (without being excessive), in ways that are acceptable to stakeholders.

Before discussing corporate governance at work in an executive remuneration context, it seems apt at this stage to acknowledge the contribution of the various committees and chairs set up since the early 1990s to review the UK corporate governance landscape and to improve in their wake both practice and debate.

A brief history lesson

High-profile corporate scandals, with which especially more recent history is littered, have often provided the pretext and impetus for the publication and amendment of corporate governance codes. Regulators around the world have responded differently to the challenges posed by the loss of public confidence typically associated with corporate failures. The US regulators, for example, have placed greater emphasis on legislation (e.g. the Sarbanes Oxley Act and the new Securities and Exchange Commission (SEC) Rules on Proxy Disclosure of Executive and Director Compensation), whilst the UK approach has been more benign and flexible.

The UK corporate governance landscape as we know it today was first formally surveyed in the early 1990s by a committee chaired by Sir Adrian Cadbury. The committee was set up to address concerns around the standard of financial reporting and accountability, brought into sharp focus by difficult economic conditions in the UK. The committee's work received further impetus through two high-profile corporate failures, BCCI and Maxwell, which coincided with its tenure.

The Cadbury Code published in December 1992 laid the foundations and defined the principles on which UK corporate governance remains firmly based until this date, and established one of the core principles at the heart of UK corporate governance – the principle of 'Comply or Explain'. The architects of the Cadbury Code held the fundamental belief that a pursuit by companies of the spirit rather than the precise letter of the Code was the key to raising governance standards. This has also been the essence and intention of subsequent extensions of the Cadbury principles over the years.

Quoting from the report: 'The effectiveness with which boards discharge their responsibilities determines Britain's competitive position. They must be free to drive their companies forward, but exercise that freedom within a framework of effective accountability. This is the essence of any system of good corporate governance.'

The recommendations of the Cadbury Committee primarily focused on board composition, the division of responsibilities between executives and non-executives, financial reporting standards and controls, and the link between shareholders, the board and the auditors, and only marginally touched on executive remuneration.

Since 1992, the recommendations of the Cadbury Committee have been added to at regular intervals – in 1995 by the Greenbury Committee and in 1998 by the Hampel Committee. The recommendations of the Greenbury Report focused on the governance of executive remuneration against the backdrop of UK privatisations and negative publicity surrounding substantial windfall gains made by directors of the newly privatised entities. The report laid down principles that should govern the setting of executive pay and long-term incentive opportunities.

In January 1998, the Hampel Committee reported its final recommendations and, drawing together the recommendations of the three committees, the Combined Code ('the Code') was published in 1998 and annexed to the Listing Rules.

Further guidance on the Code was subsequently issued – by Turnbull in September 1999, which focused on internal controls, followed in January 2003 by the publication of the Smith Report on the role of audit committees and the Higgs Report on the role and effectiveness of non-executive directors.

Following the collapse of Enron and WorldCom in the USA the Code was updated in July 2003, incorporating the recommendations from the Smith and Higgs Reports. At the same time, the UK Government confirmed that the Financial Reporting Council ('FRC') was to have the responsibility of maintaining and updating the Code, which has since undergone further limited changes in June 2006. One of the more significant changes made in June 2006 was that Code provision B.2.1 now includes the statement: 'In addition the company chairman may also be a member of, but not chair, the [remuneration] committee if he or she was considered independent on appointment.' Whilst this provision is not expected to have a material impact in practice, it formally acknowledges the chairman's role in assessing the chief executive's performance.

Throughout all of these changes, at the heart of the Code remains the principle of 'Comply or Explain', which has since been widely copied and forms the basis on which the European Union corporate governance disclosure requirements are based.

The Code applies to all companies incorporated in the UK and listed on the Main Market of the London Stock Exchange. The Code acknowledges that smaller listed companies (i.e. those below the FTSE 350 throughout the year immediately prior to the reporting year), especially those new to listing, may consider some of the Code provisions less relevant or disproportionate. However, they are nonetheless encouraged to consider their adoption. Companies listed on the Alternative Investment Market (AIM) of the London Stock Exchange are not formally required to comply with the Code. However, it is considered good practice and may even be imposed or required by investors that AIM companies comply with the Code.

A new dawn

On 1 August 2002, the Directors' Remuneration Report Regulations ('the Regulations') entered into force. The key requirements of the new legislation, which was incorporated into the Companies Act, included:

- for financial years ending on or after 31 December 2002 quoted companies are required to publish a directors' remuneration report in accordance with Schedule 7A of the Companies Act 1985 as part of their annual report and accounts; and
- the remuneration report is to be tabled for an advisory vote at the AGM of shareholders.

The advent of the Regulations is widely considered as the watershed in the governance of executive remuneration in the UK. Whilst initially embraced with a significant degree of caution, it is commonly credited with three key behavioural and structural changes:

- improved dialogue, in terms of both frequency and quality, between companies and shareholders;
- a reduction in notice periods of executive directors' service contracts; and
- a strengthened performance link in the vesting provisions for long-term incentives on a change of control.

Indeed, one could argue that the overall impact of the Regulations through their emphasis on disclosure has been to restore investor confidence in the ability of non-executive directors to discharge effectively an aspect of their monitoring role.

The governance framework around executive reward

I keep six honest serving men (They taught me all I knew); Their names are What and Why and When and How and Where and Who.

Rudyard Kipling, 'The Elephant's Child' (1902)

The framework within which remuneration committees manage and monitor executive reward is multilayered and includes, aside from the Combined Code and the Directors' Remuneration Report Regulations, the committee's terms of reference, other internal modus operandi and regular dialogue with investors and institutions.

The main Code principle (B.2) relating to the process underlying the operation of executive remuneration states that: *'There should be a formal and transparent procedure for developing policy on executive remuneration and for fixing the remuneration packages for individual directors. No director should be involved in deciding his or her own remuneration.'*

In order to meet the requirements of the Code, companies must have formal processes in place for managing the remuneration of senior executives, the starting point of which is a clear mandate and well-defined remit. In this regard, the remuneration committee's terms of reference, which form the 'constitution' by which executive reward is governed in a company, assume a central role in defining and delineating the committee's responsibilities, its membership and processes.

Remuneration committee terms of reference

The Institute of Chartered Secretaries and Administrators (ICSA) provides model terms of reference on its website (www.icsa.org.uk). The model terms are intended for guidance and only cover the basic remit of committees. It is therefore important that companies consider whether these should be added to and/or modified to suit the company's particular circumstances. Some companies may choose to adopt terms of reference which cover only the basic remit of the committee, with details being held as a separate working document, whilst others may adopt a more comprehensive approach.

Practice in this regard varies from company to company. A review by Deloitte of the terms of reference of thirty large UK companies indicates that some have clearly taken a standard template whereas others have developed more specific terms.

Whichever the approach a remuneration committee chooses to adopt, it is important that there is complete clarity about:

- the constitution of the committee;
- who attends the meetings;
- who advises the committee;
- the committee's authority and remit; and
- the processes for determining remuneration.

All of these aspects should be sufficiently documented to ensure that the committee is not only aware of the regulatory requirements but also fully aware of, and prompted to take account of, all potential areas for concern. Since the Code requires remuneration committees to make their terms of reference available, it is important that they demonstrate that the processes in place are robust, fair and transparent.

Membership of the committee

Supporting principle B.2.1 of the Code requires companies to establish a remuneration committee which should comprise at least three independent directors (at least two for companies below the FTSE 350).

The terms of reference for all but two of the thirty companies surveyed included reference to the minimum required number of members. All but five specified the minimum number of independent members but only two thirds specified that all members must be independent non-executive directors.

To avoid falling at the first hurdle, it is helpful for the terms of reference to be clear on membership criteria. There may be circumstances where, for example, members have served on the board for longer than nine years and therefore fail the Code's strict independence test. This in itself does not preclude the individual from serving as a member of the committee, as long as the individual is considered independent in character and judgment by the company and appropriate explanation to this effect is provided.

It is too early to assess the impact of the Code change now permitting the chairman to serve as a member of the committee on its membership. Notwithstanding this, we would expect that chairmen would, subject to satisfying the independence test, join the remuneration committee in the majority of companies, given their unique position on the board and their role in assessing the performance of the CEO.

Attendance at the meeting

Only two thirds of the terms of reference reviewed made specific reference to executives not being present at, or not being involved in, discussion about their own remuneration.

In our view, it should become best practice for terms of reference to include a specific provision to this effect. The inclusion of such a provision would make one of the fundamental governance principles underlying the operation of executive reward policy unambiguously clear and serve as a reminder to all protagonists involved in this process of the demarcation of their sphere of influence. Indeed, it is good practice for the committee to set aside time, for example as part of a meeting, to meet without management being present to discuss remuneration aspects and the wider strategy around executive reward, even if the discussions are not specifically about the remuneration of the individual directors.

Whilst the Code (A.1.2) requires disclosure of the number of committee meetings held during the year and the individual attendance record of its members, there is no guide in the Code as to how often a committee should meet in order to discharge its duties. Practice varies considerably from company to company and will also vary from year to year in the same company depending on the depth of review taking place and whether changes to structure or policy are being developed. Figure 7.2 provides an indication of the number of meetings currently taking place in FTSE 350 companies.

The model terms also include reference to what constitutes a quorum. This concept is useful in dealing with the increasing demands placed on committee members' time through an ever-expanding and increasingly detailed remit. For example, a quorum is helpful to conduct more procedural aspects of executive reward such as the execution of deeds of grant and the grant of long-term incentives to employees joining the company outside the normal grant cycle. However, significant decisions such as the

Figure 7.2

Number of remuneration committee meetings	Q1	Median	Q3	Average
FTSE 100	4	5	7	5
FTSE 250	3	4	6	5

Source: 'Boardstructure and Non-executive Directors' Fees', Deloitte & Touche LLP, September 2006.

setting of long-term incentive opportunities for the executive directors and senior management should, as a matter of good practice, be taken by the committee in full session.

Advisors to the committee

Executive reward touches on a wide range of fields of expertise and, whilst it is unrealistic to expect members to have deep expertise in all these fields, providing members with appropriate access to such expertise is important. Notwithstanding this, we have noted a trend over the last couple of years for remuneration committees to include a member with specific expertise in remuneration issues. Given the complexity of remuneration arrangements and the growing pace of change in the tax, legal and regulatory environment, this trend is hardly surprising.

When updating the terms of reference, companies may want to give consideration to whether a requirement for at least one committee member to have experience and/or understanding of executive remuneration should be included in the revised terms.

In order to enable the committee to discharge its duties effectively and within the time constraints associated with a non-executive role, timely access to quality information and advice are key pre-requisites. These would typically include:

- regular updates on the remuneration environment, encompassing both competitor and wider market pay practice and corporate governance;
- investor feedback received by the company on aspects of the remuneration arrangements; and
- financial updates (internal and external) to enable an assessment of performance against targets under short- and long-term incentive plans and the stretch inherent in such targets.

In addition, it is helpful to provide or make available to committee members crib-sheets summarising the characteristics of incentive arrangements, including performance conditions, vesting schedules, time frames and leaver provisions, and summaries of historical committee activity, discussion topics and key decisions.

Almost all the terms of reference reviewed stated that the committee may consult with the chairman (this reference will become redundant for companies where the chairman joins the committee as now permitted by the Code), chief executive or other executive directors.

In relation to professional advisors, the majority of the terms of reference stated that the committee is responsible for appointing external consultants, but only one third specifically note that in doing so the committee would avoid conflict of interest.

From a best practice perspective, it is clearly desirable for remuneration committees to have their own set of advisors as this will reinforce the

187

committee's ability to act as independent adjudicators. In practice, however, it is clearly not always feasible, especially for smaller companies, to engage two sets of remuneration consultants.

In circumstances where the advisors to the company are identical to those of the committee, conflicts of interest can arise, for example where the committee considers proposals developed by management with the assistance of the external advisor. What is important in such circumstances is that committee members are mindful of the risk when bringing their judgment to bear on the proposals. Another way of addressing this is for the external advisors to be the appointees and advisors of the remuneration committee in the first instance, but with a remit to work with the company's HR and compensation function. Whilst this approach, adopted by many smaller companies, is not foolproof, it provides external advisors with a clear hierarchy of loyalties within which to resolve potential conflicts of interest, if needed.

Even where separate remuneration advisors are involved, the advisors to the committee will invariably interact with the company's HR and compensation function and its advisors. In these circumstances, differences of opinion will occur from time to time which are healthy and arguably an indicator of both parties doing their job. However, a 'them and us' situation should be avoided as much as possible and efforts should be made to discuss, and, wherever possible, resolve such differences outside the forum of the formal meeting to ensure an effective use of the committee's time. Should a fundamental difference of opinion ever arise, the chairman of the company may be best placed to act as arbiter because of his or her unique insights into both sides of the fence.

Committee authority and remit

Code principle B.2.2 states that:

> The remuneration committee should have delegated responsibility for setting remuneration for all executive directors and the chairman, including pension rights and any compensation payments. The committee should also recommend and monitor the level and structure of remuneration for senior management. The definition of 'senior management' for this purpose should be determined by the board but should normally include the first layer of management below board level.

In relation to the overall remit of the committee, most companies in our review included a fairly standard statement that the committee will determine and agree with the board the appropriate policy and within that policy will have delegated responsibility to determine individual remuneration packages. However, this was not always the case, and the detail included varied substantially. In some cases it was stated that the committee determines the policy with no reference to board approval. In some cases the overall statement included details of the elements of remuneration to be determined and which individuals were covered.

We recommend that companies review the overall remit of the committee to ensure that there is absolute clarity around the 'What', the 'Who' and the 'How'.

The more detailed remit of the committee was the most varied and unclear area of the terms of reference we reviewed.

The Code states that the remuneration committee should determine the remuneration of the chairman. Only three quarters of the terms of reference specifically referred to the committee's remit in determining the chairman's remuneration. Around half of the terms stated that the company secretary came under the remit of the committee. Apart from this, there was a great deal of variation in who falls under the remit of the committee and the extent to which the committee is responsible.

In all but one company, the terms of reference specifically noted the committee's power to determine the individual remuneration of the executive directors. Most terms of reference state that the remuneration committee determines the individual remuneration for other senior executives as decided by the board. This typically includes the executive committee. Three quarters of the terms also make specific reference to recommending and monitoring the level and structure of remuneration for senior management (who comprises senior management is often not clearly defined).

All the terms of reference stated that the remuneration committee determines the contractual terms of employment, but less than half specifically require the committee to ensure that termination payments are fair, that failure is not rewarded and that the duty to mitigate is fully recognised.

The ICSA model terms of reference include a provision that the committee should give due regard to any relevant legal requirements, the Combined Code and the UK Listing Authority's Listing Rules. Only five of the companies in our review did not include this. The model terms also include a provision that the committee should oversee any major changes in employee benefit structures. A statement to this effect was included by less than half of the companies. All but two of the companies included a statement that all provisions regarding disclosure of remuneration as set out in the Regulations and the Code are fulfilled.

The model terms of reference also contain a provision stipulating that committees should review and note annually the remuneration trends across the company or group. Only around half of the companies in the review included a provision relating to the wider employee population. This ranged from reviewing all grants of options and operation of long-term incentive plans, to being kept informed of relevant aspects to the requirements to 'monitor and review the effectiveness of senior remuneration and its impact and compatibility with corporate remuneration policy and benefits

189

Figure 7.3

Remit of the remuneration committee	FTSE 100	FTSE 250	FTSE Small Cap
All matters for main board only	5%	2%	–
All matters for main board and direct reports to the main board	8%	11%	7%
All matters for main board, direct reports to the main board and the wider senior executive population	8%	9%	–
All matters for main board, direct reports to the main board, the wider senior executive population and all employees	–	2%	3%
All matters for main board and some matters for direct reports to the board	5%	6%	14%
All matters for main board and some matters for direct reports to the main board and the wider senior executive population	13%	7%	14%
All matters for main board and some matters for direct reports to the main board, the wider senior executive population and all employees	13%	25%	21%
All matters for main board and direct reports to the main board and some matters for the wider executive population	2%	11%	12%
All matters for main board and direct reports to the main board and some matters for the wider executive population and all employees	41%	20%	19%
All matters for main board, direct reports to the main board and the wider senior executive population and some matters for all employees	5%	7%	–

structures generally for employees throughout the group'. Investors and wider debate are currently focused on how remuneration of senior executives fits within the wider employee population and are looking for justification where policies for senior executives are different from those of other employees. It may therefore be appropriate to include a specific provision in the terms of reference to ensure that this is on the committee's radar.

A survey of company secretaries of FTSE All Share companies conducted by Deloitte in 2006 specifically examined the remit of the remuneration committee. Responses were received from 120 companies and Figure 7.3 indicates the wide spread of practice.

Clearly, each company must determine the appropriate remit of the committee, but the review findings suggest that there is some room for improving the clarity of the terms in this respect.

The process for determining remuneration

Our review indicated that the terms of reference were less forthcoming, in relation to the processes and the behavioural and qualitative statements, as to the manner in which (or 'How') these processes are conducted. There were very few companies that include in the terms of reference a responsibility for ensuring that the overall quantum of the package is justifiable and reasonable. A few companies included a provision that committees should ensure that executive directors are fairly and responsibly rewarded, having regard to the performance of the group.

The terms of reference of one company stated that the committee should review the remuneration of competitor companies but should not implement automatic increases.

More detail and explanation as to how committees fulfil their remit provides important context, adds colour to the charter governing a company's executive reward and helps in demonstrating that the processes are robust. The authors would argue that companies could do better in this regard. Notwithstanding this, there is clearly a balance to be struck between meaningful disclosure in this regard and being overly prescriptive, in order to safeguard the committee's ability to respond effectively to market pressures and changes in the governance environment, whilst ensuring the fairness of the outcome.

In this regard, the annual remuneration report plays an important part in communicating the processes underlying the setting and operation of executive reward. For example, it has become good practice to disclose the basis on which base salaries are reviewed and determined and annual long-term incentive opportunities are set.

As the link between reward and performance remains at the top of the shareholder agenda, the manner in which performance is measured and how this translates into tangible rewards to executives is one of the key areas in which remuneration committees remain under pressure to demonstrate the robustness of the process. This applies to the manner in which targets are set as well as the way in which payouts are determined. Particularly short-term incentives are an area where investors continue to push for more disclosure and meaningful narrative demonstrating the link between bonus levels and performance.

Since it is impossible to anticipate the future, it is prudent to consider possible outcomes when setting incentive opportunities. It has also become good practice for remuneration committees to take wider factors into consideration when determining the vesting of awards to ensure that resulting rewards are fair and appropriate.

Other provisions

One or two companies have included other provisions in the terms of reference, which other companies may find helpful. One of these is a provision to ensure that the remuneration committee and nomination committee liaise to check that remuneration packages offered on a new appointment are within the overall company policy. This could avoid potential issues of internal inequity further down the line.

Another is a specific provision requiring that any new member receives appropriate induction training on the role of a remuneration committee member.

191

Further pieces in the governance jigsaw

The terms of reference are always supplemented by internal modus operandi further detailing specific processes and cascading responsibility and accountability on reward aspects further down the organisation. Such codes of conduct embed checks and balances, reinforce consistency and ultimately ensure that the reward machinery functions across the company. Their form and content are informed by the organisational structure of a company. In highly devolved businesses, individual divisions would typically enjoy a substantial degree of autonomy in relation to the operation of remuneration policy for the senior team heading up the division. In these circumstances, the corporate centre, through the group reward governance function, would act as the 'gatekeeper'.

The corporate centre assumes a critical role both in devolved and in centralised reward systems. In a more devolved environment, it would typically provide counsels and support to the divisional reward teams through 'light-touch' governance, whilst guarding the common focus and the integrity of the system. In a more centralised system, its role would be more hands-on. Ultimately, however, the effectiveness of the system hinges on the existence of clear and rigorous processes setting out the core principles of operation, as well as clarity around the remit, authority and interaction of the different protagonists. They enforce accountability and integrity of decision making at all levels.

Some companies have 'solved' the question of the remuneration committee's remit by reference to the monetary value of the remuneration package of individuals, which is also the approach used by some companies in relation to senior appointments and new hires. Where the size of the package including salary, bonus and long-term incentive opportunity plus any relocation benefits offered, and buyouts of existing benefits and incentives, exceeds certain thresholds, the package would automatically be subject to the approval of the remuneration committee or sub-committees with relevant delegated responsibility.

In order to enable the relevant approving body to make an informed decision, it is helpful to include in the submission biographical details of the individual, interview notes as relevant, details of the current package, and internal and external benchmarks used in constructing the proposed package.

This process could be dealt with by including a relevant provision in the committee's terms of reference, or, as appears to be more common, through supplementary documentation. This approach, if operated properly, reinforces reward discipline and consistency at all levels involved in the recruitment process. It will highlight early on in the process where an individual's reward expectations are outside the company's policy and prompt consideration of how to proceed.

However good and well defined the processes, having sufficient resources at the right level in the organisation to manage these processes is another vital ingredient in the mix. The approach adopted by companies in this regard varies but it is probably fair to say that reward tends to be more often under- rather than over-resourced. Whilst it is often cost effective to outsource more process driven aspects such as equity plan administration and aspects of international assignment policies, over-reliance on external advice on the more strategic aspects of senior executive remuneration can produce sub-optimal solutions. The deep involvement of external advisors can be helpful in circumstances where the committee wishes to drive fundamental changes to the reward system through the organisation. However, in the normal course of business, bringing a balance of deep knowledge of the inner workings of the company and a fresh pair of eyes to bear on decisions will invariably serve companies best in the long run.

Another helpful instrument in the governance process is the annual remuneration committee timetable which serves as a reminder of the content and timing of the committee's annual business as well as a planning tool for more strategic reviews of aspects of the remuneration arrangements. It can be helpful for the committee chairman to review and discuss the timetable with the remuneration committee advisor at an appropriate time during the year (e.g. at the end of the financial year or following the AGM) to agree the agenda for the year ahead. This would also assist in ensuring that sufficient time is set aside to enable the committee to consider adequately all agenda items.

Annual agenda items would typically include:

- base salary reviews for the executive directors and other senior management, as appropriate;
- assessment of the individual directors' performance;
- determination of annual bonuses for the executive directors and other senior management, as appropriate;
- an update on competitor pay practice and the corporate governance environment;
- AGM feedback;
- the setting of the annual LTIPs and relevant targets for the executive directors and other senior management, as appropriate;
- an update on performance against targets of long-term incentives and determination of the vesting of maturing long-term incentive grants;
- review and approval of the annual remuneration report; and
- communication with shareholders and institutions.

Other items which the committee would commonly consider, as appropriate, during the year, would include promotions and retirement of directors and the exercise of discretion in relation to aspects of the remuneration arrangements.

In order to ensure that all t's are crossed and i's are dotted, it is important that the timetable interfaces with internal procedures and operations such as equity plan administration and the grant cycle of incentives to the wider employee population.

The external dimension

The Listing Rules require companies to make a statement of disclosure in relation to two parts of the Code:

- a statement on how the company has applied the Code principles, covering both main and supporting principles; and
- a statement on the extent to which the company has complied with the principles and, where it has not, an explanation as to the reasons for the non-compliance.

In addition, the Code requires companies to engage in regular dialogue with investors, whilst investors are urged to avoid a 'box-ticking' approach in assessing a company's corporate governance.

There is no doubt that the advent of the Regulations has made the disclosure of remuneration arrangements and the governance processes underlying them more consistent, comprehensive and informative. The length of remuneration reports has increased since then and, like a reversal of fortunes, views that less is perhaps more are gathering momentum.

The overall standard of disclosure provided by companies in remuneration reports is generally high. The disclosure of principles underlying the operation of remuneration policy has assisted committees in framing the spirit and intentions of the policy, making its application more predictable. Some companies have gone as far as providing undertakings and commitments in relation to the exercise of discretion and circumstances in which shareholders would be consulted prior to changes being implemented, even where such aspects are not formally subject to shareholder approval.

Where investors, as the primary audience of such statements, feel companies could do better is in relation to the disclosure of how performance is determined and then translated into tangible rewards to executives. This is a matter which could be addressed both through more extensive formal disclosure and through shareholder dialogue.

The annual timetable of business of some remuneration committees includes an annual meeting with investors and institutions. These meetings are used to update shareholders on the committee's thinking on key aspects of executive remuneration, to outline the issues considered by the committee over the last year and to provide shareholders with an opportunity to share their views on the remuneration arrangements and air any concerns they may have. In some cases, the chairman of the company attends the meetings to share his or her views on the remuneration arrangements from a wider business context. Such discussions are helpful in educating both parties on their respective views and the reasons driving them, to avoid investors feeling as though they are caught on the back foot in relation to changes to the remuneration arrangements, and ultimately to build trust.

As already noted by the Cadbury Committee, effective governance relies on the willingness of all players involved in the game to engage. During 2006, the FRC met with chairs of FTSE 100, FTSE 250 and Small Cap companies to solicit views on the impact of the Code and other corporate governance matters. The feedback indicated that, although companies were by and large supportive of the Code and acknowledged its benefits, companies had a number of concerns which included the cost of compliance, especially a concern for smaller companies, and a perception that some investors had reverted to a 'box-ticking approach' in applying the Code.

Arguably, the growing complexity of remuneration arrangements and the shift away from 'what does everyone else do?' to 'what works for me?' increase the need for explanation. In relation to performance measures, total shareholder return (TSR) remains by far the most common measure used in performance share plans and there is no doubt that, to a great extent, this is due to the fact that many institutional investors have expressed a preference for this measure. However, we observe a trend towards the use of more bespoke measures such as cash flow and return on capital employed, albeit such measures tend to be used alongside more standard or accepted measures such as TSR and EPS.

Professional advisors play an important role in the process of educating and supporting remuneration committees in assessing the likely external perception of, and the risk factors associated with, different choices, and, as appropriate, assist with the communication of such choices to investors and institutions. In this regard, there may be a temptation at times, encouraged by remuneration advisors, to play safe. This is not to say that remuneration advisors should urge companies towards the path of 'explanation'. Instead, the focus should be on an effective use of the flexibility provided by the Code and the willingness to use it, based on a thorough discussion and assessment of the alternatives. This will invariably stand remuneration committees in better stead of finding reward systems that succeed in balancing the three dimensions of the Bermuda triangle of executive remuneration

The Code specifically acknowledges the challenges for smaller companies in complying with specific Code provisions. Notwithstanding this, it was especially smaller companies that cited difficulties in persuading investors to engage in dialogue, which has left them under pressure to comply in circumstances where an 'explain-approach' would have better served a company's interests. Some also noted that defaulting to the Code is sometimes seen as avoiding the 'hassle factor' associated with explanation.

It is undoubtedly the case that the workload of remuneration commit-tees and of corporate governance departments of institutional investors alike has increased over the years. That said, as companies endeavour to operate executive reward within frameworks that accord to principles of good governance, with considerable time and resources being expended in the process, it is not surprising they have an expectation of constructive engagement on the part of the investors. Notwithstanding this, the chairs of FTSE 100 companies noted during the consultation with the FRC in 2006 that the voting on the remuneration reports, as the most important indication of investor views on remuneration, has thus far generally been 'comfortably supportive'.

The effective remuneration committee

> . . . good corporate governance is more than just following the Code.
> The Code is a bit like those early crude maps of the world which got the
> placing of continents roughly right but were unreliable guides in detail
> for those actually carrying out the voyages.
>
> Sir Christopher Hogg, Chair of the FRC,
> Keynote Speech at the London Stock Exchange
> Corporate Governance Conference, 26 March 2007

Any charter or regulatory framework, whether based on the force of law or on a 'comply or explain' approach, is brought to life by, and its effectiveness hinges on, the behaviours of the protagonists.

It seems therefore opportune to use the closing remarks of this chapter for a brief discussion of the behaviours and characteristics commonly asso-ciated with good governance and more specifically so, with an effective remuneration committee.

Key characteristics of effective board committees (not confined to remuneration committees) are:

- having an effective chairman;
- being well prepared;
- being aware of business needs and market practice;
- being willing to challenge and probe;
- having meetings sufficiently regularly;
- being flexible; and
- assessing how the committee is doing.

As noted elsewhere in this chapter, the workload of remuneration commit-tees has been increasing over the years and the level of public scrutiny asso-ciated with executive reward makes it one of the more high-profile board committees. Recent years have also seen a growing appetite for litigation in circumstances where payouts under incentive arrangements or termination payments were considered excessive or unjustified. Indeed, Section 1 of the revised guidelines of the Association of British Insurers (ABI) published in December 2006 states that: 'They [remuneration committees] should consider legal redress where performance achievements are subsequently found to have been significantly misstated so that bonuses and other incentives should not have been paid.'

All of this serves as a reminder of the importance of remuneration committee members not only discharging their duties effectively but also being seen to do so through appropriate and informative disclosure.

Key virtues of a good non-executive are typically considered to include the willingness to challenge proposals constructively, and a probing mind; sound judgment, integrity and high ethical standards; strong interpersonal skills and knowledge of the business, the environment in which it operates and the issues it faces. In order to enable committee members to bring these virtues to bear on decisions, having sufficient time to consider proposals and to engage in value-added discussions is as important as being provided with quality briefings and timely support from both internal and external advisors. Planning ahead through annual timetables of committee business and the provision of committee papers well in advance of the meetings are pre-requisites to enabling committee members to enter well prepared into discussions.

Aside from having a clear remit and rigorous processes in place, the committee's relationships with the chairman of the company, management and other board members are an important source from which remuneration committees leverage in their decision making. Corporate governance codes and principles are clearly important in guiding remuneration committees in the decision making process. However, it is a company's specific circumstances and competitive realities that should be the primary, albeit not sole, driver of decisions around executive reward.

Last but not least, it is good practice to undertake a regular review of the committee's overall effectiveness, including an assessment of the level and quality of support received during the year. This helps to identify gaps in the processes and procedures, enables them to be rectified in a timely manner and ensures that these processes and procedures remain relevant as the organisation and the wider market and corporate governance environment evolve.

Ultimately, governance is about trust – principals trusting the agents to conduct affairs in their best interest and agents trusting the principals to let them get on with the job and be rewarded appropriately for their efforts. As governance failures tend to make for better headlines, perception will unfortunately continue to be shaped by the few rather than the majority of companies which are run well and expertly by their respective boards. As it is equally as unlikely for the media to start championing the many rather than the few as it is for principals to give their agents a *carte blanche*, quality disclosure, constructive dialogue between companies and investors, and an effective use and application of the principles and spirit of the existing corporate governance framework hold the key to good governance in executive reward.

Glossary

The definitions in this glossary are provided to facilitate an understanding of the issues explored elsewhere in this book. Unless otherwise indicated, all references are to UK law, regulation and practice.

401(k)

A 401(k) plan is a US employer-sponsored retirement plan and named after a section of the US Internal Revenue Code. A 401(k) plan allows a worker to save for retirement while deferring income taxes on the saved money and earnings until withdrawal. The employee elects to have a portion of his or her wage paid directly, or 'deferred', into his or her 401(k) account. Employee savings are sometimes matched by employer contributions.

A-Day

Appointed day (A-Day) – 6 April 2006. The date from which the pension simplification legislation came into force in the UK, replacing a number of existing pension regimes with a single set of rules.

Admission

In relation to a flotation or IPO this refers to the point at which a company's shares are admitted and the shares begin to be traded publicly on a recognised stock market.

Alternative Investment Market (AIM)

Launched in 1995 the Alternative Investment Market (AIM) is the London Stock Exchange's 'junior' market for smaller companies that allows companies that cannot or do not wish to meet the full listing requirements to go public. To join AIM, companies do not need a specific financial track record or trading history and there is no minimum requirement in terms of size or number of investors.

Annual allowance

The pension legislation introduced in April 2006 places an annual limit on contributions to defined contribution schemes and on increases in the capital value of benefits accrued in defined benefits schemes. The annual allowance was set at £215,000 in April 2006, rising to £255,000 by April 2010.

Annual report

A yearly statement, prepared at the end of the company's financial year, of a public company's operating and financial performance. It includes:

- Directors' report
- Income statement
- Balance sheet
- Auditors' report

The annual report must be sent to all shareholders and approved at the AGM.

Approved share plans

Share plans that are approved by HMRC and which benefit from favourable tax treatment provided the plan meets certain criteria. Examples of approved share plans in the UK include:

- Company Share Option Plan (CSOP)
- Save As You Earn Scheme (SAYE)
- Share Incentive Plan (SIP)
- Enterprise Management Incentive Plan (EMI)

Articles of association

The articles of association is the document which lists the regulations that govern how a company is run. They cover things such as: main business and purposes of the company, shareholders' voting rights, directors' duties, general working and management practices. They are registered with the memorandum of association when the company is formed.

Association of British Insurers (ABI)

The ABI (Association of British Insurers) is the trade association for authorised insurance companies operating in the United Kingdom. The ABI produces principles and guidelines on executive remuneration which are considered to represent best practice. The ABI also operates the Institutional Voting Information Service (IVIS). IVIS reviews UK company annual reports and accounts and notices of company meetings for compliance with the ABI corporate governance and executive remuneration best practice guidelines. Matters for concern are identified and discussed with the company prior to the AGM.

Average

The value obtained by taking the sum of the values and dividing by the number of values. Also called the mean. See *median*.

Bad leaver

In share or share option plans, a bad leaver is an employee who leaves employment before the shares are released or the share options become exercisable, due to voluntary resignation or dismissal. Any outstanding awards would typically be forfeited. See *good leaver*.

Balanced scorecard

A model of business performance evaluation developed by Robert Kaplan and David Norton in which performance is based on a number of key indicators (typically including financial measures, customer satisfaction, internal business processes, and learning and growth). A balanced scorecard is often used as the basis of an annual bonus plan.

Balance sheet

The balance sheet is a financial statement that provides a snapshot of the company's assets (what the company owns) and liabilities (what the company owes). It is drawn up at the close of business on the last day of the company's accounting period (the balance sheet date).

Benchmarking

Benchmarking is the process of measuring something relative to a specified standard. For remuneration purposes, this will normally require the collection and analysis of data on remuneration paid to similar positions in companies of a similar nature or size to establish the market rate (i.e. the benchmark), in order to assess the competitiveness of the position being benchmarked.

Binomial model

The binomial model is used for valuing options. It was developed by Cox, Ross and Rubinstein in 1979. The binomial model calculates the value of an option by breaking down the time to expiration into a large number of time steps. A tree is produced representing all the possible paths that the share price could take during the life of the option.

It requires the same inputs as the Black-Scholes model (share price, exercise price, share price volatility, dividend yield, risk-free rate and option term). However, it is more flexible than the Black-Scholes model and can be customised to take into account specific features of an option, for example that options may be exercised before the end of the option term.

Black-Scholes model

The Black-Scholes model is used for valuing share options. The model was first published in 1973 by Robert C. Merton, enhancing work that was published by Fischer Black and Myron Scholes. The Black-Scholes-Merton formula is a closed-form model that uses an equation to produce an estimated fair value.

The Black-Scholes model is perhaps the best-known valuation model for share options and is relatively straightforward to implement, requiring determination of six inputs to the model (share price, exercise price, share price volatility, dividend yield, risk-free rate and option term / expected life).

Boiling frog

A 'scientific parable', popularised by the author Charles Handy. If a frog is placed directly into boiling water, it will feel the heat and try to escape. However, if a frog is placed into lukewarm water and the temperature is gradually increased, the frog will remain in the water, until, at 100°C, the water boils and it dies.

Buyout

In the context of hiring a new executive director, the buyout relates to compensation that the new employer offers in respect of any awards or payments promised by the current employer which will be lost if the individual leaves. See *run rate*.

Cadbury Report

The Cadbury Report was published in 1992 by a committee, chaired by Sir Adrian Cadbury, that was set up by the Financial Reporting Council, the London Stock Exchange and the accountancy profession. The committee was set up in the wake of financial scandals in the 1980s which had caused a loss of confidence in the quality of financial reporting.

The Cadbury Report, 'Financial Aspects of Corporate Governance', sets out recommendations on the structure of company boards and accounting systems to help mitigate risks and failures. The report included a code of best practice and it became a requirement for the boards of all UK listed companies to comply with the provisions contained in the code or identify and explain reasons for non-compliance.

Capital employed

Capital employed represents the debt and equity resources available to a company. It is the value of assets that contribute to a company's ability to generate revenue. It has many definitions but it is usually represented as total assets less current liabilities, or fixed assets plus working capital.

Capital employed is used in the calculation of return on capital employed (ROCE).

Capital gains tax (CGT)

Capital gains tax is the tax payable on gains made on sales of securities or other chargeable assets. Individuals are entitled to a tax-free exemption (the first £9,200 of gains for 2007/8) and may carry forward losses from previous years.

Career average plan (CARE plans)

In pensions, a career average or CARE (Career Average Revalued Earnings) plan is a type of defined benefit plan offering a pension benefit on retirement, with the benefit based not on the earnings close to retirement, but on the average earnings throughout the member's entire period of membership.

Cash balance plans

In pensions, a cash balance plan is a hybrid of a defined contribution and defined benefit plan. These plans are common in the USA but are not often seen in UK companies. Technically they are defined benefit plans but they look more like defined contribution plans in that the employer contributions are defined as a percentage of the participants' salary which is credited to a hypothetical employee account. The individual employee accounts earn a fixed rate of return and therefore the employer bears the risks and rewards of the investments. Increases and decreases in the value of the plan's investments do not directly affect the benefit amounts promised to participants.

Change of control

In employment contracts, a change of control clause entitles an employee to a specified payment or longer notice period if their employer is taken over and the takeover results in their dismissal or in a material reduction in their responsibilities leading to constructive dismissal within a specified time. In share plans, a change of control may trigger early vesting of awards.

Cliff vesting

In share schemes, cliff vesting describes a vesting schedule in which all shares or options vest or become exercisable if a single performance target is met. Cliff vesting contrasts with scaled vesting where the proportion of shares or options vesting depends on the level of performance achieved.

Co-investment plan

This is a long-term incentive plan which requires participants to make an investment in the company's shares for a specified period, which may then earn matching shares. The matching shares will vest dependent on company performance over the period. The initial investment may in many cases be satisfied in part by existing shareholdings but most plans will require at least some of the investment to be satisfied by purchasing shares, or committing shares vesting from option or other share plans. Co-investment plans are similar to a voluntary deferred bonus plan with matching shares. The main difference is that the initial investment is not dependent on corporate performance and will usually be expressed as a percentage of salary. The term also applies, and originated with, arrangements which allow private equity company employees to invest alongside other investors.

Combined Code

The Combined Code on Corporate Governance consolidates the principles and recommendations of the Cadbury, Greenbury and Hampel Reports. The Combined Code sets out standards of good practice in relation to issues such as board composition and development, remuneration, accountability and audit, and relations with shareholders.

Although compliance with the Combined Code is voluntary, listed companies are required to report on how they have applied the principles of the Code, and either to confirm that they have complied with the Code's provisions or, where they have not, to provide an explanation.

Company Share Option Plan (COSOP)

A CSOP is an HMRC approved share option plan which is a discretionary share option scheme which, if various statutory requirements are satisfied, allows a company to grant tax-advantaged options to its employees, subject to a maximum value of £30,000.

Comparator companies

In benchmarking or performance measurement, a group of companies selected for their similarity, in terms of financial size, industry and/or international reach, to a given company. Sometimes also referred to as 'competitor companies'.

Compromise agreement

A legally binding agreement that records the terms of an employee's departure and the compensation to be paid by an employer, in return for a waiver of claims.

Compulsory deferral

See *deferred bonus plans*.

Constructive dismissal

In employment law, constructive dismissal results where an employee resigns due to their employer's behaviour. Although the employee has not actually been dismissed, the employer's treatment is sufficiently bad for the employee to be entitled to regard themselves as having been dismissed. The employer's behaviour has to be such that it can be regarded as a significant breach of the employment contract.

Consumer Prices Index (CPI)

The Consumer Prices Index (CPI) forms the basis of the Government's inflation target. It is an internationally comparable measure of inflation, calculated according to rules specified in European regulations. It uses the same basic price data as the Retail Prices Index (RPI) but differs from it in some important aspects. The CPI does not include Council Tax and a number of other housing costs which are included in the RPI, but it does include charges for financial services which are not included in the RPI. The CPI is based on a wider population than the RPI, including all private households, foreign visitors and residents of communal establishments such as nursing and retirement homes and university halls of residence. Goods and services are defined for the purposes of the CPI following international standards, whereas the RPI has its own specific structure.

Correlation

Correlation represents the degree to which two or more variables show a tendency to move together. It indicates the strength and direction of a linear relationship between two random variables.

Decile (upper and lower)

A decile divides a series of ranked data into ten groups of equal frequency:

- lower decile separates the lowest 10% of data from the top 90% (i.e. the 10th percentile);
- upper decile separates the highest 10% of data from the bottom 90% (i.e. the 90th percentile).

See *median, quartile* and *quintile*.

Deferral period

In incentive plans, a specified period of time during which awards of shares are deferred and may be forfeit in the event of cessation of employment.

Deferred bonus plans

An annual bonus plan, where part, or all, of the annual bonus award is deferred for a specified period of time. This may be on a voluntary deferral basis or a compulsory deferral basis. The deferred part of the award usually takes the form of a commitment to deliver shares which may vest subject to remaining in employment and which are held in trust for the deferral period.

Matching share awards may be made at the end of the deferral period, particularly in plans where part of the deferral is voluntary. The shares held will often be matched on a one-for-one basis, although this ratio varies between plans. In some plans the participant will receive the matching award as long as they are still in employment at the end of the deferral period. More commonly the participant will only receive the matching awards if certain performance conditions are met over the deferral period.

Defined benefit plan (DB plan)

In pensions, a defined benefit plan provides a pre-determined retirement benefit to an employee, based on the employee's earnings history, years of service and age. Typically an employee accrues a proportion of their final salary for each year of service (a final salary plan). This is called the accrual rate. An accrual rate of 1/60th of salary for each year of service over a period of forty years' service would provide a pension in each year of retirement of two thirds of final salary. See *pension accrual*.

Defined contribution plan (DC plan)

In pensions, a defined contribution plan is a scheme in which contributions are defined on a fixed basis, and the final benefits payable are dependent on the performance of investments made with contributions to the plan, any management charges and the cost of buying an annuity. These plans are sometimes referred to as money purchase plans.

Dilution

An increase in the number of a company's issued shares.

In employee share schemes, dilution is caused when a company issues new shares to satisfy awards under share plans. The ABI guidelines on executive remuneration contain specific guidance on the dilution limits that should apply to company share schemes.

Directors' Remuneration Report Regulations 2002

In 2002 the Directors' Remuneration Report Regulations were incorporated into the Companies Act 1985 as Schedule 7A. The Regulations require the directors of a listed company to prepare a directors' remuneration report which includes:

- details of the remuneration committee;
- a policy statement for future years with details about any long-term incentive arrangements;
- a performance chart which illustrates the five-year TSR performance of the company against a broad market index;
- amount of each director's remuneration in the preceding financial year.

The Regulations also require the remuneration report to be approved by shareholders each year. The vote is advisory, giving shareholders an opportunity to express a view on the remuneration policy and practice, and the quality of the disclosures.

Discount rate

The discount rate may refer to the time value of money (i.e. taking into account the net present value of future income) or the risk-free rate of return.

Dividend

Dividends are regular distributions to shareholders, typically twice a year (interim dividends are paid following the announcement of half-year performance and final dividends are paid following the declaration of full-year results).

Dividend yield

Dividend yield is the income an investor receives from a company in return for the capital invested in it. It is calculated as the annual dividend income per share divided by its current share price and expressed as a percentage. The ratio can be used to compare dividend rates for different companies.

The average yield for UK shares has been between 2% and 3% over the past ten years.

Domicile

Broadly speaking, an individual is domiciled in the country where they have their permanent home. This is different from residency. An individual can only have one domicile at any given time. Non-UK-domiciled individuals have advantageous tax treatment.

Due diligence

The process by which the buyer of, or an investor in, a company investigates the records of the target company to support the value of the company. Professional reports from accountants and solicitors are frequently an important component of this process. Due diligence may include a detailed assessment of the organisation's financial stability, legal risks, technical capacity, human resource policies and infrastructure. The due diligence process is normally conducted by a potential buyer after providing confidentiality undertakings. Any open issues will be subject to negotiations with the vendor, and the buyer will seek warranties and indemnities.

Earnings cap (1989)

The earnings cap was introduced by the Finance Act 1989 and was a limit on the amount of remuneration on which benefits and contributions could be based for those members of pension schemes established on or after 14 March 1989 and for all new members of earlier schemes joining on or after 1 June 1989. The limit increased each year in line with inflation. The earnings cap has now been replaced by the annual and lifetime limits contained in new pension legislation that came into effect in April 2006. However, a notional cap has been maintained in many plans and is set at £112,500 for the year 2007/8.

Earnings per share (EPS)

Earnings per share (EPS) is calculated as earnings divided by the weighted average number of shares in the year of measurement. It is disclosed at the bottom of the income statement in the annual report. EPS is shown on a diluted or an undiluted basis. For undiluted EPS the weighted average number of shares is based on shares that are issued throughout the year. Diluted EPS takes into account any potential dilution that would be suffered by shareholders, for example when outstanding warrants and options are exercised.

EBITDA

EBITDA is a measure of a company's profit during a financial period. It stands for earnings before interest, tax, depreciation and amortisation. It measures the fundamental earning power of the company before taking into account non-cash expenses, financing expenses or taxation. It essentially represents the operational performance of the company during the year. EBITDA is often thought of as a measure of approximate cash flow during the period. It provides a more 'smoothed' measure of annual cash flow than the cash flow statement because large one-off capital expenditures are excluded.

Economic profit

Economic profit is net operating profit after tax less a charge for the capital used in the business.

Economic profit = Net operating profit after tax – capital employed × weighted average cost of capital (WACC)

Economic profit is the absolute amount of profit made during a financial period, over and above that which is required to satisfy all investors in the company at their required rates of return. It can be thought of as the 'value added' profit.

Employee benefit trust

An employee benefit trust (EBT) is a discretionary trust which holds assets for the benefit of employees. A trust is a legal arrangement by which one person owns assets on behalf of somebody else. An EBT can be operated for pensions, share schemes or employee insurances.

Enhanced protection

Under the pension legislation introduced in April 2006, two forms of transitional protection were introduced to allow employees to protect the benefits they have accrued to A-Day: primary protection and enhanced protection. The choice of protection method is based on individual circumstances.

Under enhanced protection, pre-A-Day pension rights are ring-fenced, provided the employee ceases active membership of all registered schemes from A-Day, although defined benefits can continue to grow by reference to future pay increases and defined contribution plans may continue to receive investment returns within limits. This route is available to members with benefits both above and below the lifetime allowance at April 2006. The protection ceases if active membership resumes in any registered scheme.

Enterprise Management Incentive Plan (EMI)

An Enterprise Management Incentive Plan ('EMI') is a tax-efficient share option scheme designed for use by smaller quoted or unquoted companies, provided they meet certain qualifying conditions. It is normally offered as a targeted incentive to selected employees, but there is no limit on the number of employees who may participate in an EMI Scheme (subject to an overall limit of £3 million on the value of shares that may be offered under option).

Employees are granted the right to purchase company shares in the future at a price set at the date of grant. There is no tax on grant or exercise (provided the options are granted at market value at the date of grant) and any gain is instead subject to capital gains tax.

Equity dilution

See *dilution.*

Equity settled stock appreciation rights (ESARs)

In share schemes, a stock appreciation right (SAR) is the right to receive cash equal to the difference between the market value of an award at vesting/exercise and the market value at the date of grant (or the exercise price if different). In equity settled SARs, the difference between the market value of the award at vesting and grant is paid in shares rather than cash.

Executive director

An executive director is an individual who is appointed to the board of directors under procedures contained in the Articles of Association and who is responsible for the day-to-day administration of the business.

Exercise

In share plans, the act of acquiring shares underlying an option by paying the exercise price (if any) once any conditions relating to performance, employment or time have been met.

Exercise period

In share plans, the period which starts when an option first vests or becomes exercisable (i.e. when any conditions relating to performance, time or employment have been met) and ends when the option expires. In the UK, options generally expire after ten years from the date of grant.

Exercise price

In share plans, the price an option holder must pay to acquire the underlying shares subject to an option at the time of exercise. In listed companies, this is usually the market price at the date of grant but there are specific situations where options are granted with an exercise price at a discount to the market price. Some awards under performance share plans are structured as 'nil-cost' options, where the awards are made as options with an exercise price of nil.

Ex gratia

A payment made where there is no contractual or statutory requirement to do so, e.g. by an employer to an employee.

Expatriate

In employment, an employee who is seconded to work abroad.

Expatriate benefits

Certain additional benefits such as cost of living, housing and schooling allowances provided to expatriates when they are required to live and work outside their country of residence, to take account of additional expenses or differences in the cost of living.

Expected life

Although there is usually a long period in which an option can be exercised, in practice individuals do not always hold the options until the end of this period. The expected life of an option is an estimate of the length of time between the grant of the option and the point during the exercise period when an employee is expected to exercise his/her option, and is an important factor in calculating the fair value of an award.

Expected value

In the context of valuing and comparing elements of remuneration across a number of companies, the expected value of an award of shares considers the likelihood of meeting any performance or service conditions and the value of the shares. The expected value is the sum of the probability of each possible outcome multiplied by the potential value. It therefore represents the value which might be expected, on average, if the same situation was repeated many times.

Fair value

The fair value is the amount at which an asset (or liability) could be bought (or incurred) or sold (or settled) in a current transaction between willing parties, in an arm's-length transaction.

Final salary plan

See *defined benefit plan.*

Financial Reporting Council (FRC)

The Financial Reporting Council (FRC) is the UK's independent regulator responsible for promoting confidence in corporate reporting and governance. Its activities include promoting high standards of corporate governance; setting, monitoring and enforcing accounting and auditing standards; setting actuarial standards; statutory oversight and regulation of auditors; operating an independent investigation and discipline scheme for public interest cases; and overseeing the regulatory activities of the professional accountancy and actuarial bodies.

Financial Services Authority (FSA)

Established in December 2001, the United Kingdom Financial Services Authority (FSA) is an independent non-governmental body that regulates the UK financial services industry. Almost every type of financial services firm must get permission from the FSA to do business in the UK. The FSA regulates banks, building societies, credit unions, insurance and investment firms (stockbrokers and fund managers) and independent financial advisors. It has powers to investigate, discipline and prosecute.

Fixed compensation

The term 'fixed compensation' is used to describe the sum of all remuneration elements that are guaranteed and not dependent on company or individual performance, i.e. base salary and pension. Also see *variable compensation.*

Flotation

Flotation is the process by which a company's shares are admitted for trading on a public market. There are three types of flotation: an introduction raises no new money and is used if enough of the company is already in public hands (for example this method may be used for a move from the Alternative Investment Market to the London Stock Exchange's main market); a placement offers shares to selected institutional investors; an initial public offering (IPO) offers shares to private and institutional investors. The latter is the most common method of flotation and is also the most expensive route to market. As part of the flotation process, the company will need to produce a document (called a prospectus or listing particulars) for prospective investors providing key information about the business.

Forfeiture

In share plans, forfeiture means that a share award lapses or is taken away from the award holder, for example as a result of the award holder ceasing employment with the company before the end of the vesting period or as a result of performance conditions not being met.

Forfeiture period

In share plans, the period during which an award can be forfeited if certain conditions relating to employment or performance are not met.

Free shares

The term 'free shares' most commonly refers to shares given for free under a Share Incentive Plan (SIP).The term is sometimes used to refer to awards of shares given for nil consideration under a performance share plan. See *Share Incentive Plan (SIP)*.

FRS20

Financial Reporting Standard 20 Share-based Payment is the UK version of IFRS 2.

FTSE

FTSE Group (FTSE) is an independent company owned by the *Financial Times* and the London Stock Exchange. FTSE create and manage over 100,000 equity, bond and hedge fund indices.

FTSE 100 is an index weighted by market capitalisation and representing the performance of the 100 largest UK 'blue chip' companies.

FTSE 250 is an index weighted by market capitalisation and representing the performance of the mid-cap capital and industry segments of the UK market not covered by the FTSE 100 index.

FTSE 350 is an index which combines the FTSE 100 and FTSE 250 companies.

FTSE SmallCap comprises those companies in the FTSE All-Share index which are not constituents of the FTSE 350.

FTSE All-Share is an index which combines the FTSE 100, FTSE 250 and FTSE Small Cap indices. It represents around 700 companies.

Funded Unapproved Retirement Benefit Schemes (FURBS)

A funded retirement benefit scheme to provide additional pension benefits outside an approved retirement benefit scheme. Many companies responded to the introduction of the earnings cap in 1989 by putting in place FURBS or Unfunded Unapproved Retirement Benefits Schemes (UURBS) to provide for benefits on salary in excess of the earnings cap for a limited number of senior executives. Since April 2006 the earnings cap is no longer in force; however, many companies continue to maintain a notional cap on pensionable salary. FURBS previously benefited from reduced tax rates which have now been removed and many employers are now favouring cash supplements on earnings above the notional cap.

Furlough

A term for a leave of absence, also sometimes used to refer to a longer period of absence, such as a sabbatical or career break, as well as to opportunities to return to the home country for an expatriate.

Gardening leave

The term used for a period during which an employee continues to receive their normal salary and to be bound by their contract of employment but is requested, usually under an express clause in the service contract, not to attend the office or contact clients or customers. Employers typically use gardening leave during an employee's notice period to prevent the employee from having further contact with customers, clients and staff and to prevent the employee from working for a competitor.

Gearing

Gearing is the financial term used to describe the relationship between a company's debt and equity financing. It is calculated by dividing the company's debt by equity capital. Gearing is a measure of financial leverage, demonstrating the degree to which a company's activities are funded by owner funds versus creditor funds. If the company has low levels of debt compared to equity it has a low gearing ratio. Conversely, a high debt-to-equity ratio would be a highly geared company.

Good leaver

In employee share plans, a good leaver is an employee who leaves employment before the end of the vesting period due to specified circumstances which typically include injury, disability, redundancy or retirement (subject to any age discrimination issues). In these situations, the share or share option awards commonly vest. The remuneration committee will often have discretion to determine the level of vesting and will typically reflect the extent to which performance conditions have been met and the reduced period of time between grant and vesting. See *bad leaver*.

Greenbury Report

The Greenbury Study Group, chaired by Sir Richard Greenbury, was set up on the initiative of the Confederation of British Industry (CBI) in 1995, in response to public and shareholder concerns about pay and remuneration of directors of UK companies. It followed on from the work of the Cadbury Committee. The terms of reference were to 'identify good practice in determining Directors' remuneration and prepare a Code of such practice for use by UK PLCs'. The report of the Study Group in July 1995 established the fundamental principles of accountability, transparency and performance and these were encapsulated in a Code of best practice. The Code covers four main areas:

- the role of the remuneration committee;
- disclosure and approval;
- remuneration policy;
- service contracts and compensation.

Following publication of the Code it was appended to the London Stock Exchange Listing Rules, and the Listing Rules required companies to include a statement about compliance with the Code or to explain and justify any areas of non-compliance. The framework of corporate governance was further developed by the Hampel Report which culminated in the publication of the Combined Code in 1998. This was updated as a result of the Higgs and Turnbull Reports in 2003.

Hampel Report

The Hampel Committee was established in 1996 to review and revise the earlier recommendations of the Cadbury and Greenbury Committees. The final report emphasised principles of good governance rather than explicit rules in order to reduce the regulatory burden on companies and avoid 'box-ticking', so as to be flexible enough to be applicable to all companies.

Higgs Report

In 2002 the Department of Trade and Industry commissioned Sir Derek Higgs to lead a review of the role and effectiveness of non-executive directors. The report resulted in a number of changes to the Combined Code relating to board structures and policies, independence of directors, the role of the non-executive director, succession planning, recruitment and appointment of directors, performance evaluation, the role of the remuneration committees and directors' remuneration, the relationship with shareholders and the role of the institutional investor.

At the same time the Department of Trade and Industry set up the Co-ordinating Group on Audit and Accounting Issues (CGAA) to consider the wider issues of accountancy and audit reform. The interim report of the CGAA proposed the creation of a separate group, chaired by Sir Robert Smith and under the auspices of the Financial Reporting Council, to develop existing Code guidance for audit committees. These were also incorporated into the revised Combined Code.

The revised Combined Code was issued in July 2003 and updated in June 2006.

HM Revenue & Customs (HMRC)

HM Revenue & Customs (HMRC) was formed on 18 April 2005, following the merger of Inland Revenue and HM Customs and Excise departments. It is responsible for collecting and administering direct and indirect taxes and paying and administering certain benefits and tax credits.

Holding period

In incentive plans, a specified period during which, once vested, awards must be further retained until they can be exercised or the shares sold.

Incumbent

The term for an individual currently holding an office or post.

Indemnity

Security against damage, loss or injury. Generally, an undertaking by one party to meet a specific potential legal liability of another. An indemnity commonly entitles the indemnified party to a payment if the indemnified event takes place.

International Accounting Standards (IAS)

International Accounting Standards (IAS) were issued by the International Accounting Standards Committee (IASC) between 1973 and 2000. The IASC was replaced by the International Accounting Standards Board (IASB) in 2001. Since then IASB has amended some IAS, replaced some IAS with new International Financial Reporting Standards (IFRS) and adopted or proposed new IFRS on topics for which there were no previous IAS.

International Financial Reporting Standard 2 (IFRS 2)

International Financial Reporting Standard 2 Share-based Payment is the international accounting standard that sets out how companies should account for share-based payments.

The standard requires that companies recognise the 'fair value' of all share-based payments as an expense in the income statement, spread over the vesting/performance period. It applies to the financial statements of companies listed on the London Stock Exchange for accounting periods beginning on or after 1 January 2005, to all share awards which were granted on or after 7 November 2002, which had not vested prior to 1 January 2005.

International Financial Reporting Standards (IFRS) are standards and interpretations adopted by the International Accounting Standards Board (IASB).

Intrinsic value

The amount by which the fair value of the underlying stock exceeds the exercise price of an option.

IPO

See *flotation.*

Key performance indicator (KPI)

Key performance indicators (KPIs) are the indicators which are considered to be the most effective in measuring the delivery of the strategy of the company and the management of the business, both financial and non-financial. Incentive plans are often based on the KPIs of the company.

Lifetime allowance

The pension legislation introduced in April 2006 places a limit (the 'lifetime allowance') and an annual limit (the 'annual allowance') on the amount of pension savings in a registered pension scheme that can attract favourable tax treatment. The lifetime allowance is the maximum value of the fund a pension scheme member can accumulate under all registered pension plans without incurring a tax charge. If the value of a member's benefits when they are drawn exceeds the lifetime allowance, a tax charge will be made against the excess. The lifetime allowance increases annually. It was set at £1.5m in 2006, £1.6m in 2007, rising to £1.8m in 2008.

The limit applies to the capital value of a pension fund, so for a defined contribution plan it is the accumulated contributions and investment returns net of incurred costs. For a defined benefit plan, the legislation provides a formula which applies a multiplier to the annual pension which is promised.

Linear regression

Linear regression is a statistical method of determining the relationship between two variables. In remuneration terms, the variables would typically be the remuneration of an individual in relation to the size of the role the individual holds. A linear regression analysis calculates the best possible straight line through a series of data points. *See also regression analysis.*

Liquidated damages

When an executive contract is terminated it is common for the company not to want the executive to serve the full notice period. The company is then breaching the terms of the contract and it is necessary to settle on an appropriate termination payment. Liquidated damages are an agreement at the outset on the amount that will be paid by the company to the executive in the event of severance. Liquidated damages must be calculated as a genuine pre-estimate of probable loss arising from termination, otherwise they can be considered to be a 'penalty clause' and, as a result, unenforceable.

The advantages of such provisions are that they provide certainty over the level of payment and they ensure that the company is acting in accordance with the terms of the contract and can therefore enforce any restrictive covenants. From an employee's point of view it takes no account of the duty to mitigate during the notice period and is therefore a real advantage if they find alternative employment early.

Listing Rules

All companies are subject to Company Law, but publicly listed companies are also subject to rules governing listing on the Stock Exchange. These are called the 'Listing Rules' and are administered by the UK Listing Authority (UKLA) which is part of the Financial Services Authority (FSA). There are three sets of rules:

- The prospectus rules which dictate the contents of the prospectus on flotation.
- The disclosure and transparency rules which dictate ongoing disclosure obligations such as the disclosure of price-sensitive information and share transactions by those employees discharging managerial responsibility.
- The rules which set out the rules for listing applications, the listing principles, continuing obligations such as the documents requiring shareholder approval, the content of proxy forms, the content of the annual report and the preliminary statement of annual results, disclosure of directors' remuneration, details of the notification of transactions, dealing in own securities and the content of circulars. The Listing Rules include the Model Code which sets out the rules on share dealing by employees discharging managerial responsibilities.

Long-term incentive plan (LTIP)

An arrangement under which an individual may receive an asset in the future (e.g. cash or company shares) provided certain conditions related to performance and service are met over a predetermined time period. LTIP is a generic term which describes any incentive plan which is based on performance over a period longer than one year. This may include share option plans. However, in some situations it may be used to describe a long-term incentive plan other than a share option plan. In the Listing Rules, the definition of a long-term incentive plan which would require prior shareholder approval is a plan in which one or more executive directors may participate and in which performance is measured over more than one financial year.

Long-term performance

In remuneration terms, long-term performance generally relates to long-term incentive plans where awards are subject to performance conditions being met over a predetermined time period, typically three years for UK long-term incentive plans. The Listing Rules define a long-term incentive as any plan which measures performance over a period greater than one year.

Main market

The London Stock Exchange's main market for UK and international listed securities.

Lifetime allowance

The pension legislation introduced in April 2006 places a limit (t allowance') and an annual limit (the 'annual allowance') on the pension savings in a registered pension scheme that can attract tax treatment. The lifetime allowance is the maximum value of pension scheme member can accumulate under all registered pe without incurring a tax charge. If the value of a member's be they are drawn exceeds the lifetime allowance, a tax charge w against the excess. The lifetime allowance increases annually. I £1.5m in 2006, £1.6m in 2007, rising to £1.8m in 2008.

The limit applies to the capital value of a pension fund, so f contribution plan it is the accumulated contributions and investr net of incurred costs. For a defined benefit plan, the legislatio formula which applies a multiplier to the annual pension which i

Linear regression

Linear regression is a statistical method of determining the between two variables. In remuneration terms, the variables wo be the remuneration of an individual in relation to the size of individual holds. A linear regression analysis calculates the l straight line through a series of data points. *See also regression*

Liquidated damages

When an executive contract is terminated it is common for the to want the executive to serve the full notice period. The con breaching the terms of the contract and it is necessary to settle priate termination payment. Liquidated damages are an agre outset on the amount that will be paid by the company to th the event of severance. Liquidated damages must be calculate pre-estimate of probable loss arising from termination, other be considered to be a 'penalty clause' and, as a result, unenfor

The advantages of such provisions are that they provide the level of payment and they ensure that the company is ac dance with the terms of the contract and can therefore enfor tive covenants. From an employee's point of view it takes no a duty to mitigate during the notice period and is therefore a rea they find alternative employment early.

Listing Rules

All companies are subject to Company Law, but publicly lis are also subject to rules governing listing on the Stock Excha

Matching shares

See *deferred bonus plan and Share Incentive Plan (SIP)*.

Mean

For any given data set, the value obtained by adding the values up and dividing by the number of values. Also called average.

Median

The middle point of a ranked set of numbers. See *quartile, quintile* and *decile*.

Mitigation

Entitlement to damages for early termination of a service contract is subject to the director's duty to mitigate his/her loss by seeking further employment and thereby reducing the damages payable by the company by the amount the director may be reasonably expected to earn. The duty to mitigate is made easier by the fact that the director is entitled to restrict his/her search to positions at a similar level, offering similar salary and benefits. After a period, an individual might be expected to look at a lower level. An increasing number of companies now make the duty to mitigate a specific provision in the contract and may also include a provision which allows the termination payments to be phased, or paid in monthly instalments, which would reduce or cease if the director were to find alternative employment. See *payment in lieu of notice (PILON)*.

Money purchase plan

See *defined contribution plan*.

National Association of Pension Funds (NAPF)

The National Association of Pension Funds (NAPF) is the UK body providing representation and other services for those involved in all aspects of pension provision. As part of their representation, the NAPF engages with, and is consulted by, companies on corporate governance matters such as board structures and executive remuneration. It promulgates a Corporate Governance Policy which is based on the provisions of the Combined Code. It is associated with Research Recommendations Electronic Voting (RREV) which provides pension funds with corporate governance research and voting recommendations on matters submitted for share approval at AGMs.

Net asset value (NAV)

The net asset value (NAV) is a term used to describe the value of an entity's assets less the value of its liabilities. NAV growth may be used as a performance measure.

Nil-cost options

Performance share awards may be structured as nil-cost options with the exercise price set to nil (or close to nil), thereby replicating a free share award. The option can be exercised at any time after the end of the performance period up until expiry (usually up to ten years from grant). This structure has the advantage that, under UK law, it provides the employee with the choice of when to crystallise the tax charge (i.e. with the exercise of the option typically being the tax point).

Non-executive directors

A director who is not an employee of the company and who only dedicates a proportion of his time to the company. A non-executive director is usually an individual with particular skills or experience who holds a seat on the board to provide an independent opinion on board decisions. His legal obligations to the company and creditors are the same as those of an executive director. Essentially, the role of the non-executive director is to:

- constructively challenge and contribute to the development of strategy;
- scrutinise the performance of management and monitor the reporting of performance;
- satisfy themselves that financial information is accurate and that financial controls and systems of risk management are robust;
- determine appropriate levels of remuneration for executive directors and have a prime role in appointing and removing senior management and in succession planning.

Notice period

In employment law, a contract of employment normally includes a specified period of notice required to be given by the employer to the employee and by the employee to the employer. The notice period to be given by the employer must be at least the minimum required in law (one to twelve weeks depending on service). The notice period to be given by the employer and the employee may be different. For an executive director it would be typical for the contract to require twelve months' notice to be given by the employer and either six months', or twelve months', notice to be given by the director.

Option pricing model

A number of different models have been developed to price / assign a value to share options. The most commonly used option pricing models are the Black-Scholes model and the binomial model.

Option term

Option term is the period of time during which an option holder may exercise the options granted (although there may be conditions restricting the exercise for a period following grant). Most options have an option term of ten years.

Ordinary resolution

A resolution that has been passed by a simple majority of members, or their proxies, who are entitled to vote at a company general meeting of which notice has been properly given.

Organic growth

A company is said to be growing organically when it grows or increases the financial size of its existing business rather than growing by acquiring another company.

Outlier

For a set of numerical data, any value that is markedly smaller or larger than other values and is not representative of the general trend.

Partnership shares

See *Share Incentive Plan (SIP)*.

Payment in lieu of notice (PILON)

A payment in lieu of notice clause allows an employer to terminate someone's employment instantly on making a payment in lieu of salary, and sometimes benefits, during a notice period. PILONs are normally used for senior executives who are bound by restrictive covenants. Payment in lieu will normally be at the discretion of the company but it is important that any PILON clause is drafted very carefully, as even when the payment is said to be discretionary there have been cases where the courts have decided the employee can receive the appropriate sum with no deduction for mitigation or accelerated receipt. Although not common, the provision may be drafted so that the payment in lieu may be made in instalments which reduce or cease if the employee finds new employment. See *mitigation*.

PBIT

Profit before interest and tax.

Pension accrual

The accrual rate is the rate at which pension rights are built up in a salary-related, or defined benefit, plan. This is typically 1/60th of salary each year – which would result in an accrual of 2/3 of salary after forty years of service, or 1/30th of salary for senior employees, which would result in a pension of 2/3 of salary after twenty years of service. The accrued pension is the pension payable based on service already completed.

Pension deficit

When a pension scheme is valued by an actuary, an assessment is made of its assets and liabilities. Where the liabilities exceed the assets, this is referred to as a pension deficit. Many companies have accumulated pension deficits because people can now expect to live longer.

Performance conditions

In remuneration, this term refers to the performance measures and targets on which the vesting of incentive awards depends. In annual bonus plans, the most typical performance measure is profit. In long-term incentive plans, typical performance measures are total shareholder return (TSR) and earnings per share (EPS).

For the purpose of accounting for share-based payments, this term refers to any condition which affects the vesting, exercisability, exercise price or other pertinent factors used to determine the fair value of an award, relating to both service and performance.

Performance share plan (PSP)

A performance share plan is the most common type of long-term incentive plan used in UK companies. An initial award is made to a participant at the beginning of a performance cycle. This award is usually determined as a percentage of basic salary and will take the form of the right to receive a specified number of shares, some or all of which will be earned ('vest') at the end of the performance period depending on the performance of the company over this period. The value of the final award received will therefore depend on both the performance of the company and the movement of the share price over the performance period. The number of shares may be adjusted to reflect accumulated dividends over the performance period, or a supplementary cash payment may be made.

Perquisite ('perk')

An incidental benefit provided to an employee in addition to his/her salary, such as a company car, medical insurance and free products.

Phantom options

These plans are analogous to a share option plan but the growth in value of the share price is paid in cash when the options are exercised. These plans are not common in UK listed companies, and are most often used where conventional options are not considered appropriate. Most plans will incorporate performance conditions in the same way as a standard share option plan.

Power of attorney

A power of attorney is legal authorisation that allows a person to act on behalf of another party for a given period of time, either for a specific purpose or in general. Any contract of employment containing a power of attorney must be set out as a Deed.

Present value

The current capital value of a future income, calculated by a process of discounting future cash flow at a predetermined rate of interest.

Price/earnings (P/E) ratio

$$\text{P/E ratio} = \frac{\text{Share price}}{\text{EPS}}$$

The P/E ratio is also referred to as the earnings multiple and is a measure of the price paid for a share relative to the income or profit per share earned by the company. A higher P/E ratio means that investors are paying more for each unit of profit.

Primary protection

Under the pension legislation introduced in April 2006, two forms of transitional protection were introduced to allow employees to protect the benefits they had accrued to A-Day: primary and enhanced protection. The choice of protection method is based on individual circumstances but it was possible to register for both where benefits exceed the lifetime allowance at A-Day.

Under primary protection, a member registers the capital value of their pre-A-Day pension rights expressed as a percentage of the lifetime allowance (it must be more than 100%). On retirement a penalty tax (the 'recovery charge') is only paid on pension funds where the value exceeds this percentage of the lifetime allowance at retirement. The lifetime allowance increases from £1.5 million in 2006/7 to £1.8 million in 2010/11 providing an annual increase of nearly 5%. Benefit increases would therefore be subject to the recovery charge on amounts in excess of this level.

Private equity

Private equity is a generic term that includes management buyouts and buy ins, venture capital and other forms of 'private equity' investment. Private equity businesses raise funds from a number of sources and invest those funds in large holdings in companies, sometimes together with other similar businesses. Private equity businesses generally receive a return on their investment at an 'exit' point which will usually be through an IPO, a sale or merger of the company they control, or by re-financing the company. Private equity can provide high returns but the investment is medium- to long-term and can be high-risk. Typically, private equity businesses are funded by a combination of debt and equity, often with a higher proportion of debt.

Projected value

The projected value is the value of the remuneration package in a given set of circumstances. Typically this approach considers the value of the element assuming that on-target performance is achieved and that this would be accompanied by share price growth of $x\%$, or by assuming that outstanding performance is achieved and that this would be accompanied by a higher share price growth. Assumptions still need to be made about the probability of achieving performance targets but the level of vesting that would be achieved for this level of performance is usually readily available. For a given level of performance and an assumed share price growth, it is then possible to calculate the value at the end of a given period.

Quartile (upper and lower)

A quartile divides a series of ranked data into four groups of equal frequency:

- lower quartile separates the lowest 25% of data from the top 75% (i.e. the 25th percentile);

- upper quartile separates the highest 25% of data from the bottom 75% (i.e. the 75th percentile).

See *median, quintile* and *decile*.

Quintile (upper and lower)

Upper quintile is the point 80% through an array of data; the lower quintile is the point 20% through an array of data. See *median* and *quartile*.

Quoted company

Any company whose shares are listed on an official stock exchange.

Ranking analysis

One of the main methods of remuneration analysis which relies on grouping remuneration data into bands of companies or jobs of a similar size by ordering companies or jobs from the largest to the smallest. For each band, the median, quartiles and sometimes deciles can be calculated for all of the data within that band.

The most common way of measuring relative TSR performance also relies on the ranking methodology in order to determine the position of the company relative to the comparator group and the resulting level of vesting.

Regression analysis

One of the main methods of remuneration analysis which finds the relationship between one variable (typically salary) and one or more other variables (e.g. company size). See *linear regression.*

Remuneration committee

A sub-committee of the board of directors with delegated responsibilities including: setting the policy for the remuneration of the executive management; determining targets for performance-related pay or share schemes; and determining the total individual remuneration package of each executive director including, where appropriate, salary, bonuses, pensions, incentive payments and share schemes. The Combined Code recommends that the remuneration committee consists exclusively of independent non-executive directors. The remuneration committee has a chairman who is normally different from the chairman of the company as a whole. The chairman and/or CEO are usually invited to meetings to comment on other executive directors' pay, but not their own.

225

Repatriation

In employment, this is the return of an employee who has lived and worked overseas to their country of residence. See *expatriate.*

Research Recommendations Electronic Voting (RREV)

See *National Association of Pension Funds (NAPF).*

Restricted shares or stock

A share where the sale is prohibited for a specified period of time. In the case of most grants of shares to employees, these may be described as non-vested shares because the limitation on sale is due to the fact that the shares may become forfeit if the employee does not satisfy the necessary service or the required performance condition(s) to earn the rights to the shares.

Restrictive covenant

A restrictive covenant is an obligation imposed on an employee or director preventing the employee/director from doing something during or after his employment has terminated. For example it may prohibit an employee from engaging in competitive businesses or poaching staff or customers for a specified period following the termination of employment. When drafting these terms in employment contracts, it is important to remember that they will only be enforceable if very carefully drafted.

Retail Prices Index (RPI)

The Retail Prices Index (RPI) is the most familiar general-purpose domestic measure of inflation in the United Kingdom. It tracks changes in the prices of a basket of goods and services. The RPI includes virtually all types of household spending, with some exceptions such as savings and investments and charges for credit. It includes mortgage interest payments, although an additional index, RPIX, exists which excludes mortgage interest payments. It is designed to be representative of the 'typical' household and therefore the expenditure of the people in the households with the top 4% of incomes and low-income pensioners are excluded.

The RPI is often used as the basis of wage negotiations for the workforce. In UK share plans, it is common practice for target measures of company performance, such as growth in earnings per share, to be defined as growth in excess of RPI, or 'real' growth.

However, the Government now prefers to use the CPI as its key measure and it is the CPI which the Bank of England uses to make interest rate decisions.

Re-testing

The process of re-measuring or re-assessing a performance condition, if not met over the initial performance period, over a further period of time. See *rolling re-testing*.

Return on capital employed (ROCE)

$$\text{ROCE} = \frac{\text{Profit before interest and tax}}{\text{Average capital employed}}$$

ROCE represents the capital efficiency with which profit is generated because it measures profit achieved relative to the company's assets.

Return on equity (ROE)

$$\text{ROE} = \frac{\text{Profit after tax (PAT)}}{\text{Average equity}}$$

ROE measures the rate of return on the shareholders' ownership interest. The key difference to ROCE is that ROE only measures return to shareholders rather than the return to all investors in the company.

Risk-free rate

The risk-free rate is usually accepted to be the interest rate on the safest investments. In practice it is likely to be based on short-term Government bonds. In the USA, US Treasury Bills are used. These securities are considered to be risk-free as the likelihood of the Government defaulting is very low, and, because they are short-term, the investor is protected from the risk that the interest rate will go up after the bond is purchased thereby causing the investor to miss out on a higher interest rate before the bond matures and can be reinvested at the higher interest rate. An investor will expect any additional risk taken with an investment to be rewarded with an interest rate higher than the risk-free rate. The risk-free rate may sometimes be described as the 'discount rate'.

Rolling re-testing

Usually found in share option plans, this refers to the practice of allowing performance targets to be re-measured over any consecutive three-year period during the life of a share option. This means that, during the ten-year life of the option, there would be eight opportunities to meet the performance target (years 1 to 3, then 2 to 4, etc). This practice does not comply with best practice guidelines and it is now rare to see this feature in share option plans.

Run rate

When used in the context of the hiring of a new executive director, the run rate is the remuneration an individual will earn each year if he remains with the current employer, as opposed to the 'buyout' which relates to accumulated awards or payments which will be lost if the individual leaves.

The run rate can also refer to the average annual dilution from share awards and share option grants measured over the most recent three-year periods. In the USA the run rate is recorded in the annual report. See *buyout*.

Save As You Earn (SAYE)

SAYE plans are HMRC approved arrangements. They must be offered to all eligible employees on a similar basis and allow them to commit to saving monthly from their pre-tax earnings, up to a maximum limit, currently £250 per month, into a fixed return contract. At the end of the contracted period, the individual can have the savings returned as cash with pre-determined interest; or alternatively can choose to exercise an option over shares at an exercise price set at the commencement of the savings period. The exercise price can be discounted to 80% of the market value of the shares at the date of grant.

Scaled vesting

In share plans, this refers to plans where the number of shares vesting at the end of the performance period can vary depending on the level of performance achieved. A threshold level of performance will normally be identified, at which point a proportion of the award will vest. Full vesting will occur if more stretching performance targets are met.

Schedule 7A

See *Directors' Remuneration Report Regulations 2002*.

Securities and Exchange Commission (SEC)

The United States Securities and Exchange Commission (SEC) is a United States Government agency. Its primary responsibilities are enforcing the federal securities laws and regulating the securities industry / stock market.

Service agreement

A service agreement is a contract of employment between the executive and his/her employer. The contract includes normal employment terms, such as remuneration, duties and responsibilities, details of benefits and holiday entitlement, and termination arrangements. An executive directors' service contract must be made available for inspection by shareholders.

Shareholder value

Shareholder value is the combination of movement in share price and dividends.

Shareholding

Many UK companies now require executive directors, and in some cases non-executive directors, to maintain a specified holding of company shares. For executive directors this is likely to be a holding equal to at least annual pre-tax salary.

Share Incentive Plan (SIP)

A SIP is an HMRC approved share plan which must be offered to all eligible employees on a similar basis. Under a SIP, employers can either award free shares up to a maximum value or allow employees to purchase shares out of their pre-tax salary (partnership shares) up to a maximum value, and the employer may also award up to two free matching shares for each partnership share bought. Employers can also offer the reinvestment of up to £1,500 of cash dividends per year paid on Free, Partnership and Matching Shares into dividend shares to be held under the SIP.

Share options

A share option gives the holder the right, but not the obligation, to purchase shares at a fixed or determinable price for a specified period of time.

Many companies granting share options to executives will operate both a UK HMRC approved and an unapproved plan. Commonly, option plans will comply with the broad principles set down in the ABI guidelines. The exercise price of these options will usually be equal to the market value at the date of grant and they will generally be granted on an annual basis. Most plans incorporate an annual limit on the number of options that may be granted to an individual each year, usually expressed as a percentage of salary. In the majority of plans, the options will not vest for three years, and only then if specified performance conditions have been met over this period. In a growing number of plans the vesting is scaled so that the proportion of the total number of options that may be exercised depends on the level of performance achieved.

Some performance share plans (PSP) are structured as 'nil-cost' option plans. See *nil-cost options*.

Short-term performance

Short-term performance usually refers to performance measured over one financial year. Measures of short-term performance are typically used to determine the level of payout under annual incentive plans. See *long-term performance*.

Special resolution

A special resolution is a resolution that must be passed by 75% of shareholders of a company. See *ordinary resolution*.

Spot price

This refers to the current share price on a particular day or at a specific time. In the context of remuneration, this contrasts with taking an average of the share price over a period of time to smooth out share price fluctuations.

Stock appreciation rights (SARs)

In share schemes, a stock appreciation right (SAR) is the right to receive cash or shares equal to the difference between the market value of an award at vesting/exercise and the market value at the date of grant (or the exercise price if applicable). The difference between the market value of the award at vesting and grant may be paid in cash or in shares. See *equity settled stock appreciation rights*.

Stock options

See *share options*.

Termination payments

A termination payment is a payment made to an employee on the termination of their employment. It usually includes payment of the contractual salary and benefits for the period up to the date of termination. The contracts of executive directors may also specify payment in respect of the bonus, which may be defined in a number of ways, including the equivalent of the target bonus, 50% of the maximum bonus or an average of previous bonuses. The rules regarding what happens to long-term incentive share and share option awards held by the employee are usually contained in the rules of the plan and dealt with separately. The termination payment may be contractually agreed (see *liquidated damages*) but this is not generally considered best practice by shareholders. Termination payments can be subject to mitigation and, although not commonly, may be paid on a phased basis, or in monthly instalments which are reduced, or cease, once alternative employment is found. See *notice period* and payment in lieu of notice (PILON).

Term sheet

A term sheet summarises all the important financial and legal terms related to a transaction. Once the term sheet is agreed, it serves as the basis on which the legal documents are drafted. The term sheet allows the parties involved in a deal to focus on the important conditions of the deal prior to commencing the legal drafting.

A term sheet can also be helpful when hiring a senior executive. It can be used to summarise all the details of the negotiations around the components and value of the remuneration package that the candidate will receive. The term sheet will then form the basis of the contract.

Time value

The time value of money is based on the premise that it is better to receive a payment of a fixed amount of money today rather than an equal amount in the future. The present value of a sum of money is greater than the present value of the right to receive the same sum of money at a time in the future because the sum paid now could be invested and yield interest. This is important in remuneration terms, particularly when valuing a remuneration package, as, when calculating the value of a future award, a discount factor should be applied in order to establish the 'present' value of the award.

Total cash

Total cash is a term used in remuneration surveys which usually refers to the annual cash compensation that may be paid to an employee. This typically includes salary and bonus payments where these are made in cash. Annual bonus payments made in shares which are deferred for a period of time but are not dependent on any further performance conditions being met will usually be included in total cash. The specific elements included in total cash may vary between different survey providers.

Total direct compensation

Total direct compensation is a term used in remuneration surveys which usually refers to the total cash compensation plus the annualised 'fair value' of any long-term share or share option awards.

Total remuneration

Total remuneration is a term which typically refers to the annualised value of all elements of the remuneration package, including salary, bonus, the annualised value of share awards, the value of the pension benefit and any other non-cash benefits.

Total shareholder return (TSR)

Total shareholder return (TSR) measures the growth in share price with dividends reinvested and provides an external market view of the company's success. TSR is usually measured against a group of relevant comparator companies with vesting dependent on the ranked position against those companies (relative TSR).

Transfer value

In pensions, the transfer value of a defined benefit pension promise is calculated by an actuary and refers to what would be paid by one pension plan to another in order to enable the liability for the payment of accrued benefits to be moved between plans. The Directors' Remuneration Report Regulations require that the transfer value for each individual director participating in a defined benefit plan is disclosed in the remuneration report.

Treasury shares

Since 1 December 2003 UK companies have been able to buy shares and hold them in their own name as treasury shares without the need to cancel those shares.

UK GAAP

The Generally Accepted Accounting Principles in the UK, or UK GAAP, were, up until 2005, the standard framework of guidelines for financial accounting and the preparation of financial statements for all UK companies. From 2005, listed companies in the UK have been required to report under International Accounting Standards (IAS).

Underpin

In incentive plans, the term 'underpin' (sometimes referred to as a 'hurdle' or 'threshold') relates to a threshold level of performance that must be met before any of the award will vest or be paid. This is most commonly seen in long-term incentive plans based on total shareholder return (TSR) performance relative to a comparator group of companies. In order to ensure that the TSR performance reflects underlying financial performance, it is considered best practice to include a condition relating to an internal financial measure which requires a threshold level of performance to be met. Once this level of performance is achieved, the shares will vest dependent on the ranking of TSR against the comparator group.

Unfunded Unapproved Retirement Benefit Schemes (UURBS)

An UURBS is an unapproved pension scheme used to provide top-up benefits for employees who were affected by the 1989 pensions cap. An UURBS is a covenant to provide a future retirement benefit and typically replicates a defined benefit arrangement. The intention would be to provide a pension to an individual affected by the earnings cap that would be the same as if the individual were not capped. Following the introduction of the new pension legislation in April 2006, both FURBS and UURBS are non-registered schemes.

Variable compensation

The term 'variable compensation' is used to describe the sum of all remuneration elements that are dependent on company or individual performance, i.e. short- and long-term incentives. See *fixed compensation.*

Vest

In share plans, awards vest when any conditions relating to performance, employment or time have been met and the award holder becomes entitled to the underlying award.

Vesting period

In share plans, the time during which an award remains subject to unsatisfied conditions (time, performance or service) and during which the award holder is not allowed to dispose of or exercise the award.

Volatility (share price)

A measure of the amount by which a financial variable, such as a share price, has fluctuated (historical volatility) or is expected to fluctuate (expected volatility) during a period.

Voluntary deferral

See *deferred bonus plans.*

Weighted average cost of capital (WACC)

The weighted average cost of capital (WACC) represents the average return required by all investors in the company. It takes into account the after-tax cost of debt and the rate of return / dividend yield expected by shareholders. It is the return a company must earn on existing assets to keep its stock price constant and satisfy its shareholders and creditors.

Index

Entries in **bold** denote main entries.
The following abbreviations are used:

ABI	Association of British Insurers
AGM	Annual General Meeting
AIM	Alternative Investment Market
CARE	career average revalued earnings
CBI	Confederation of British Industry
CEO	Chief Executive Officer
DB	defined benefit
DC	defined contribution
DRR	directors' remuneration report
DTI	Department of Trade and Industry
EBITDA	earnings before interest, taxes, depreciation and amortization
EEA	European Economic Area
EMI	enterprise management incentive
EPS	earnings per share
EU	European Union
FRC	Financial Reporting Council
FTSE	Financial Times Stock Exchange
FURBS	funded unapproved arrangements
HMRC	Her Majesty's Revenue and Customs
HR	Human Resources
IAS	International Accounting Standards
ICSA	Institute of Chartered Secretaries and Administrators
IP	Intellectual Property
IPO	pre-initial public offering
LEAP	Leadership Equity Acquisition Plan
LSE	London Stock Exchange
LTIP	long term incentive
NAPF	National Association of Pension Funds
NYSE	New York Stock Exchange
PAT	profit after tax
PBIT	profit before interest and tax
PILON	payment in lieu of notice
PSP	performance share plan
ROCE	return on capital employed
ROE	return on equity
SARs	stock appreciation rights
SAYE	Save As You Earn
SEC	Securities and Exchange Commission
SIPs	Share Incentive Plans
TSR	total shareholder return
UK	United Kingdom
US	United States
UURBS	unapproved unfunded arrangements
WTR	Working Time Regulation (1988)